1998

This book is the first in-depth investigation of Coleridge's responses to his dreams and to contemporary debates on the nature of dreaming, a subject of perennial interest to poets, philosophers and scientists throughout the Romantic period. Coleridge wrote and read extensively on the subject, but his richly diverse and original ideas have hitherto received little attention, scattered as they are throughout his notebooks, letters and marginalia. Jennifer Ford's emphasis is on analysing the ways in which dreaming processes were construed, by Coleridge in his dream readings, and by his contemporaries in a range of poetic and medical works. This historical exploration of dreams and dreaming allows Ford to explore previously neglected contemporary debates on 'the medical imagination'. By avoiding purely biographical or psychoanalytic approaches, she reveals instead a rich historical context for the ways in which the most mysterious workings of the Romantic imagination were explored and understood.

CAMBRIDGE STUDIES IN ROMANTICISM

General editors

Professor Marilyn Butler *University of Oxford*
Professor James Chandler *University of Chicago*

Editorial board
John Barrell, *University of York*
Paul Hamilton, *University of London*
Mary Jacobus, *Cornell University*
Kenneth Johnston, *Indiana University*
Alan Liu, *University of California, Santa Barbara*
Jerome McGann, *University of Virginia*
David Simpson, *University of California, Davis*

This series aims to foster the best new work in one of the most challenging fields within English literary studies. From the early 1780s to the early 1830s a formidable array of talented men and women took to literary composition, not just in poetry, which some of them famously transformed, but in many modes of writing. The expansion of publishing created new opportunities for writers, and the political stakes of what they wrote were raised again by what Wordsworth called those "great national events" that were "almost daily taking place": the French Revolution, the Napoleonic and American wars, urbanization, industrialization, religious revival, an expanded empire abroad, and the reform movement at home. This was an enormous ambition, even when it pretended otherwise. The relations between science, philosophy, religion, and literature were reworked in texts such as *Frankenstein and Biographia Literaria*; gender relations in *A Vindication of the Rights of Woman* and *Don Juan*; journalism by Cobbett and Hazlitt; poetic form, content, and style by the Lake School and the Cockney School. Outside Shakespeare studies, probably no body of writing has produced such a wealth of response or done so much to shape the responses of modern criticism. This indeed is the period that saw the emergence of those notions of "literature" and of literary history, especially national literary history, on which modern scholarship in English has been founded.

The categories produced by Romanticism have also been challenged by recent historicist arguments. The task of the series is to engage both with a challenging corpus of Romantic writings and with the changing field of criticism they have helped to shape. As with other literary series published by Cambridge, this one represents the work of both younger and more established scholars, on either side of the Atlantic and elsewhere.

For a complete list of titles published see end of book

CAMBRIDGE STUDIES IN ROMANTICISM 26

COLERIDGE ON DREAMING

Le médecin,

Pourquoi diable mes malades s'en vont ils donc tous?......... j'ai beau les saign...
les purger, les droguer......... je n'y comprends rien !

Lithograph by Honoré Daumier, plate 15 from 'L'imagination' series. 'Le Médecin' was first published in the periodical *Le Charivari* in 1833. Daumier produced the fifteen plates in the series in 1832, while serving a prison sentence. Four of them deal with medical problems: plate 6 depicts colic, for instance. In plate 15, imagination is perceived as the disorder of the doctor: but does the imagination also deceive the patient? Mesmerists and magnetists in the closing decades of the eighteenth century utilised the powers of the imagination to cure and sometimes inadvertently to cause disease.

Reproduced with kind permission of Yale University, Harvey Cushing/John Hay Whitney Medical Library, Clements C. Fry Print Collection.

COLERIDGE ON DREAMING

Romanticism, Dreams and the Medical Imagination

JENNIFER FORD

CAMBRIDGE
UNIVERSITY PRESS

PUBLISHED BY THE PRESS SYNDICATE OF THE UNIVERSITY OF CAMBRIDGE
The Pitt Building, Trumpington Street, Cambridge CB2 1RP, United Kingdom

CAMBRIDGE UNIVERSITY PRESS
The Edinburgh Building, Cambridge CB2 2RU, United Kingdom
40 West 20th Street, New York, NY 10011–4211, USA
10 Stamford Road, Oakleigh, Melbourne 3166, Australia

First published 1998

Printed in the United Kingdom at the University Press, Cambridge

Typeset in 11 on 12.5 point Baskerville [CE]

A catalogue record for this book is available from the British Library

Library of Congress cataloguing in publication data
Ford, Jennifer
Coleridge on dreaming: Romanticism, dreams, and the medical imagination / Jennifer Ford.
p.   cm. – (Cambridge studies in Romanticism: 26)
Includes bibliographical indexes and index.
ISBN 0 521 58316 0 (hardback)
1. Coleridge, Samuel Taylor, 1772–1834 – Knowledge – Psychology.
2. Dreams in literature. 3. Poets, English – 19th century – Psychology.
4. Poetry – Psychological aspects. 5. Dreams – History – 18th century.
6. Dreams – History – 19th century. 7. Romanticism – England. 1. Title.   11. Series.
PR4487.D73F67   1998
821'.7 – dc21   96–5764   CIP

ISBN 0 521 58316 0 hardback

Contents

Acknowledgements

Special thanks to the Department of Manuscripts in the British Library, London, for permission to quote from Coleridge's unpublished notebooks and marginalia. Financial assistance to travel to London to work with Coleridge's unpublished materials would not have been possible without the Kathleen Margaret Karnaghan, F. A. Elgar and A. J. A. Waldock Scholarship, offered by the University of Sydney. The bulk of this work was written with the assistance of an Australian Postgraduate Research Award.

My thanks for critical comments from Will Christie, Judith Barbour, Peter Otto and Jonathan Wordsworth. Comments from Marilyn Butler and my two readers at Cambridge University Press have been particularly useful. Many friends humoured and helped me along the way in writing this work. Matthew Dillon and Lynda Garland provided assistance with Coleridge's Greek and Latin translations. My parents, Lance and Marie, Margaret (Peg) Butler, and Rachel Smith all helped with proofreading at various stages. Justine Larbalestier's invigorating friendship spawned numerous enlightening discussions on aspects of Coleridge's dreaming experiences, helping me to see many of his dreams in a new light. My deepest thanks are extended to Deirdre Coleman who was always enthusiastic about my ideas, insightful in her criticisms, and patient in commenting on the many drafts of each chapter. Very special and warmest thanks also to Timothy Clark, who provided valuable criticisms on draft chapters, and who has for many years been an unwavering source of inspiration and encouragement in my studies of Romanticism. Most of all, my gratitude and love to Lawrence Fan, who persevered with me throughout the seemingly endless stages of writing this work and whose friendship and support continue to be a source of inexhaustible strength.

Abbreviations

BL	*Biographia Literaria.* Ed. James Engell and W. Jackson Bate. 2 vols., 1983. Vol. 7 of *The Collected Works of Samuel Taylor Coleridge*, gen. ed. Kathleen Coburn. Bollingen Series LXVV. London and New York: Routledge & Kegan Paul, Princeton University Press, 1969– .
CKK	S.T. Coleridge, *Christabel; Kubla Khan, A Vision; The Pains of Sleep*, London, 1816. Woodstock Books Facsimile, Ed. Jonathan Wordsworth. Oxford and New York: Woodstock Books, 1991.
CL	*Collected Letters of Samuel Taylor Coleridge.* Ed. E. L. Griggs. 6 vols., Oxford and New York: Oxford University Press, 1956–71.
CM	*Marginalia.* Ed. George Whalley. 3 vols. published, 1980– . Vol. 12 of *The Collected Works of Samuel Taylor Coleridge.*
CN	*The Notebooks of Samuel Taylor Coleridge.* Ed. Kathleen Coburn. 4 vols. published, London and New York: Routledge & Kegan Paul, 1957– .
Coleridge's Library	Ralph J. Coffman, *Coleridge's Library. A Bibliography of Books Owned or Read by Samuel Taylor Coleridge*, Boston: G.K. Hall & Co., 1987.
Confessions	Thomas De Quincey, *Confessions of an English Opium-Eater and Other Writings.* Ed. Grevel Lindop. Oxford University Press, 1989.
F	*The Friend.* Ed. Barbara Rooke. 2 vols., 1969. Vol. 4 of *The Collected Works of Samuel Taylor Coleridge.*

L	*Logic.* Ed. J. R. de J. Jackson, 1981. Vol. 13 of *The Collected Works of Samuel Taylor Coleridge.*
LB	*Lyrical Ballads.* Ed. R. L. Brett and A. R. Jones. 2nd edn., London and New York: Routledge, 1991.
Lectures	*Lectures on Literature 1808–1819.* Ed. R. A. Foakes. 2 vols., 1987. Vol. 5 of *The Collected Works of Samuel Taylor Coleridge.*
Lectures 1795	*Lectures 1795, on Politics and Religion.* Ed. Lewis Patton and Peter Mann, 1971. Vol. 1 of *The Collected Works of Samuel Taylor Coleridge.*
LR	*The Literary Remains of Samuel Taylor Coleridge.* Ed. H. N. Coleridge. 4 vols., London 1836.
LS	*Lay Sermons* [being *The Statesman's Manual* and *A Lay Sermon*]. Ed. R. J. White, 1972. Vol. 6 of *The Collected Works of Samuel Taylor Coleridge.*
N	MS Notebook, held in the British Library.
Notes	S. T. Coleridge, *Notes, Theological, Political and Miscellaneous.* Ed. Derwent Coleridge, London, 1853.
Omniana	Robert Southey and S.T. Coleridge, *Omniana; or Horae Otiosiores.* Ed. Robert Gittings. Fontwell, Sussex: Centaur Press, 1969.
PLect	*The Philosophical Lectures of Samuel Taylor Coleridge.* Ed. Kathleen Coburn. London: Pilot Press, 1949.
PW	*The Complete Poetical Works of Samuel Taylor Coleridge.* Ed. E. H. Coleridge. 2 vols., Oxford: Clarendon Press, 1912.
Remorse	S.T. Coleridge, *Remorse. A Tragedy, in Five Acts*, 2nd edn, London, 1813. Woodstock Books Facsimile, ed. Jonathan Wordsworth. Oxford and New York: Woodstock Books, 1989.
SWF	*Shorter Works and Fragments.* Ed. H. J. Jackson and J. R. de J. Jackson. 2 vols., 1995. Vol. 11 of *The Collected Works of Samuel Taylor Coleridge.*
TT	*Table Talk.* Ed. Carl Woodring. 2 vols., 1990. Vol. 14 of *The Collected Works of Samuel Taylor Coleridge.*

W   *The Watchman.* Ed. Lewis Patton, 1970. Vol. 2 of
               The Collected Works of Samuel Taylor Coleridge.

NOTE ON PRIMARY MATERIALS

Manuscript materials consulted in this book are located at the British Library; call numbers are given in every instance, as several collections were consulted. All manuscript materials are quoted with the kind permission of the Department of Manuscripts, British Library, London.

EDITORIAL SYMBOLS USED IN MANUSCRIPT AND PUBLISHED NOTEBOOKS

\<word\>	A later insertion by Coleridge
[?word]	An uncertain reading
[?wood/word]	Possible alternative readings
~~word~~	Coleridge's correction
[word]	A word editorially supplied
[. . .]	An illegible word

Introduction

> I have long wished to devote an entire work to the Subject of
> Dreams, Visions, Ghosts, Witchcraft, &c. in which I might first
> give, and then endeavour to explain the most interesting and
> best attested fact of each, which has come within my knowl-
> edge, either from books or from personal testimony.
>
> <div align="right">(<i>F</i> ɪɪ 117, ɪɪ 145)</div>

In spite of Coleridge's remarkable dedication to understanding
dreams and dreaming, there have been very few studies dealing with
his writings on dreams. There is no single collection of all of his
dream cogitations; his thoughts remain scattered throughout his
marginalia, notebooks, letters and formal writings. Nor has there
been a comprehensive or contextual study of these dream writings.
This book seeks to explore what Kathleen Coburn in 1979 rightly
called a 'subject in itself'; the 'richness and variety of Coleridge's
notes on sleep and dreaming'.[1] His insightful observations on the
'most interesting' features of dreams, visions and ghosts, gathered
together in the following pages, reveal the extent to which he utilised
his own dreaming experiences as well as those he encountered
through his wide reading. My emphasis throughout is on discovering
what Coleridge's contemporaries wrote and thought about dreams
and dreaming, and the ways in which his own experiences often
challenged these contemporary theories. I particularly focus on
Coleridge's exploration of dreams and dreaming states in his notebooks, because these have not yet been systematically studied, and
because they yield the richest, the most surprising and most
comprehensive discussion of dreams in his writings.

Certainly, there have been some scholarly commentaries on
Coleridge's thoughts on dreams. But such investigations have on the
whole been essentially biographical; they are, for example, set in the
context of his so-called opium addiction[2] or they have primarily

attempted to divine his character, or psychopathology, through a Freudian analysis of his dreams. Elisabeth Schneider's *Coleridge, Opium and Kubla Khan* (1953) identified two of his important eighteenth-century dream sources, Andrew Baxter's *Enquiry into the Nature of the Human Soul* and Erasmus Darwin's *Zoonomia*, but unfortunately she concluded that Coleridge was unoriginal in his approach to dreams.[3] Patricia Adair's *The Waking Dream* (1967) also refers to texts which the poet read on dreams, but her emphasis remains narrowly focussed.[4] Alethea Hayter's *Opium and the Romantic Imagination* (1968), though more substantially concerned with the dreams themselves, trivialises their importance by attributing all their features to opium.[5]

Norman Fruman, in *Coleridge, the Damaged Archangel* (1971), offers a detailed psychoanalytical reading of the poet's dreams which disparages his achievements and investigations in this field (Coleridge 'saw no *moral* connection between his dreams and waking life . . . he rigorously kept these two realms of his experience in separate compartments of the mind, thereby shutting off all possibility of achieving any revolutionary grasp of the meaning of dreams or any genuine understanding of himself').[6] Paul Magnuson, in his study, *Coleridge's Nightmare Poetry* (1974), discusses *The Rime of the Ancient Mariner*, 'Kubla Khan', *Christabel* and *Remorse* as poetic nightmares personal to Coleridge, rather than as part of a wider contemporary debate on dreaming.[7] David Miall's essay, 'The Meaning of Dreams: Coleridge's Ambivalence' (1982),[8] acknowledges the importance of placing Coleridge's thoughts on dreams 'in the context of his period', and uses his historical insights to challenge the judgements of Schneider and Fruman.[9] But while Miall touches upon the importance of Coleridge's contemporary writers on dreams, he does not explore sufficiently closely the detailed observations and wide scope of the poet's penetrating notes on dreams, or the extent to which his medical understanding of the topic challenged his notion of the poetic imagination.

In a general study of the Romantic period, J. R. Watson has argued that the Romantic poets were strongly interested in dreams because dreams recaptured a precious childhood; they revealed the Romantic imagination as 'sovereign, untrammelled and unquestioned'.[10] Watson refers to the writings of some of Coleridge's contemporaries, but denies himself genuine historical insight by adopting a post-Freudian and psychoanalytic point of view and in the process risks etherialising and infantilising the Romantic imagination.

In recognition of the value of exploring Coleridge's thoughts on dreams and dreaming in the historical context of the late eighteenth and early nineteenth centuries, both the intellectual context of contemporary medicine and the close relevance of that medicine to an understanding of concepts of the imagination are key issues of my study. This book explores the fascinating ways in which Coleridge draws on and contributes to some of the major scientific, medical and philosophical issues of the eighteenth and early nineteenth centuries. In pursuing the topic over four decades of great significance in the history of science and medicine, he read widely and deeply across a staggering range of works; and he was often engaged with various theories and topical controversies which were directly relevant to his enquiries into dreams and dreaming. Although his concept of the imagination is frequently discussed in relation to a poetic sphere, it is clear from his engagement with a variety of medical and scientific works that the imagination for Coleridge is also medical, physical. His own diseased body figured predominantly in both his experience and his understanding of dreams, and is a constant presence throughout the bulk of his dream writings. He clearly acknowledged the close connections and associations between dreaming and the poetic, imaginative creativity and genius. But this ethereal, spiritual, idealistic concept of the imagination was not the only construction of it that he acknowledged. In adopting a fundamentally physiological doctrine of the source and production of dreams, Coleridge was also able to explore the physiological, medical nature of the imagination.[11] This uniquely physiological approach to dreams and the imagination is certainly, as Coleridge himself acknowledged, one of the 'most interesting' features of his projected enquiry into the subject of dreams and dreaming.

Throughout the Romantic period, many poets, prominent scientists and philosophers were intrigued by dreams and dreaming processes. Sir Humphry Davy, a close life-long friend of Coleridge's, kept a dream journal. Although he had a fervent interest in the subject and intended to write a major work on dreams as well as a short novel, 'The Dreams of a Solitary', neither project was ever completed.[12] Bristol physician Thomas Beddoes had a keen interest in dreams, giving serious discussion to the topic in his *Hygeia* (1802–3), and assisting Coleridge in treating certain cases of extreme nightly disturbances and reverie (*CL* I 257). Robert Southey kept records of his dreams, detailing a series of disturbing and often amusing ones in a 'dream-book'.[13] He recorded his dreams throughout 1807 and 1808, then lost his dream-book until 1818, when he again resumed the task. Unlike Coleridge, Southey viewed his dreams as curiosities, taking more interest in recording than in analysing them. Thomas De Quincey claimed that he penned his *Confessions of an English Opium-Eater* more to reveal the mysteries and potential grandeur of dreams than to outline the dangers and pleasures of opium (*Confessions* 87).

Percy Bysshe Shelley began to write an essay on dreaming, but was allegedly forced to stop because he was 'overcome by thrilling horror'.[14] The poet's general efforts to understand processes of mind and dreams are evidenced in his poems: many contain elaborate dream sequences and visionary moments (notably *Alastor*, and *Prometheus Unbound*). Leigh Hunt, William Hazlitt and George Crabbe also joined in speculation as to the origin and meaning of dreams.[15] John Keats displayed his interest in dreams and sleeping states in poems such as *Endymion* and *Sleep and Poetry*. When he met Coleridge in 1819, he recorded that they talked about many things, including different types of dreams, nightmares and nightingales.[16] Recognition of Coleridge's understanding and experience of dreams is also suggested by Joseph Blanco White's dedication of a poem on dreams and night visions to him.[17]

The eminent scholar of dream history, Ludwig Binswanger, has suggested that there have been three great periods of heightened interest in and debate surrounding dreams: the classical Greek era, the Romantic era, and the era marked by the publication of Freud's *Interpretation of Dreams*.[18] Coleridge was perceived by many of his contemporaries to be an embodiment of this rekindled interest and fascination with dreams and processes of mind. To many of the second generation of Romantic poets, Coleridge was 'a good-natured wizard, very fond of earth, but able to conjure his aetherialities about him in the twinkling of an eye'.[19] He was the man who wrote 'Kubla Khan', 'The Pains of Sleep' and *Christabel*. The Shelleys, Lord Byron and John William Polidori read aloud from the poems of the as yet unpublished *Christabel* volume as they wrote and discussed ghost stories and recent medical and science discoveries in Geneva.[20] Coleridge was a man Thomas De Quincey described as a poet, a philosopher, an opium-eater, a prolific dreamer: a man whose poetry was 'shrouded in mystery – supernatural – like the "ancient Mariner" – *awfully* sublime'.[21] Leigh Hunt remarked that Coleridge's body was 'very metaphysical and very corporeal'; his countenance was 'boy-like', which Hunt considered 'very becoming to one who dreams as he did when he was a child'.[22]

Dreams and dreaming were topics which attracted intense scrutiny and endless conversational exchange; the subject was a frequent topic at dinner parties. At one such gathering in 1812, Coleridge lectured guests 'for some time' on the reasons why distressing circumstances always seem doubly afflicting at night, when the body is in a horizontal position. He told his listeners that 'the effect originated in the brain, to which the blood circulated with greater force and rapidity than when the body was perpendicular'.[23] Years later, in a lecture of 1818, he noted how the 'mind is never perhaps wholly uninformed of the circumstantia in Sleep – by means of the feeling, the temperature / &c. – People will awake by removing Lights' (*Lectures* II 207). The singling-out of the physical and physiological, characteristic of Coleridge's thinking on dreams, adds a complex dimension to his thoughts on dreaming. Dreams for him were very physical, bodily experiences, and at times pathological – even though he also used them to symbolise the powers of the poetic imagination. The imagination was not, then, merely the evoker of sublime dream visions, as noted by Charles Lamb and many others:[24] in essence, as this book will reveal, the Coleridgean imagination also partook of a corporeal, physiological and often diseased existence. In the earliest of his notebook dream writings, Coleridge presents his dreams as intimately connected with his (diseased) bodily processes.

The most familiar concept of the Coleridgean imagination is one which is spiritual, poetic, idealist. Read with sections from *Biographia Literaria*, Coleridge's notions of the imagination have been chiefly thought to be expounded through a handful of poems, including *The Rime of the Ancient Mariner*, *Christabel*, 'Kubla Khan' and the conversation poems. This imagination unites reason with sense and understanding; it achieves a 'heightened awareness', a 'creative insight into truth'.[25] It is an idealist, transcendent imagination, firmly located in the theoretical, the intangible.[26] However, what clearly unfolds throughout this book is that the predominance of the corporeal in Coleridge's dreams has significant implications for our understanding of the imagination. It is through a contextual study of an astonishing array of specialised materials in the notebooks and marginalia that the truly complex nature of the imagination emerges. Coleridge's understanding of it was deeply influenced by contemporary medical debates throughout the last decades of the eighteenth century and the first decades of the nineteenth. These debates centred on discoveries of new natural forces; on medical experiments which revealed that some bodily processes continue after life is apparently extinguished; on processes of body and mind and the role of voluntary and involuntary components of both body and mind processes. Impassioned debates took place between medical men such as John Brown and William Cullen in the 1790s and John Abernethy and William Lawrence from 1814 to 1820 on the nature of life, physiology and anatomy; and there was increasing speculation regarding the role of nerves, spirits and fibres within the human body.[27]

Coleridge's profound intellectual affinities from the early 1790s are with medicine and the organicist life sciences for which the body and the senses, and their relatedness to the mind, were matters of central concern and spirited debate. He read many works which clearly demonstrated the imagination in a medical capacity, capable of both curing and causing disease. This medical notion of the imagination was hotly debated throughout the last decades of the eighteenth century and particularly in the decade leading up to the publication of Wordsworth's and Coleridge's *Lyrical Ballads*. As I explore in greater detail in later chapters, what is particularly fascinating throughout the later part of the eighteenth century is that both poets *and* medical writers entered the debate concerning the nature of the imagination. On this score there was no clear distinction between theorists and practitioners of medicine and those of poetry. A medical man might also be a poet, and vice versa, and topics that engaged medical men were equally interesting to poets: Mark Akenside, Tobias Smollett, Oliver Goldsmith, Erasmus Darwin and Thomas Beddoes were all prominent men of letters who were also medical practitioners by training.[28] What emerges from this book is that by looking at the historical contexts of Coleridge's thinking about his dreams, about the body, and in particular his preoccupations with his own disease and pain, all his work, including his literary work, can be seen in a new perspective.

It is in his private notebooks that he most explicitly and frequently explores dreams and dreaming states. Many notebook entries are characterised by ellipses, a sense of urgency, a sceptical and ironic playfulness, or a note of personal despair. They are often couched in a rhetoric of uncertainty, evasion, self-contradiction and self-justification. Perhaps it is because of the complexity and unusually private, raw nature of Coleridge's many notebooks that so few studies have been primarily concerned with them. Nevertheless, they constitute a rich, diverse and unique resource of his many interests: the notebooks are the place where he queries, argues, jokes, despairs and partially resolves concerns about his dreams. The specialised notebook form proved the best suited for his exploratory design; in his notebooks he arrives at his complex and remarkable understanding of the physical and medical nature of dreams, dreaming and the imagination.

Because Coleridge's dream writings are exploratory and meditative, they often raise many more questions than they answer. For this reason, I do not argue that Coleridge had a cogent *theory* of dreams. The experience of his dreams is quintessentially private, impervious to outside theories. To write, record and discuss dreams is to remain captive within their internal, uncertain frameworks, with all the ambiguous things they present and re-present. This is a problem that Coleridge faced as he attempted to analyse and record his own dreams with an objectivity that could never escape their purely subjective nature.[29]

Coleridge's opinions on the nature of dreaming changed and shifted in emphasis many times over the course of his lifetime as he attempted to understand dreams as a totality rather than as isolated instances. His vicissitudes render a chronological, progressive study of his thoughts on dreaming problematic. He never claimed he had stumbled upon the one true theory which would explain his dreams or dreaming in general. On the contrary, he was often frustrated by the continual perplexity of his dreams; he struggled with their mysteries, but never claimed that he had unriddled them. At times, it is as though he was too painfully aware of the complexity of dreams, the intricately internal nature of dreaming, the plethora of possible explanations, and his own limitations as an interpreter or theoriser:

O vanity! I have but a few hours back announced myself to my friend, as the author of a SYSTEM of Philosophy on Nature, History, Reason, Revelation; on the Eternal, and on the Generations of the Heaven and the Earth, and I am unable to solve the problem of my own Dreams! After many years' watchful notice of the phaenomena of the somnial state, and an elaborate classification of its *characteristic* distinctions, I remain incapable of explaining any one Figure of all the numberless Personages of this Shadowy world. (*CL* VI 715)

This letter was written in November 1827, after Coleridge had one of his 'terrific' and 'fantastic' dreams, an experience so vivid and unsettling that he exclaimed that he 'would have required tenfold the imagination of a Dante to have constructed it in the waking state'. Yet, as this book aims to show, the deeply problematic nature of the material and the irresolvable dilemmas it afforded him did not prevent him from studying the 'shadowy world' as few others have done. Many of Coleridge's 'characteristic distinctions' on the subject of dreams are for the first time here critically discussed, including the pivotal role that his body played in dreaming: the body as a cause of dreams, as a feature of the language in which dreams were expressed, and as an undeniably real part of the distressing nightmares he so frequently endured.

The following chapters explore some of the 'most interesting' (*F* II 117) features of Coleridge's explorations of dreams and dreaming. In chapter 2, his observation that dreams occur within their own unique space, and that time, distance and touch are altered in this dreaming space is discussed. Other chapters consider Coleridge's deliberations on the language of dreams and his investigations into the many differing types of dreams and dreaming experiences. His efforts to understand the origins of his dreams and the peculiar role his body and the imagination played in them are explored in the later chapters. And it is in these later chapters that the unique role of the imagination in his dream writings is revealed: the imagination is both poetic and medical and plays a crucial role in dreaming states. Debates concerning the medical powers of the poetic imagination throughout the latter half of the eighteenth century are contextualised within Coleridge's explorations of his dreams and reveal the extent to which the imagination belongs just as much to medical theory as to poetic theory. What follows is a portrait not only of how Coleridge interpreted his dreams according to contemporary theories, but also of the fascinating ways in which he attempted to construct for himself a distinctly personal account of the many still unresolved mysteries of the shadowy world of dreams and dreaming.

CHAPTER ONE

Dreaming in the eighteenth and nineteenth centuries

> Dreams in their development have breath,
> And tears, and tortures, and the touch of joy;
> They leave a weight upon our waking thoughts,
> They take a weight from off our waking toils,
> They do divide our being; they become
> A portion of ourselves as of time,
> And look like heralds of eternity;
> They pass like spirits of the past, – they speak
> Like Sibyls of the future: they have power –
> The tyranny of pleasure and of pain;
> They make us what we were not – what they will,
>   . . . What are they
> Creations of the mind?

This questioning opening to Byron's 'The Dream',[1] written in 1816, succinctly touches upon many of the fundamental and often contradictory opinions on the nature of dreams and dreaming during the Romantic period. In the late eighteenth and early nineteenth centuries, there was no consensus on the origin and meaning of dreams. Some argued that they were miraculous, potentially divine events. Many believed that dreams revealed the powers of the imagination and that dreaming was a form of poetic inspiration.[2] Others argued that they were entirely attributable to the dreamer's physical or psychological constitution. In seeking to formulate his own answers, Coleridge turned to the writings of antiquity as well as those of his contemporaries. From ancient writers he gleaned the notion that dreams have the potential for prophecy and can 'speak like Sibyls of the future'. In the works of some of his contemporaries he encountered the theory that dreams are caused by spirits taking possession of the dreamer for short periods during sleep. Other contemporary writers emphasised the ethical dimension of dreams, claiming that they could impart moral lessons, while others

9

maintained that dreams derived from the digestive process. Contemporary writers he consulted included Andrew Baxter, Erasmus Darwin, David Hartley, and men he labelled 'Scotch Metapothecaries': Dugald Stewart, Thomas Reid, Adam Smith and Dr John Brown (*CN* IV 5360 and n; see also *CL* II 767–8). He also found in contemporary medical texts, works of physiology, philosophical treatises, mystic and magical writings enduring topics which touched upon his broad interest in dreams: the nature of pain, the relations between mind and body in dreaming states, and the role of psychological and intellectual processes, including the imagination, in causing and curing diseases. These ideas were all vigorously discussed throughout his lifetime, but particularly during the 1790s.

Some of Coleridge's earliest sources were Aristotle, Plato, Cicero and Galen, and the influential interpreter of dreams, Artemidorus. Two broad approaches in the classical world still had credibility in the eighteenth century.[3] The first was supernatural, sometimes termed irrationalistic:[4] dreams were thought to be messages from gods; they could take the form of visions or oracles; and their importance was evidenced by the intrinsic role of incubation and ritual. The second major understanding was a rationalistic one, in which dreams were seen as natural phenomena, the result of the dreamer's physical and physiological processes.[5]

In Homer's *Odyssey*, dreams are given to humans via two dreaming gates. In describing her dream, Penelope tells Odysseus that dreams may originate from either a gate of ivory or a gate of horn:

dreams verily are baffling and unclear of meaning, and in no wise do they find fulfilment in all things for men. For two are the gates of shadowy dreams, and one is fashioned of horn and one of ivory. Those dreams that pass through the gate of sawn ivory deceive men, bringing words that find no fulfilment. But those that come forth through the gate of polished horn bring true issues to pass, when any mortal sees them.[6]

This powerful and enduring schema of two dreaming gates could not easily resolve the question of which dreams were deceptive and which were potentially valuable, prophetic. As Homer's Penelope suggests, dreams were sometimes too awkward and confusing to be definitively categorised. The challenge was to differentiate between those that were significant and those that were not.[7]

Because the Greeks regarded dreams so highly, they and the

messages they contained were sought after. Soothsayers, augurs and dreamers were consequently held in high esteem.[8] The most striking example of the importance of dreaming is seen in the cult of incubation – the ritual invoking of dreams, usually for medical purposes, by sleeping in the temple of a particular god or hero. Although incubation was only one of many methods used by the Greeks to solicit dreams, it was the most widely practised and most highly regarded.[9]

The cult was practised for several centuries in Greece, but by the end of the fifth century AD, its popularity was beginning to decline.[10] One of the primary reasons for this was the emergence of a rational attitude to dreaming which replaced seeing the dream as a purely 'divine' phenomenon. Some of the changes that occurred in their general understanding of dreams can be traced to the gradual emergence of a distinction between the theory of dreams and their interpretation.[11] Oneirocriticism, the art of interpreting the symbolism of dreams, was beginning to emerge. Medical men, including Hippocrates, argued that 'he who has learnt aright about the signs that come in sleep will find that they have an important influence upon all things'. For instance, Hippocrates wrote that when a dream contradicts the waking actions or thoughts of the dreamer, a 'disturbance in the body' was present. To dream of the sun, moon or stars as clear and bright indicated physical health; but if the celestial bodies appeared murky, Hippocrates recommended a diet and regime which would encourage the patient to perspire, thus relieving the body of its excess moisture.[12]

Galen, the second-century Roman physician, also believed that dreams could contain messages of healing and offered his own interpretations of dream symbols. For him, dreams were symptomatic of humoral imbalances in the body.[13] Only a skilled physician could interpret dreams: accordingly, skills of interpretation became increasingly valued.[14] For Hippocrates and Galen, food and digestive processes were also foregrounded as explanations for a particular type of dream.

Other writers such as Plato, Aristotle and Cicero (primarily in his *De Divinatione*) argued that dreams were not prophetic. Somewhat inconsistently, Plato sometimes argued that they were true evidence of prophecy or divine intervention in the lives of humans, but elsewhere he maintained that they were the reflections of the savage and terrible side of man's soul.[15] Aristotle argued that dreams were not god-sent but a natural phenomenon, residual movements of past sensations in the body. He explained sleep as the rising to the head of 'vapours' from digestive processes.[16] Dreams could be explained by their relation to the material world and to waking thoughts, and not as a result of prophetic messages from gods.

The growing interest in the classification and interpretation of dreams is seen in the enormous growth of dream-books in later Greek and early Roman societies. These dream-books have proved to be tremendously popular and are a striking illustration of the impact of the classical world's approach to dreams on the ways in which they have been interpreted over many centuries. Dream-books were manuals for interpreting dreams and offered standard interpretations for a variety of common dream symbols. They were also often published with various fortune-telling techniques. One of the most influential of ancient dream-books to survive into the eighteenth century was Artemidorus' *The Interpretation of Dreams*.[17] Coleridge probably knew of Artemidorus' work (*CN* III 4409), as it was translated into English many times, and between 1606 and 1740 no less than twenty-four editions appeared.[18] An extremely popular edition of 1644 also included essays on dreams by English writers.[19] The interpretations of dream symbols and events in all these editions tended to remain constant over many generations. Other dream-books included the equally popular *Dream Book of Daniel*, which appeared in English as early as 1542. Like so many other dream-books, *The Dream Book of Daniel* attempted to distinguish between divine, natural and diabolical dreams.[20] Interpretation tended to be straightforward: to dream of swimming in tempestuous waters was a sign of impending trouble, to dream of gold indicated the prospect of riches. On special occasions and anniversaries, dream-books were consulted and their advice strictly followed. For instance, the popular *Mother Bridget's Dream Book and Oracle of Fate*, a best-seller for many decades in the seventeenth century, offered the following advice for young women on Candlemas Eve:

On this night let three, five, seven, or nine young maidens assemble in a square chamber. Hang in each corner a bundle of sweet herbs . . . Then mix a cake of flour, olive-oil and white sugar . . . Afterwards it must be cut into equal pieces, each marking the piece as she cuts it with the initial of her name. It is then to be baked one hour before the fire, not a word being spoken the whole time . . . Each cake is then to be wrapped up in a sheet of paper, on which each maiden shall write the love part of Solomon's song. If she puts this under her pillow she will dream true. She will see her future husband and children, and will know besides whether her family will be poor or prosperous.[21]

The assumption that the dream will be 'true' and prophetic under-pinned many similar superstitions. The influence of such dream-books and the interpretations they offered were also utilised by Romantic poets: John Keats added exquisite touches of irony and scepticism to his account of 'The Eve of St Agnes' while still relying on the premise that the dream could be interpreted broadly as a prophetic agency. The strength of many similar superstitions rested heavily on the notion, derived from ancient civilisations, that dreams contained messages about the future.

This prophetic potential of dreams has been a dominant feature of many dream theories since ancient times and throughout the middle ages it continued to be debated.[22] A vast assortment of dream texts from the middle ages still survives, clearly revealing the diversity of approaches to dreams during this time: erudite works of theory, vernacular popularisations of theoretical material, suggestions for interpreting various dream symbols. Medieval poets also utilised dreams within long narrative pieces, and the extremely popular dream vision genre was commonly used with great effect.[23] The growing influence of Christianity added complexity and sometimes confusion to approaches to dreaming from the fourth century to the Renaissance.[24] The Bible often validated the use of dreams as predictive tools (the Old Testament stories of Joseph and Daniel, the appearance of God's angel to Joseph in the New Testament), but at times the Bible also lent its authority to a suspicious attitude towards dreaming. For instance, in Deuteronomy, dreams are strongly con-demned: 'Neither let there be found among you any one . . . that consulteth soothsayers, or observeth dreams and omens, neither let there be any wizard, Nor charmer, nor any one that consulteth pythonic spirits, or fortune-tellers, or that seeketh the truth from the dead. For the Lord abhorreth all these things.'[25] This tension between taking dreams seriously and disregarding them as irrelevant could not be resolved. They continued to be both scorned and desired and were often employed in a variety of literary forms to create tension or suspense, or to add a supernatural – sometimes even tragic – element to the narrative.[26]

The debate on the origin, interpretation and significance of dreams did not abate in the eighteenth century. Interpretation and understanding underwent consistent evolution, as the ideas of ancient writers were constantly compared with more recent theories. Modern explanations of dreams also nestled uneasily with persistent traditions of superstition and folklore.[27] Significantly, in the eighteenth and early nineteenth centuries there was a revival of interest in dreams and dreaming, as is indicated by the numbers of medical treatises written on the subject as well as by the numbers of poems and other literary works devoted to and often celebrating dreaming. Some authors steadfastly maintained a belief in the prophetic and divine nature of dreams.[28] Others argued that they were not to be 'considered as having any necessary connection with futurity' and that the only useful thing about them was that they might 'serve to exercise the faculties and improve the temper of the mind'.[29] Some saw dreams as powerful diagnostic tools in both physical and psychological disturbances, as undeniable proof of the immortality of the human soul,[30] while others perceived them to be nothing more than a different mode of thinking.[31] Specific dreams, such as the nightmare, or *incubus*, were classified in one of the earliest British treatises on nightmares as being caused by 'difficult respiration, a violent oppression of the breast, and a total privation of voluntary motion'.[32] The dream had progressed from a Hippocratic diagnostic tool to a disease in its own right.[33] The bewildering and enigmatic nature of dreams was no closer to being explained but, increasingly, what fascinated those who wrote on the subject was the *process* of dreaming.

One reason why dreaming and the process itself became such topical areas of discussion had to do with the perceived unsatisfactory mechanical and associationistic explanations of dreams offered by John Locke, David Hartley, George Berkeley and others. Interest in the forces and features of psychic life began to increase, and a concept of the 'unconscious' mind began to emerge.[34] Furthermore, the development of empiricism, primarily through the works of Kant and Hume, cast significant doubts on whether or not the five senses could ensure an accurate perception of the world outside the self, or indeed of the self.[35] A major component of this scepticism – in philosophical as well as medical circles – entailed various speculations into the nature and origins of dreams, and the general, broader question of the nature of fundamental life processes including sleeping, waking, digestion, disease. What is particularly interesting is the startling array of treatises and scholarly dissertations: discussions of dreams and many differing types of dreaming states were as likely to be found in medical texts as in philosophical ones. Throughout the eighteenth and early nineteenth centuries, many physicians of all calibres included a discussion of nightmares, dreams and visions in their treatises, regarding such phenomena as the domain of medicine.

Many contemporary medical works cited as a cause of bad dreams the eating of a heavy meal too close to bedtime. The physician William Buchan writes:

That light suppers cause sound sleep is true even to a proverb. Many persons, if they exceed the least at that meal, are sure to have uneasy nights: and, if they fall asleep, the load and oppression on their stomach and spirits occasion frightful dreams, broken and disturbed repose, the night-mare, &c. Were the same persons to go to bed with a light supper, or sit up till that meal was pretty well digested, they would enjoy sound sleep, and rise refreshed and cheerful.[36]

This explanation emphasises the role of the body's digestive processes as an influence on the images and feelings experienced during sleep. The remedy for nightmares and other manifestations of 'disturbed repose' is simple: a light supper must be eaten, so that its contents can be thoroughly digested before sleeping. Thomas Hobbes observed that dreams could be generated from sensations of appetite or aversion to pain, and that 'cold doth in the same manner generate fear in those that sleep, and causeth them to dream of ghosts, and to have phantasms of horror and danger'.[37] The physician Erasmus Darwin established the cause of dreams in the workings of the arterial and glandular systems, and in the internal senses of hunger, thirst and lust. Nightmares were caused by indigestion. All of these physiological systems 'are not only occasionally excited in our sleep, but their irritative motions are succeeded by their usual sensation, and make a part of the farrago of our dreams'.[38] The philosopher David Hartley argued that the body's position in dreams 'suggests such ideas, amongst those that have been lately impressed, as are most suitable to the various kinds and degrees of pleasant and painful vibrations excited in the stomach, brain, or some other part'.[39]

In all these texts, the emphasis is not on how the dream may be interpreted but rather on understanding the physiological and psychological processes of dreaming phenomena. Part of the reason for this intense medical interest can be explained by the scientific controversies of the later decades of the eighteenth century, particularly the medical and physiological controversies resulting from advancing anatomical studies.[40] Such controversies raised problematic questions as to the nature of physiological processes and the interaction between body and mind. Coleridge followed these controversies in the 1790s and continued to maintain a keen interest in the ways in which advances in anatomical and physiological studies could or could not account for his dreams and the physiological processes he observed in dreaming states.

Many years after Coleridge began recording his dreams in his notebooks, he declared that 'modern Hartleio-Locklean Metaphysics, with its Impressions, Ideas, and Sensations, and its Jack of all Trades, Association' could never hope to explain the complexities of dreams and the dreaming process (*CN* IV 5360; also *CL* VI 715). Although he had also earlier stated in a series of letters at the beginning of 1801 that he had 'overthrown the doctrine of Association, as taught by Hartley' (*CL* II 706), it was not until many years later that he could confidently write that he had also discarded associationistic doctrines of dreams.

In a notebook entry from 1826, Coleridge specifically voices his dissatisfaction with dream readings offered by 'Hartley, Condillac, Darwin' and the 'Scotch Metapothecaries' (*CN* IV 5360).[41] The problem with these 'Scotch Metapothecaries' was that they eliminated from the process of dreaming what was potentially personal and psychological, mysterious and worth while. They eliminated the potential to explore the perplexing physiologies of dreams and the ways in which dreaming mind and body are related. Dreams were not perceived by Locke and Hartley as divine phenomena, nor as windows into the psychological depths of the mind, nor as examples of its creative powers. In Locke's words, dreams were 'all made up of the waking man's ideas, though for the most part oddly put together'.[42]

The limitations of Locke's arguments, and others who thought like him, were particularly evident to Coleridge, as his interest lay in discovering the psychological, subjective processes of dreams and the complex links between subjective and physiological processes. Hartley dismissed dreams as 'nothing but the Imaginations, Fancies, or Reveries of a sleeping Man'.[43] They are caused by the ideas received by the brain from the previous day, or by the 'State of the

Body, particularly of the Stomach and Brain', or by the action of associative ideas. He discriminates between the effects of the imagination in reveries and its effects in dreams. Reverie differs from imagination only in that a person will be 'more attentive to his own Thoughts, and less disturbed by foreign Objects, more of his Ideas are deducible from Association, and fewer from new Impressions'. But in both cases, thoughts 'depend in part, upon the then State of Body or Mind . . . a pleasurable or painful State of the Stomach or Brain, Joy or Grief, will make all the Thoughts warp their own way'.[44] In Hartley's philosophy, the body is given equal weighting with what was more often than not a passive mind: 'the then State of Body *or* Mind' (my emphasis). What actually concurs or differs between the two is vague, and Hartley offers no insight into the dependence of a 'pleasurable or painful State of the Stomach or Brain' on various types of thoughts or dream contents. The relationship between the dreaming mind and the sleeping body, between psychological process and physical manifestation, is not considered. Nor is the role of the active intervention of the mind broached in Hartley's philosophy. His failure to account for the relationship between body and dreaming mind was one of the main reasons why in later years Coleridge came to reject such dream theories, labelling them 'the scant & ragged Breeches of the modern Hartleio-Lockean Metaphysics' (*CN* IV 5360).

Coleridge also included Etienne Bonnot de Condillac, David Hume, Thomas Reid, Adam Smith, Dr John Brown, James Mackintosh, Dugald Stewart and Erasmus Darwin in the grouping of 'Scotch Metapothecaries' whose theories failed to explain dreams. His objections to such a wide range of writers were based on both medical and philosophical concerns. In Dugald Stewart's *Elements of the Philosophy of the Human Soul* (1791), dreams are seen as the product of the imagination, which is the tendency in the 'human mind to associate or connect its thoughts together'.[45] The thoughts and scenes of dreams are the result of the 'general laws of association', slightly mediated by bodily sensations and the 'prevailing temper of the mind'.[46] The will, or volition, is suspended in sleep, the 'extravagance and inconsistency of our dreams' being 'sufficient proof' of this. Stewart concludes that the most striking feature of a dream is its ability to reveal the actions of association.[47] A similar theory of dreaming was offered by the respected and pioneering surgeon, John Hunter, who claimed that dreams are 'always independent of the

relative connexion between body and mind'. This 'perfect' indepen-
dence allows the mind to 'distinguish perfectly what is sensation and
what is only thought, without which all would be a dream'.[48]

With the mind's emphasis on association and the implied passivity
of its dreaming actions, it is no wonder that Coleridge continually
searched for explanations and studies of dreams which better suited
his own experiences and understanding. One of the most influential
dream texts for him was Andrew Baxter's *Enquiry into the Nature of the
Human Soul; Wherein the Immateriality of the Soul is Evinced From the
Principles of Reason and Philosophy*, published anonymously in 1733 and
in a two-volume second edition in 1737 with Baxter named as
author.[49] Coleridge had read Baxter's work by 1795 (*CN* 1 188 and
188n). Many years later, in 1827, whilst writing an account of an
annoying and 'almost' amusing dream in his notebook (N35, fo. 35v),
he was reminded of Baxter's work on dreams:

Bye the bye, I must get my Baxter . . . back, which I have never seen since
in my 24th year I walked with Southey on a desperate hot Summerday
from Bath to Bristol with a Goose, 2 Vol. of Baxter on the Immortality of
the Soul, and the Giblets, in my hand – I should not wonder if I found that
Andrew had thought more on the subject of Dreams than any other of our
Psychologists, Scotch or English. (N35, fo. 36)

Although Coleridge's edition of Baxter was lost around 1796 it is
apparent that many of Baxter's ideas became deeply infused into his
habitual modes of thinking and writing on the subject of dreams. The
arguments Baxter uses in his discussion are as fresh in Coleridge's
mind in 1827 as they were in 1795. What was so memorable about
Baxter's writings on dreams was his explanation of their origin: that
they are external to the soul and are caused by 'Beings' outside us.

According to Baxter, dreams are not the product of the mind, or
of the soul. Scenes and visions experienced in a dream are *offered to*
the soul by external spiritual beings who gain access to the dreamer's
sleeping consciousness. Because the body is resting, these spirits are
able to enter the soul with relative ease, and they have substantial, if
not complete, control over the senses.[50] Part of the mystery of
dreams has always been their novelty: how is it that one can dream
of things never before seen, or people never before encountered?
Baxter's concept of dream-spirits explains this. His syllogism is quite
simple: dreams presented to the soul during sleep are both strange
and new, sometimes disturbing and frightening. The soul can never

be without consciousness of acting or creating, neither can it willingly frighten itself. The dream visions must, therefore, originate from outside the soul: 'there must be living Beings existing separate from matter; . . . they act in that state; that they act upon the matter of our bodies, and prompt our sleeping visions'.[51]

Although Baxter does not directly acknowledge the implications of the causal presence of these external spirits, his theory implies that the dreamer must be distanced from any moral awareness or responsibility. In support of this externalisation theory, he continually asks how, and more importantly why, the soul would willingly terrify and delude itself with visions encountered in dreams. There must be, therefore, spirits which 'force' dreams upon the soul.[52] These living beings act upon our minds and bodies, and *prompt* our sleeping visions: this suggests that, to some extent at least, the visions are in some form already present in the mind.

These spiritual beings who bring visions to the sleeping soul must actually have possession of the body during sleep. Baxter writes that the 'Eastern philosophers' 'took it so much for granted that the transactions which are carried on with us in our sleep, were to be ascribed only to the efficiency of separate spirits, that they gained both *authority* and *probability* to their doctrine, by delivering it under the form of *vision* or *dream*, wherewith they were prompted by some friendly intelligence'.[53] Dreams can be ascribed as a divine visitation, a direct means of communicating with God, as argued by many ancient writers. Dreams were proof of the higher, spiritual side of human nature. But the visions in sleep, those sights and sounds which are forced upon the soul, also have a potentially dangerous aspect, for possession of the soul was, at the time of Baxter's treatise, one of several definitions of madness.[54] Madness and dreaming are seen as remarkably akin to each other, for the soul is exposed to very similar experiences in both states. Madness becomes a type of sleep, or delirium. Baxter claims that '*dreaming may degenerate into possession;* . . . the cause and nature of both is the same, differing only in degree: for *dreaming* is but *possession in sleep*, from which we are relieved again when we are awake'.[55]

Once these ideas of possession, degeneration and sleeping are linked, it is very easy to continue the associations until one appears to cause, or even is, the other. He notes the explicit links between madness and the nightmare. It was not a novel notion to see the nightmare in this way. Baxter calls the nightmare the *'Incubus'*, a disease accompanied with 'frightful, ghostly apparitions, which are then obtruded on the imagination; so that the dreamer fancies that the distemper itself proceeds from *their* pressing him down with a weight like to stifle him' (his emphasis).[56]

Baxter underpins his classification of the incubus as antithetical to normal dreams by referring the reader to an entry in *Chambers' Cyclopedia*, a common general reference in the eighteenth century.[57] The entry in Chambers to which he refers suggests that sleeping in general and dreams in particular are analogous to diseases, and should be treated as a type of disease. One of the most striking features of Chambers' description is the physicality of the nightmare experience, the sense of breathlessness and suffocation, such that the nightmare is:

a disease, by the English called the *night mare*, and the Latin, *incubus*: chiefly affecting persons asleep, when laid on their back, and having the stomach loaded with food of difficult digestion. . . . The disease does not arise, as was anciently imagined, from gross vapours filling the ventricles of the brain: but chiefly from too great repletion of the stomach, which hinders the motion of the diaphragm, and of consequence, the dilation of the breast necessary for respiration. . . . The pressure of the cerebrum on the cerebellum, and that of the full stomach on the descending trunk of the aorta, seem also to be concerned in this order: for neither of these can happen without affecting the nerves that pass to the muscles of respiration. Without supposing one or both of these, it will be hard to assign a reason, why persons should be rather affected when laid on the back, than in any other posture.

. . . they are but rarely affected with this disorder who use a laudable diet, and sup sparingly: lying on the side, with the head pretty high, generally prevents it. The Arabs call it, the *nocturnal epilepsy*, because, when habitual, it usually generates into the epilepsy, being the usual forerunner thereof, especially in young people. – In the old, it frequently terminates in an apoplexy. . . . Menjoitius accounts for its being most usual in boys, from their being too voracious, and eating more than they can digest. Aurelianus assures us, it has killed several; adding from Symmachus, that there was a contagious, or epidemic *ephialtes* at Rome, which over-ran numbers, like a plague.

Baxter's allusion to this entry is of interest in itself, for Chambers suggestively and provocatively links possession, dreaming, disease and physiology: the incubus becomes an epidemic, 'like a plague'. The nightmare is seen as a phenomenon which takes control over the dreamer's body.

This notion of dreams as possessing the dreamer provides a rich source of anxiety and thoughtful deliberation for Coleridge and many others who ventured into the often hostile territory of the dream. Dreams were involuntary events and could not be controlled: often the dream itself was perceived as the controlling force. Ronald Thomas has recently commented upon this notion of possession, noting that for many Romantic writers, accounts of dreams and dreaming characteristically assume the shape of a possession: Percy Bysshe Shelley refers to enchantment by the 'fierce fiend of a distempered dream', and in Byron's poem 'The Dream' the poet cannot deny the 'power' of dreams to make 'us what we were not'.[58] George Crabbe, afflicted with frequent terrifying dreams, turned to a notion of alien possession to account for them, and specifically refers to the spirits who possess him as 'Baxter's sprites'.[59] Thomas De Quincey's battle with his dreams in his *Confessions* also reveals the underlying assumption that the dream can possess the dreamer: he asserts on more than one occasion that he has *triumphed* over his dreams.[60] The tendency to perceive dreams as caused by external spirits, and therefore able to possess the dreamer, is perfectly illustrated on a number of levels in Wordsworth's dream of the Arab in *The Prelude*. The source of the dream is generally acknowledged to have been provided by Coleridge, who in turn drew from Descartes' account of a dream he recorded in the now lost *Olympia* manuscript.[61] What is intriguing is that although suggested by Coleridge, in later versions of the poem Wordsworth claims the dream is his own, rather than that of a friend. By doing this, Wordsworth seeks to claim the dream for himself rather than have it claim and possess him. He is not entirely successful in this endeavour: for in both the 1805 and 1850 versions of *The Prelude* sleep is described as seizing the dreamer, irrespective of whether the dreamer is Wordsworth's friend, or Wordsworth himself. In the 1805 version, Wordsworth claims it is his friend who was 'seized' by sleep and then 'passed into a dream'. In the 1850 version, he attempts to claim the dream as his own, but is still forced to admit that 'Sleep seized me, and I passed into a dream.'[62] The power of this belief in possession was as potentially frightening as it was undeniable.

Baxter's ideas on the subject remained well known for over one hundred years, but they had a mixed reputation amongst his contemporaries.[63] The strongest indication of the awareness of his ideas is evident in one of the most frequently consulted texts on dreams during Coleridge's lifetime: the *Encyclopedia Britannica*.[64] The *Britannica* authors define dreams as 'all those thoughts which people feel passing through their minds and those imaginary transactions in which they often fancy themselves engaged, when in the state of sleep'.[65] Nine known 'facts' of dreaming are mentioned, but these characteristic 'facts' do not provide reasons for the existence of dreams. Instead, the authors refer to four major writers on dreams, one of whom is Andrew Baxter.[66] However, after devoting consider-able discussion to Baxter's ideas, the editors of the *Encyclopedia* reject his 'ingenious' endeavour to explain dreams as the 'agency of some spiritual beings, who either amuse or employ themselves seriously in engaging mankind in all those imaginary transactions with which they are employed in dreaming'. Baxter's view is 'implausible' and 'entirely beyond the limits' of knowledge. The only conclusion the editors can reach is that:

dreams are affected by the state of our health, by the manner in which we have passed the preceding day, by our general habits of life, by the hopes which we most fondly indulge, and the fears which prevail most over our fortitude when we are awake. From recollecting our dreams, therefore, we may learn to correct many improprieties in our conduct.[67]

What has changed, subtly but definitely, in the *Britannica*'s definition of dreams is to be observed in many other writings around this time: dreams became the domain of the psychological and the subjective. A moral dimension is also added: from dreams, we may 'learn to correct many improprieties in our conduct'. Vanished is the notion of divine intervention: the editors of the above extract unhesitatingly perceive dreams to be fond indulgences of hopes, or left-over anxieties of the preceding day.

Another influential writer with whom Coleridge disagreed and whom he described as unable to offer a solution to the 'mysterious Problem' of dreams was Erasmus Darwin (*CN* IV 5360). In Darwin's works he found an intriguing combination of exciting, new physio-logical theory and investigations into dreaming and sleeping states. Although Coleridge came to classify Darwin's *Zoonomia, or the Laws of Organic Life* (1794–6) and *The Botanic Garden* (fourth edition, 1799) as examples of inadequate dream theorising, these works nonetheless contain many examples of popular eighteenth-century dream psy-chology and physiology. Coleridge would have been familiar with many of the features of Darwin's discussion, on medical and literary and dream matters.[68] Initially an admirer of Darwin's work, he quickly found inadequacies and contradictions in the scientist's philosophy. But while his philosophy may have been contemptible to Coleridge, *The Botanic Garden* and *Zoonomia* were key texts for Coleridge on the nature and causes of dreaming.[69]

Coleridge claimed he met Darwin in 1796 and that they had, within hours of meeting, discussed philosophy, art and religion (*CL* 1 177). It is highly probable that the subject of dreams and sleeping arose in their conversations, especially as Coleridge had already read *Zoonomia* and *The Botanic Garden*.[70] In his *Early Years and Late Reflections*, Clement Carlyon devotes a lengthy section to dreams, and the conversations he had with Coleridge and others on the subject. Carlyon suggests that the reader who 'wishes to enter philosophically upon this subject, will find a great deal of valuable information in the Zoonomia of Darwin'.[71] The ideas expressed in Darwin's works were undoubtedly well known to Coleridge and his circle, particularly during the years Coleridge was at Bristol.

The Botanic Garden and *Zoonomia* both express very similar ideas on the nature of sleeping and dreaming. Two of the main features of their presentation of the subject are the absence of surprise in dreams and the comparison of the dreaming experience with that of the theatre. The issue of lack of surprise is raised in the first Interlude of *The Botanic Garden*:

we are perfectly deceived in our dreams: and that even in our waking reveries, we are so much absorbed in the contemplation of what passes in our imaginations, that for a while we do not attend to the lapse of time or to our own locality; and thus suffer a similar kind of deception, as in our dreams. That is, we believe things present before our eyes, which are not so.[72]

The introspective self-absorption of the mind during the dream or reverie enables the mind to believe that what it sees and experiences is actually real. The imagination becomes a world unto itself, oblivious to the demands and conditions of the outside world: we do not 'attend to our own reality'. The world of the dreamer and the world outside are presented in sharp opposition. This absorbing introspection causes the dreamer to 'suffer'. Darwin's general approach relies heavily on the implication that because dreams are a delusion, they are consequently untrustworthy and should be disregarded. If, as he argues, the dreamer is deluded and deceived, the dream becomes something to be avoided, as it contains irrational elements; it represents something inherently to be mistrusted.

This notion of deception is one of the chief characteristics of dreams presented in *The Botanic Garden*, and Darwin's explanation of it gained immense popularity:

There are two circumstances which contribute to . . . complete deception in dreams. First, because in sleep the organs of sense are closed or inert, and hence the trains of ideas associated in our imaginations are never interrupted or disserved by the irritations of external objects, and cannot therefore be contrasted with our sensations. On this account, though we are affected with a variety of passions in our dreams, as anger, love, joy, yet we never experience surprise. – For surprise is only produced when any external irritations suddenly obtrude themselves, and dissever our passing trains of ideas.[73]

Darwin later emphasises that the organs of sense are only temporarily closed or inert, and that this closure can be instigated by a variety of causes. The images seen in the dream are, however, instigated purely by associative processes. The 'trains of ideas' act upon each other associatively, and the continuing yet diverging train of dream sensations is only 'dissevered' by an external irritation. This notion of dissevering the imagination from its self-created reverie is a welcome one: to dwell too long in 'complete deception' endangers the dreamer.

A second reason offered by Darwin as to why delusion is experienced during the dreams is that:

in sleep there is a total suspension of our voluntary power, both over the muscles of our bodies, and the ideas of our minds; for we neither walk about, nor reason in complete sleep. Hence, as the trains of our ideas are passing in our imaginations in dreams, we cannot compare them with our previous knowledge of things, as we do in our waking hours; for this is a voluntary exertion, and thus we cannot perceive their incongruity.[74]

These two causes of the mind's deception in dreams are the essential features of Darwin's approach. In *Zoonomia* he also claimed that in our dreams 'our power of volition is suspended, and the stimuli of external objects are excluded'.[75] Further commenting on this in his poem *The Botanic Garden*, he notes that the senses are never completely lost, never entirely 'dead': they are 'only precluded from the perception of external objects, by their external organs being rendered unfit to transmit to them the appulses of external bodies'.[76] The mind Darwin presents in this dialogue is a passive one: those pleasant 'trains of ideas' are said to 'pass' in the imagination. The ideas themselves are 'of' the mind, the preposition 'of' suggesting that the idea and the mind are somehow disparate entities. This lack of surprise, characteristic of dreams, was used by Darwin as an illustrative analogy of the problems of drama and theatrical experience, even of aesthetic experience in general.

The intimate connections between dreaming, literature, painting, and the loss of volition are well illustrated in the third canto of Darwin's 'The Loves of the Plants' in his *Botanic Garden*. As Laura flees from the troubled grove, she speaks in fury with 'words *unwill'd*, and wisdom not her own'. Her strange possession is likened to Henry Fuseli's painting:

> So on his NIGHTMARE through the evening fog
> Flits the squab Fiend o'er fen, and lake, and bog,
> Seeks some lover-wilder'd Maid with sleep oppress'd,
> Alights, and grinning sits upon her breast.
> – Such as of late amid the murky sky
> Was mark'd by FUSELI's poetic eye;
> Whose daring tints, with SHAKESPEAR's happiest grace,
> Gave to the airy phantom form and place. –
> Back o'er her pillow sits her blushing head,
> Her snow-white limbs hang helpless from the bed.   (lines 51–60)[77]

Darwin and Fuseli were friends, and Fuseli's engraving of 'The Nightmare' was included in the 1789 edition of 'The Loves of the Plants'.[78] The relationship between the two artists was a close one personally, and aesthetically. Laura's nightmare is laden with imagery from Fuseli's painting, but also with language from Darwin's enquiries into the nature of sleep:

> Shrieks of captur'd towns, and widows' tears,
> Pale lovers stretch'd upon their blood-stained biers,
> The headlong precipice that thwarts her flight,
> The trackless desert, the cold starless night,
> And stern-eye'd Murderer with his knife behind,
> In dread succession agonize her mind.
> O'er her fair limbs convulsive tremors fleet,
> Start in her hands, and struggle in her feet;
> In vain to scream with quivering lips she tries,
> And strains in palsy'd lids her tremulous eyes;
> In vain she *wills* to run, fly, swim, walk, creep;
> The WILL presides not in the bower of SLEEP!   (lines 63–74)

The secluded bower of sleep, earlier seen as a potentially threatening delusionary world, here becomes the pure embodiment of terror: the terror caused primarily by the fact that the 'WILL presides not in the bower of SLEEP!' In a footnote to Canto III of 'The Loves of the Plants', Darwin claims that 'Sleep consists in the abolition of all voluntary power, both over our muscular motions and our ideas', and that the nightmare, or incubus, is specifically due to 'a painful desire to exert the voluntary motions'. This loss of volition and the potential for terror render the experience of sleep and dreaming a subhuman one: Darwin prides himself on his model of man as one in which reason and volition are dominant.

Darwin's insistence on the terror of involuntary thoughts, the fear of possession by the dream, and the power of irritations to create and prevent dreams is deeply influenced and informed by debates surrounding physiological discoveries and theories in England, France and Germany in the later eighteenth century. Interest in dreams as illustrations of involuntary or suspended powers was correspondingly high in educated and medical circles as those debates flourished. The last decades of the century saw an exciting rise in interest in the life sciences, or what would now be termed theories of physiology and the physical sciences. Many scientists at this time were concerned with understanding living processes, the meaning of health and sickness, the relations of mind and body. Now discredited and often forgotten scientific fields of enquiry gained popularity and often notoriety: phrenology, mesmerism and physiognomy all emerged in mid-century and were, in differing ways, concerned with unravelling the mysteries of life processes. These scientific debates and discoveries had far-reaching impacts on other intellectual debates of the period – debates about the origin and meaning of dreams, contemporary notions regarding the nature of the imagination, concepts of creativity, taste, sensibility and genius. Enlightenment scholar and historian G. S. Rousseau has superbly demonstrated the common ground between the belief advanced by key physicians such as Edinburgh professors Robert Whytt and William Cullen in the centrality of the nervous system as the cross-point between physiology and psychology and the notions of sensibility championed by late-Enlightenment novelists and literary figures. Rousseau has also emphasised the ways in which concepts of the imagination towards the end of the eighteenth century drew from both medical and scientific thinking.[79]

This close connection between medical discovery and literary theorising was crucial in Coleridge's approach to his dreams and in his concept of a medical imagination. His interest in theories of life and life sciences can be traced back to his young adult life: to his days in Bristol during the 1790s, when he was debating the question with John Thelwall (*CL* I 294–5) and Thomas Beddoes, and when in Germany between March and June 1799 he attended Blumenbach's 'delightful' lectures on physiology and natural history (*CL* I 494). His interest continued well into the second decade of the nineteenth century and is evidenced in his essay, 'Theory of Life' (*SWF* I 482–3). His reading included the most influential writers on this new science from Britain, Germany and France: works by John Brown, John Hunter, Albrecht von Haller and Marie François Bichat – writers at the frontier of the new theories of physiology, anatomy, the relations between mind and body, and the nature of life itself. Many of these also wrote on dreams and dreaming. Coleridge's early readings in the science of life and his rejection of the mechanistic view expounded in many of the works he read contributed significantly to his fascinating explorations of dream and body, imagination and disease (*CN* I 388, *CN* IV 4825 and 4825n, for example). These works formed a rich background for him as he attempted to understand whether or not dreams were the creations of his own mind, the creations of supernatural, external spirits, or perhaps revelations of deeply complex physiological processes; and they provided him with numerous illustrations of the ways in which dreams could be treated and understood as diseases, and the imagination understood as a medical faculty: a psychological, intellectual faculty which could both cure and cause diseases.

In both Germany and Britain, debates concerning the nature of life had immense impact across many intellectual debates and fields of enquiry. Studies of psychological and physiological life processes were eagerly pursued, and dreams were studied as instances of both. Hermann Boerhaave (1668–1738), professor of medicine at Leiden University, was at the forefront of the new discoveries in physiology. He argued that the body was composed of a series of vessels through which vital bodily fluids ebbed and flowed. It was the movement of these fluids which caused disease: if they were obstructed, certain diseases arose. If the fluids stagnated, another type of disease was manifest. Albrecht von Haller (1708–77) critically developed Boerhaave's theories by further dividing animal organs and tissues according to their reactive properties; according to 'sensible' and 'irritable' parts. He discovered that nerves could respond to stimuli arising from muscular action through a force or property that he called 'sensibility'. These investigations into sensation and the sensibility of nerves were revolutionising physiology in the second half of the eighteenth century.[80] Haller's research led to a number of other enthusiastic physicians and scientists adopting his principles, including the Scottish physician John Brown (1735–88).

Brown had studied medicine at Edinburgh and was once a student of the celebrated physician William Cullen. His modifications of Cullen's teachings on physiology, which became known as the Brunonian system, were first expounded in Brown's *Elementa Medicinae* in 1780. It was subsequently translated by him into English and published with additional commentaries in 1787 and 1788. The central principle in this system is that of excitability. Excitability is a basic quality inherent in or given to all living matter. It is a capacity to perceive outside impressions and to be able to respond to them. Under normal physiological conditions, excitability decreases throughout the body from childhood to old age. The implications of this theory are profound: Brown argued that life is produced only when outside influences act upon excitability. External stimulants utilise excitability and the response to their actions is the combined product of both stimuli and excitability. Brown calls this a life force. Life is not, therefore, a spontaneous or independent phenomenon: it is only a response to external influences. It is not defined by the presence or absence of a soul or any spiritual matter. Life is constituted in and through physiological changes in the organs. External stimulants are constantly needed to maintain the body in order to avoid disease and death.[81] Excitability, located in the medullary portion of the nerves, had to be maintained in proportion to the stimuli acting on the system, or illness would ensue. Diseases should therefore be treated so as to adjust the stimuli and restore proper balance. Opium and alcohol were thought to be stimulants in Brown's system and were prescribed for those diseases which were characterised by a deficiency of stimulation, including some kinds of nightmares and dreams.[82] As one supporter argued, Brown's theory was brilliant in its effort to reduce 'the whole phaenomena of life . . . to one simple cause . . . excitability'.[83]

Brunonian theory highlighted the importance of the environment in shaping organic life and experience. The theory and its implications caused widespread acrimonious debate in medical, theological and political arenas: debate became so intense at one point that it was deemed necessary to pass a law which forbade duelling, and in Germany, debate almost turned into violent rioting.[84] But as well as being controversial, Brown's stress upon external powers as the active force governing life and bodily functions enjoyed a burst of popularity amongst other physiologists and physicians. Brunonian principles were applied across several other critical studies, including dreams and dreaming phenomena. Several prominent physicians adopted Brown's ideas, including the Bristol physician Thomas Beddoes. Beddoes published a long biographical Preface to the 1795 English translation of the *Elementa Medicinae*, in which he argued that Brown's achievement was to have solved the problem of life: 'avoiding all useless disquisition concerning the cause of *Vitality* [Brown] confines himself to the phaenomena'.[85]

Beddoes was amongst the first and was probably one of the most influential medical practitioners Coleridge befriended. He arrived in Bristol in 1793, in part because his sympathy for the French Revolution had made a professorship in chemistry at Oxford untenable.[86] Beddoes' political tendencies would have appealed to the young Coleridge at this time, and the two men met in Bristol in 1795.[87] Coleridge was soon reading many of Beddoes' books on science, philology and philosophy, including German philosophers such as Kant (*CN* I 389n).[88] Many works which Coleridge and Beddoes read contained discussion of questions of life and life processes. Brown had argued that life exists only as a response to external influences, and although Beddoes was clearly a supporter of the doctrine, Coleridge quickly became dissatisfied with this simplistic and deeply unsatisfying approach. If he was temporarily swayed by Brown's theories during the late 1790s, and took opium as a cure for various ailments or was prescribed it by Beddoes, he later spoke of the Brunonian system as a 'false theory', and by 1807 had repudiated its 'tyranny of the mechanic system in physiology' (*BL* I 163).[89]

These life-science debates were topics to which Coleridge frequently returned throughout his life (*SWF* I 481–557). The depth of his dissatisfaction with Brown's theory and the materialist implications of his arguments become clear when questions concerning dreams and dreaming are raised (*CN* IV 5360). Dreams could be explained as illustrations of involuntary excitability, certainly not as instances of divine intervention or of left-over thoughts from a tiring day. According to Coleridge, Brown and many others who subscribed to the excitability theory treated dreams and dreaming slightly and superficially, explaining the dreaming process merely as an illustration of external sensory processes. Even Beddoes, whose ideas on dreaming phenomena were well known to Coleridge, had argued that dreams were the result of excitement upon the nervous system during sleeping states.[90] Another prominent subscriber to materialist physiology, Albrecht von Haller, heavily based his theory about the origin of dreams and sleep on physiological principles, couching his explanation in terms of the sensitivity of organs and nerves to external events:

> dreams we judge to be rather referable to disease, or to some stimulating cause that interrupts the perfect rest of the sensorium. Hence we see, that intense cares of the mind, or the strong impression of some violent idea received in the memory, hard indigestible food, abounding, in its quantity, with any uneasy posture of the body, are the most usual causes that excite dreams.[91]

The entire human body is physiologically interlinked, even in sleep, and the actions of the digestive system are able to cause dreams. External sensations impinge upon the sleeping brain and it is these sensations which cause dreams as well as disease. In Haller's system, dreams are involuntary productions of an unstimulated nervous system. Restful sleep is sleep attained when no external sensations are received and consequently no dreams are experienced. Brown argued that sleep was the result of decreasing excitement upon the nervous system: sleep was the point where the 'degree of excitement, necessary to constitute the waking state, no longer exists'. Dreams were evidence that a small degree of excitement was reaching the nervous system.[92] Dugald Stewart also argued that the cure for waking dreams (reveries) was 'bleeding, purges, and low diet, when the epulse indicates undue excitement in the arterial system'. Too much excitement in the arterial system led to disturbing day-dreams and was a sign of impending disease.[93]

Theories of dreams as dependent on excitement or stimulation of the nervous system aroused intense interest in medical circles, and were discussed in terms of other general questions surrounding the nature of life processes. Coleridge's interest in the implications of new discoveries in physiology and the life sciences, encouraged by Beddoes during his Bristol years, complemented his interest in dreams and dreaming states. In discussions and through his reading, he must have considered that dreams could be seen as another illustration of the remarkable way in which the human body responds to stimulation or irritation. His interest in such issues remained long after his residency in Bristol. The question of the nature of life and its processes was again topical between 1814 and 1820, when physicians John Abernethy and William Lawrence had public and, at times, heated debates on the subject.[94] Not only was Coleridge aware of these debates, he consciously participated in them (*SWF* I 532).

His continuing interest in life theories, in the treatment of diseases and the nature of pain complemented his fascination with dreams. His reading in medical texts and his interest in new treatments for painful conditions were both academic and personal. He wrote to various doctors, asking for their advice: his suggestions about what form his own treatment might take revealed substantial knowledge (*CL* III 508–9; *CL* V 45–50; *CL* VI 721–3); and he often diagnosed friends and acquaintances (*CL* V 392). He was, for instance, keenly interested in the causes and potential cures for many kinds of hysteria, and was as informed of developments in the treatment of hysteria as he was in many other aspects of medicine. It was his interest and understanding of hysteria that once prompted him to refer to a particular bout of illness that Wordsworth suffered as an illustration of male hysteria, or hypochondriasis (*CN* I 1826).[95]

This general interest in medicine and science, coupled with frequent bouts of ill-health, ensured that Coleridge maintained throughout his lifetime an eager interest in many of the latest suggested cures for particular ailments. His friendship with Beddoes marked the beginning of a number of close and intellectually stimulating friendships with medical men. Nosologies which particularly attracted him often included those which advocated a role for the imagination or the power of involuntary thoughts: mesmerism and the theory of maternal impressions were prime illustrations of this, as I discuss in later chapters. Coleridge's intensive medical reading has been noted by other critics,[96] but it has not been hitherto linked with his investigations into dreams and dreaming. Futhermore, the implications of his medical knowledge on his poetry have not been fully explored. His medical knowledge embraced many of the accepted ideas of his day, but he also began to question and to experiment with his own bodily ailments and with the effects of certain treatments and drugs on his body and mind. Most obviously, opium provided an opportunity for experimentation, and was probably prescribed to Coleridge as a cure for the numerous rheumatic and circulatory complaints he laboured under from his early adulthood. Marginalia in a book from Thomas Poole's library at Nether Stowey reveals that he had also studied the effects of betel.[97] He was also a keen participant in experiments at the Pneumatic Institute with Humphry Davy.[98]

Many of the works Coleridge read certainly provided him with a distinctively physiological explanation for the origin of dreams, which were often treated as specific diseases. But in spite of recent medical and physiological discoveries, many ailments and diseases, including nightmares and other nightly disturbances, were often still approached and treated according to superstitious beliefs.[99] Disease was still often thought to be a divine punishment for an immoral action, or an immoral agency within a community, the result of maleficium (spells cast by witches) or of demonic possession.[100] Nightmares were often thought to be the result of a temporary demonic possession, and were sometimes believed to be a prelude to epilepsy, insanity or apoplexy.[101] Both dreams and diseases were mysterious and could be explained in terms of a 'spirit theory' such as that advocated by Baxter (*CN* IV 5360). This shared characteristic of dreams and disease – that they could be explained in terms of superstition or current medical science and that they both revealed the powers of the imagination – was one means by which Coleridge was able to perceive similarities between his dreams and his bodily infirmities.

CHAPTER TWO

Dramatic dreaming spaces

Coleridge often referred to his dreams as being like dramas, with their own characters, costumes, settings, and temporal and spatial conventions. The most essential quality likening dreams to drama was that both required the suspension of volition. From his earliest recorded thoughts on dreams, Coleridge considered the suspension of volition as one of the fundamental qualities of dreaming. Following from this, the illusory qualities inherent in watching a play are similar to the illusory qualities of a dream. He also often perceived his dreams as being performed on a stage – a space within which the actions and characters of the dream unfolded. He termed this theatrical dreaming space 'Somnial or Morphean Space' (*CN* IV 5360), and carefully recorded many of its features throughout his lifetime.

Both Andrew Baxter and Erasmus Darwin argued that in sleep the faculty of volition is suspended and therefore the many strange visions encountered in dreams are not considered surprising. Coleridge often remarked that when we are awake, the will is in control of all that is reasonable, creating the potential for the mind to be surprised by odd and unusual sights. The faculty for surprise exists in the waking state. In dreams, however, there is no sense of surprise, for all that happens is accepted without question (*CN* I 1250): the dreamer is bereft of a controlling sense of judgement, and no image or event is unlikely or surprising. This suspension of certain faculties requires the 'voluntary Lending of the Will' (*CL* IV 642). The question of the extent of the voluntary suspension of reason and volition is at the heart of Coleridge's analogy between the theories of drama and of dreaming.

In notes to *The Tempest*, Coleridge argues that a dreamer cannot take the dream for reality because the comparative powers of the will and volition are suspended, and no judgement 'either way' on the often bizarre occurrences within dreams is possible. The 'highest' example of the suspension of disbelief is found in dreaming states. For Coleridge, this analogy depends as much on the qualities and nature of sleep as it does upon the conventions of drama:

It is laxly said, that during Sleep we take our Dreams for Realities; but this is irreconcilable with the nature of Sleep, which consists in a suspension of the voluntary and therefore of the comparative power. The fact is, that we pass no judgement either way – we simply do *not* judge them to be real – in conseq. of which the Images act on our minds, as far as they act at all, by their own forces as images. Our state while we are dreaming differs from that in which we are in the perusal of a deeply interesting Novel *in the degree rather than in the Kind*, and from three causes: First, from the exclusion of all outward impressions on our senses the images in sleep become proportionally more vivid than they can be when the organs of sense are in their active state. Secondly, in sleep the sensations, and with these the Emotions & Passions which they counterfeit, are the causes of our Dream-images, while in our waking hours our emotions are the effects of the images presented to us. . . . Lastly, in sleep we pass at once by a sudden collapse into this suspension of Will and the Comparative power: whereas in an interesting Play, read or represented, we are brought up to this point, as far as it is requisite or desirable, gradually, by the Art of the Poet and the Actors; and with the consent and positive Aidance of our own will. We *chuse* to be deceived. . . . But this . . . depends on the degree of excitement in which the mind is supposed to be. (*Lectures* ii 266)

Coleridge's analogy between some states of dreaming and an 'interesting Play' has been noted by Elisabeth Schneider, who has also elaborated upon his use of Erasmus Darwin's *Zoonomia* and A. W. Schlegel's *Lectures on Dramatic Art and Literature* in the formulation of these ideas.[1] However, the close exploration of the implications of the drama/dream analogy which Coleridge embarks upon is not mentioned by Schneider. The notion of the mind choosing to be gradually deceived when reading or watching an interesting play is contrasted with the 'sudden collapse' of volition which characterises sleep. This is similar to Coleridge's concept of 'that willing suspension of disbelief for the moment, which constitutes poetic faith' (*BL* ii 6). There is a strong suggestion of control implied with a 'willing suspension of disbelief', that is simply not present in the 'sudden collapse' of the will in the sleeping state. This fundamental distinction between the extent of control the dreamer perceives himself as having and that of the spectator accounts for the unmitigated terror of the many nightmares Coleridge experienced.

In a letter to Daniel Stuart of May 1816 Coleridge commented further on this feature of dreams and theatrical experience: the true 'Theory of Stage Illusion' rests on the 'voluntary Lending of the Will' to the suspension of judgement (*CL* IV 642).[2] He argues that it is not 'strictly accurate' to state that 'we believe our dreams to be actual while we are dreaming' (*CL* IV 641). Rather, he suggests that we 'neither believe or disbelieve' the dream. In sleep, Coleridge argues, reason, will, fancy and the understanding are fundamentally altered. Optimal waking states enjoy full control of these faculties. Many years later, he still grappled with the consequences of the altered roles of reason, will and understanding in sleeping as opposed to waking states. In an unpublished notebook entry of December 1827, he adopts a more subjective position. His obvious confusion in this entry testifies to the potentially troubling, but not completely articulated, conclusion that the complete loss of the will in dreams indicates disturbances in the very concept of the self:

In our waking state the Will so far controls and influences the products of Fancy ([?the] more effectively and easily from the bedimming of them ~~and the only~~ the more vivid impressions thro' the Organs of Sense, both by effect of comparison or [?relatively] and *positively* by expenditure of Sensation & activity and consequent subtraction from the acts & products of the Fancy) ~~as~~ In our w. st., I say, the influence of the Will aided by the [. . .] influx thro' the Senses tends to Subjectivize the products of the Fancy, makes the Fancy [. . .] from a point nearer the Understanding, as shown by the partial substitution of Words for *Pictures*, – images, and [?this/ thus] diminishing their Objectivity softens their antithesis to the *Ich* in it. But in Dreams the Fancy shifts. (N36 fo. 7v)

Here, Coleridge's explanation is an uneasy combination of reliance upon the physical processes by which our senses receive knowledge of the world, and the desire to understand the subjective process which allows for the partial substitution of words for pictures in dreams. The fundamental difference between the influence of the will in waking states and that in dreaming states also has serious ramifications with regard to the perception of objects as subjective or objective. This, in turn, relates to Coleridge's careful distinctions concerning the many different levels of dreams, reverie, and consciousness (see also *Lectures* I 130). Poetry was an instance of a 'rationalized dream' (*CN* I 2086), which suggests that the creation of poetry requires the magnitude of loss of volition as experienced in dreams, with the crucial qualifier that there is still some reason present. This is a rationalising presence, which is not discernible in other states of dreaming. And it is the lack of that shaping will and reason in many dreams which creates a potential uneasiness, a disturbing shift in objectivity and subjectivity of the 'I' who dreams.

One of the most striking illustrations of Coleridge's use of the analogy between drama and his dreams is discernible in his state-ment that he often saw his dreams *as* dramas, rather than simply as being *like* dramas. In a notebook entry from April 1826, he termed the characters of his dreams 'Dramatis Personæ' (*CN* IV 5360). He noted how spontaneous their beings and actions were, and how 'detached' they were from the dreamer. This entry reveals his use of the dream/drama analogy in such a way as to highlight the visual quality of the characters in dreams: they were like characters in a play, with lives of their own and a theatrical space within which they moved.[3] The dreamer watches their performances as though they form part of a play: and the characters who perform seem not to breathe, nor are they conscious of breathing. This apparent lack of consciousness of breathing fascinated Coleridge. It was one of the most intriguing features of the dream characters: the dreamer 'never' supposes the 'Men & Women of the Dream to breathe' but neither does the dreamer 'suppose them *not* to breathe' because the 'thought is wholly *suspended*' and absent from the dreamer's consciousness (*CN* IV 5360).

Coleridge further develops his notion of dramatis personæ in a later unpublished notebook entry, written on 25 November 1827. In this entry he calls the characters in his dreams 'Personœ Sominis', or '*Dreamatis* Personæ' (N35, fo. 48v, his emphasis). The dramatis personæ of the April 1826 entry have become, more appropriately, dreamatis personæ: a subtle alteration which stresses the similarities between the figures in dreams and dramatic characters. In notebook entries after November 1827, Coleridge always refers to the figures in his dreams as dreamatis personæ. Although he did not formally coin the term until 1827, it is clear from his dream writings that the concept had been in his mind for many years. The 'dreamatis personæ' comprise not only the characters of people he knew and saw in his dreams (such as Dorothy Wordsworth, *CN* I 1250, *CN* III 3912; or Hartley, his son, *CN* I 1620), but people whom he did not personally know (Duns Scotus, *CN* I 1824, or Emanuel Swedenborg, *CN* IV 5360). Furthermore, these characters were fundamentally different from the 'vivid thoughts & half-images of poetic Day-dreaming' (*CN* IV 5360). The primary reason for this qualitative difference was that Coleridge firmly believed there to be distinct and special types of dreams, and that for each type there were general dreamatis personæ. For instance, in dreams of sleep, but not in dreams of poetic day-dreaming, the dreamatis personæ have their 'own center', and this renders them 'perfectly detached' from the dreamer (*CN* IV 5360, cf *CN* IV 4714).

This necessary detachment meant that one character who always emerged in his dreams was himself. It is necessary to differentiate between Coleridge the dream character, and Coleridge the man who experiences the dream and writes it down in a letter or in his notebooks. For this reason, I use the term 'dream-Coleridge' when discussing the character of Coleridge in a dream. The need to differentiate between the dream-Coleridge and the historical Cole-ridge is supported by the Notebook 35 entry quoted above: here he argues that dreamatis personæ are distinct characters within the dream because dreams invoke a split between the self as an object and the self as a subject (N35, fo. 48v). In dreams, conscience becomes the '*real*' antithesis of the 'I', and the dream and its characters oppose this conscience. The split between the 'I' who dreams and the 'I' in the dream is further occasioned by the motives and passions of the dreamer (N36, fo. 5v).

Coleridge's dreamatis personæ are both literal and figurative constructions. He meets, confronts, converses with and creates different characters in his dreams. When, after a frightening night-mare, he exclaims, 'Creatures of my dreams, you may make me feel you as if you were keeping behind me/but you cannot speak to me', he seems to be referring to the creatures he has dreamt about as well as the creatures he believes may have caused the dream in the first instance. Equally likely to appear as both figurative and literal constructions is the 'fiendish crowd' of 'The Pains of Sleep' (*CKK* 62). The dreamatis personæ include an aged Adam, who was taken for a 'Madman' and slaughtered by his own descendants (*CN* I 1698); a servant maid, a gardener and some 'Gentlemen' (*CN* II 2418); a cunning and mischievous 'Devil' who was faced with the task of performing astronomical mathematical sums without 'paper or slate' (*CN* II 2455); and a shipwrecked Robinson Crusoe (*CN* II 2489).

The perception of dreamatis personæ demands that the dream has a spatial dimension to it, within which the dream-stage is placed, and upon which the characters play. His earliest dream writings indicate his strong belief that dreams occupy a very specific, and very private, space within the mind. He calls it 'Somnial or Morphean Space' (*CN* IV 5360). When he describes a dream he does so in terms which involve a conceptualisation of it as both a physical and a psychological place within his mind. Once the dreaming experience is conceived in this way, a major ethical consideration ensues: if the mind is likened to a physical dreaming place, then the potential for the mind to split from aspects of its own self as well as from the dreamer's body is also metaphorically possible. In many of his writings on dreams, Coleridge moves towards a recognition of the existence of an ontological fracture between waking and sleeping existences.[4] The existence of a dreaming space also involved a fundamental alteration in the conception and experience of time in dreams.

There seemed no doubt in Coleridge's mind, after years of enduring the hideous and tormenting forms of his dreams, that a part of his consciousness (and conscience) was hidden and obscured. He describes the soul never as *being* while dreaming; rather, the soul 'lives in *approaches* touched by the outgoing pre-existent Ghosts of many feelings' (*CN* II 3215). Dreams become the primary site of the proof that the soul can only be glimpsed, and as such form only one part of the entire development of the concept of self and of the individual psyche. Dreams also exist in their own mental space, and can detrimentally divide the psyche.

On many occasions, Coleridge images his mind as having a physical existence: an existence which in a sense houses dreams and which can be entered at certain times. That the mind was conceived as a place that can be revisited was not unusual in Romantic thinking.[5] Once the mind is seen in spatial terms, it is possible for its perceived limits to be transgressed. Coleridge's presentation of his mind as a dreaming place that can be visited and experienced spatially is intimately linked to his explorations into an individual's moral constitution and into the nature and origin of evil. He once commented that 'the greater & perhaps nobler certainly all the subtler parts of one's nature, must be solitary – Man exists herein to himself & to God alone / – Yea, in how much lies *below* his own Consciousness' (*CN* I 1554). The employment of a spatial metaphor here implies that the mind is unknown, and also potentially insidious and threatening: for what lies *below* consciousness may be noble and refined, but it might also be dark and brutish (*CL* III 310). Thomas

De Quincey described this potentially dark area of the mind as an 'infinite' chamber which, from time to time, throws into waking hours 'dark reflections from eternities below all life' (*Confessions* 88).

The spatial image of the mind which Coleridge constructs, with depths and an alternative consciousness that can be below waking consciousness, immediately introduces an image which contains specific compartments, unique spaces for differing psychological characteristics. The need for borders, divisions, specific domains and the going out of, going beyond such liminalities, is thus created: the mind is likened to something which has an above and a below. What can then be defined in metaphoric spatial terms must also have spaces and nominal borders which can be expanded upon, and certain areas which are specific to certain psychological activities or thoughts. Once he begins conceptualising the mind in this way, it is not difficult for Coleridge to conceive that the phenomena of dreams occupy and occur within a unique space.

Coleridge often describes the experience of falling asleep as requiring the dreamer to enter into the physical and psychological space of the dream. In a notebook entry of 1805, he describes himself passing on and into 'the other side of the confine of Dozing' (*CN* II 2542). The idea expressed in the passing from one side of consciousness to another may be a common one, but what is ultimately being expressed is that the dream belongs to another 'confine', to another place within the mind. In a note to Southey's *Life of Bunyan*, Coleridge images the mind as having another depth, in this case, an other 'side', specifically in relation to the particular writing processes which he terms 'manual somnambulism' (*LR* III 397). In describing how a writer's pen can become the 'tongue of a systematic dream', he differentiates between that type which exhibits a 'single-mindedness' and that type of writing which is 'one-side-mindedness' (*LR* III 397). He suggests that dreams occur within this physical space of the mind, that they are never entirely under the conscious control of the dreamer, never without the potential to impinge upon waking life. This notion of the dream as paradoxically independent yet dependent on waking thoughts is one which he never resolved (as in *CN* II 2537).

In 'Suspira de Profundis', De Quincey exquisitely articulated the schema of dreams as both independent and dependent upon waking thoughts. Both writers explored the delicacy of this somnial phenomenon: Coleridge primarily in his private notebooks, and De Quincey in his published autobiographical writings:

Everlasting layers of ideas, images, feelings have fallen upon your brain as softly as light. Each succession has seemed to bury all that went before. And yet in reality not one has been extinguished . . . countless are the mysterious handwritings of grief or joy which have inscribed themselves successively upon the palimpsest of your brain; and, like the annual leaves of aboriginal forests, or the undissolving snows on the Himalaya, or light falling upon light, the endless strata have covered up each other in forgetfulness. But by the hour of death, but by fever, but by the searchings of opium, all these can revive in strength. They are not dead, but sleeping. (*Confessions* 144–5)

The gently evocative ebbings of the 'strata' of ideas, images and feelings are noticeable in times of fever, delirium caused by opium, but also in dreams. It is highly appropriate that De Quincey claims that such ebbings and inscriptions upon the brain are 'not dead, but sleeping': it is in the dreams of sleep that they are likely to re-emerge. For Coleridge and De Quincey, those moments were also likely to emerge in times of illness. The links between illness and certain qualities of dreams were recognised by both writers.

The initial moments of falling asleep and beginning a dream stand for Coleridge as the most accessible illustrations of the mind's ability to house and to experience a space for dreaming: a 'somnial space' (*CN* IV 5360). In a notebook entry from early 1803, he toys with these ideas, claiming:

To *fall* asleep – is not a real *event* in the body well represented by this phrase – is it in *excess*, when on first *dropping* asleep we *fall* down precipices, or *sink* down, all things *sinking* beneath us, or *drop down*, &c – Is there not a Disease from deficiency of this critical sensation/when people imagine, that they have been awake all night/& actually lie dreaming, expecting & wishing for this critical Sensation? (*CN* I 1078)

Entering into a dreaming state of consciousness necessitates entering a special place within the mind. Coleridge differentiates between events in the body and linguistic representations of the psychological event when first falling asleep. This distinction points towards his later ideas of the mind as being as tangible a place as a particular house or natural landscape. That he describes the dreamer in such terms as falling, 'sinking', dropping down, can only be possible if the dream has a place *to be* within the mind. He combines the language used to describe the experience of falling asleep with the common sensations of falling experienced during a dream itself, those dreams of falling down precipices. Potentially, insomnia can also be explained using this metaphoric vocabulary, for Coleridge suggests that it is the perception of falling, of sinking into the depths of the mind, and letting the entire body be engulfed by the physical and psychological feelings of sinking, which allows sleep to occur at all. If the feeling of this metaphoric falling is not experienced, then it is assumed that little or no sleep has occurred. This accounts for his thinking that in order to fall asleep, a falling sensation is both wished for and expected.[6]

Again, it was Thomas De Quincey who commented upon the sensation of falling into dreams and into the dreaming world. Like Coleridge, what De Quincey found in that world was not always palatable and pleasant. In his *Confessions*, he writes that his dreams were 'accompanied by deep-seated anxiety and gloomy melancholy, such as are wholly incommunicable by words. I seemed every night to descend, not metaphorically, but literally to descend, into chasms and sunless abysses, depths below depths, from which it seemed hopeless that I could ever re-ascend. Nor did I, by waking, feel that I *had* re-ascended' (*Confessions* 68). It is significant that, like Coleridge, the deep-seated anxiety and guilt De Quincey experiences in his dreams seem to linger uneasily into waking life. There is no sense of relief from the dream upon awakening; the somnial space itself seems as much a part of waking thoughts and life as of somnial experiences. De Quincey's claim that he literally descended, each night, 'into chasms and sunless abysses, depths below depths', firmly establishes the existence of a dreaming space.

The sinking into sleep is welcome, but the critical falling and sinking sensation has ominous overtones. Adam and Eve fell from the grace of God, and from the Garden of Eden; and in *Paradise Lost*, an extremely influential text in Coleridge's reading, John Milton utilises Eve's dream as a prefiguration of her temptation. The sensation of waiting to fall asleep often provided Coleridge with a poignant metaphor for the fall into moral uncertainty and sin. The guilt and suffering that he experienced in many dreams partly hinge on his recognition that he could just as easily fall into morally murky waters whilst dreaming as he could fall into pleasant streams and happiness. Falling in either direction required the existence of a somnial space.

But the somnial spaces were not always dark and threatening. In a well-known notebook entry of December 1803, Coleridge suggestively presents one of his dreams as a commentary upon the processes of poetry. Another idea also expressed in this notebook entry – that of the mind as harbouring a specific dreaming place – has received less attention:

When in a state of pleasurable & balmy Quietness I feel my Cheek and Temple on the nicely made up Pillow in Cælibe Toro meo, the fire-gleam on my dear Books, that fill up one whole side from ceiling to floor of my Tall Study – & winds, perhaps are driving the rain, or whistling in frost, at my blessed Window, whence I see Borrodale, the Lake, Newlands – wood, water, mountains, omniform Beauty – O then as I first sink on the pillow, as if Sleep had indeed a material *realm*, as if when I sank on my pillow, I was entering that region & realized Faery Land of Sleep – O then what visions have I had, what dreams – The Bark, the Sea, ~~the~~ all the shapes & sounds & adventures made up of the Stuff of Sleep & Dreams, & my Reason at the Rudder/O what visions, <μαστοι> as if my Cheek & Temple were lying on me gale o'mast on – Seele meines Lebens! – & I sink down the waters, thro' Seas & Seas – yet warm, yet a Spirit – /

<οῖ>

Pillow=mast high (*CN* I 1718)

The suggestion here of a material realm of sleep is tentatively offered: '*as if* Sleep had indeed a material realm' (my italics), but the surrounding text implicitly supports this suggestion. Coleridge describes sinking on his pillow, an image which directly refers to the physical action of lying down and preparing to sleep, but which also suggests that a psychological feeling of sinking is occurring simultaneously. Once this sinking feeling is experienced and finalised – the past tense, 'I sank' – he describes himself as 'entering that region & realized Faery Land of Sleep'. The journey into the somnial space is psychic and physical. He imagines himself entering into this magical 'region', and confirms this through a sudden and subtle change of tense: instead of designating this land of sleep as something that is to be realised, or perhaps as something which may be realised, he describes it as *already* having been 'realized'. There is no doubt that the land of sleep and dreams exists and has been entered, for Coleridge proceeds to describe the potential pleasurable visions that are to be experienced once this point is reached: 'O *then* what visions have I had, what dreams' (my emphasis).

The entry is hurried and almost telegrammatic in its urgency. Such rapidity creates a very specific humour and pun. The dreamer enters into the space of the dream, partakes of its forbidden pleasures (the description of, presumably, Sara Hutchinson's breasts as 'mast-high' is a Greek etymological pun from μαστοι: mast-high and mast-

οῖ) and exposes the boundaries of conscious mental activity.[7] To dream is to enter into a region of the mind, of the self, that is not, and cannot always be, accessible. This region is partially realised, and perhaps may not even exist, for it is 'as if' sleep had a spatial character. The sinking-down is not merely descriptive of the vessel sinking down into the sea; it is a psychological sinking into the realm of sleep. This sinking is distinguished by a tangible souvenir of the world above the dreamer, something 'warm', but something which is also 'spirit'. It is also potentially comic and lewd: to sink from the poetic and grandiose opening of the entry to the pun at its close. To dream is to retreat within and to enter the mind's space, a space which also belongs to a world of magic, of poetry, of visions, of sexual fantasy, the 'Stuff of Sleep & Dreams'.

It was not only that Coleridge perceived dreams as occupying a definite space within the mind: dreams themselves had their own unique spatial laws and characteristics. Late on Wednesday night, 26 April 1826, after one of the 'most grievous and alarming' dreams he had ever experienced, he noted 'the qualities & relations of Somnial or Morphean Space – which I now must content myself by MEM-ing' (*CN* IV 5360). This incomplete and teasing notebook memo on the subject of 'Somnial or Morphean Space' is itself an indication of how important, and how difficult, the subject was for him. He is concerned not only with the qualities of this space, what distinguishes it from other spaces, for instance, but also with its relations, presumably, with other somatic and psychological spaces. The two terms Coleridge uses, 'Somnial or Morphean', are interchangeable: 'Somnial' simply meaning of or relating to dreams, and 'Morphean' deriving from Ovid's name for the god of dreams, Morpheus.

Somnial space is a space in which objects 'make no resistance and neither occupy Space than fill it up' (N39, fo. 33v). Magnitude and distance are tangibly different from their waking and rational counterparts (see also *CN* II 2402). In an unpublished notebook entry, Coleridge describes a type of dream in which he feels that he is 'immense', gigantically tall and foreboding, towering over all that surrounds him such that the 'prodigious height of the vast Temples & Palaces' becomes tiny stepping-stones (N36, fo. 4v). Dreams allowed him an uninhibited exploration of the spatial world of the under/sub-consciousness of his identity. This Morphean space was one which knew no boundaries and followed its own laws: on one occasion Coleridge describes himself as flying within it (N41, fo. 1);

on another he has a vision of a world of fairies and paradisiacal meadows (N35, fo. 35v). In a nightmare, he becomes the victim of an evil creature who wanders through the psychological, somnial space, threatening to claw him to death (*CN* III 4046). This space was often seen to include the powerful effects of opium and the beauties of poetry (*CN* I 1823). Terrifying Piranesian buildings also readily appear along with other ghastly and gothic buildings (N39, fo. 33v).

It is tantalising to speculate that Coleridge regularly discussed such features of dreams, with De Quincey in particular. Both men encountered similar features in their dreams and the processes of dreaming were of perennial interest to them. The opportunity to discuss such topics was readily available after the two men met in 1807, and especially in their conversations of autumn 1809, a result of which was a memorandum by Coleridge suggesting that De Quincey make a survey of scientific publications on psychology and the senses.[8] De Quincey does record that he and Coleridge at least discussed the concept of space in dreams in relation to Piranesi's drawings. His account of the resemblance of Coleridge's description to his own terrifying architectural dreams is a testament to the similarities between the two men's dreams, but also to the influence that Coleridge's reading and perspicacious understanding of dreams had on De Quincey's own conceptions:

Many years ago, when I was looking over Piranesi's Antiquities of Rome, Mr Coleridge, who was standing by, described to me a set of plates by that artists, called his *Dreams*, and which record the scenery of his own visions during the delirium of a fever. Some of them (I describe only from memory of Mr Coleridge's account) represented vast Gothic halls: on the floor of which stood all sorts of engines and machinery, wheels, cables, pulleys, levers, catapults, &c &c expressive of enormous power put forth, and resistance overcome. Creeping along the sides of the walls, you perceived a staircase; and upon it, groping his way upwards, was Piranesi, himself: follow the stairs a little further, and you perceive it come to a sudden abrupt termination, without any balustrade, and allowing no step onwards to him who had reached the extremity, except into the depths below. Whatever is to become of poor Piranesi, you suppose, at least, that his labours must in some way terminate here. But raise your eyes, and behold a second flight of stairs still higher: on which again Piranesi is perceived, but this time standing on the very brink of the abyss. Again elevate your eye, and a still more aerial flight of stairs is beheld: and again is poor Piranesi busy on his aspiring labours: and so on, until the unfinished stairs and Piranesi both are lost in the upper gloom of the hall. – With the same power of endless growth and self-reproduction did my architecture proceed in dreams. (*Confessions* 70)

De Quincey's retelling of Coleridge's description is a striking illustration of the everlasting layers of ideas, images, perception and experience in dreams themselves: not only has Piranesi been narrated by Coleridge, he and his dreams have also been narrated by De Quincey in the same way that a dream is retold, reinterpreted as it is recorded.[9]

Somnial space can therefore easily accommodate endless growth and self-reproduction and was recognised as possessing these qualities by both writers. Time also undergoes radical changes in somnial space: it is 'suspended'. This suspension fundamentally alters other properties usually taken as unalterable; once it has happened, physical bodies that are normally immutable in their composition can become fluid, creating the illusion of endless growth, as in Piranesi's drawings.[10] Some of the most important phenomena of sleep and dreams can be explained by the 'transmutation of the *succession* of *Time* into the *juxtaposition* of *Space*' (*CL* II 974). In following chapters this complex idea is discussed more fully, but it should be noted here that the fundamental concept of transmutation depends upon the unique existence of a somnial space. Again, De Quincey also found the alteration of the sense of time in dreams a common and frightening occurrence. Whereas Coleridge approached the concept of altered time in dreams as a metaphysical and philosophical one, pondering the effects of both time and space, De Quincey uses these strange alterations of time as an illustration of the ways in which childhood memories and experiences repeatedly recur in dreams. For De Quincey, the 'minutest incidents of childhood . . . were often revived' in dreams, particularly during illness (*Confessions* 69). Additionally, he writes of the feeling that he seemed to have 'lived for 70 or 100 years in one night; nay, had feelings representative of a millennium passed in that time'.

As De Quincey also found, the dream journey inwards – into the depths, sides, and undersides of the mind – was not always a pleasant one. What lay *'below* . . . Consciousness' (*CN* I 1554) was a conglomeration of ideas, images, sensations and emotions that spasmodically emerged in dreams, or in dream-like states. Sometimes these ideas emerged with a life completely their own. Coleridge once called this area of the untapped imaginative self a 'storehouse' of raw material for dreams, poetry and metaphysical speculation. After a protracted illness in the winter of 1800–1, he wrote to Thomas Poole that he would look back on his 'long & painful Illness only as a Storehouse of wild Dreams for poems, or intellectual Facts for metaphysical Speculation' (*CL* II 668). The condition of the diseased body allows for entry into the usually inaccessible regions, those that Coleridge describes elsewhere as down, or under the mind. These regions can, he claims, be entered, apparently at will.

Some poems did arise from that long illness, most notably 'The Pains of Sleep'. Thomas Poole commented that 'The Pains of Sleep' was a 'magnificent poetical description of disturbed sleep'.[11] But other poems included with the publication of 'The Pains of Sleep' may also have arisen from the illness. Christabel, too, becomes the subject for a poetical discussion of disturbed sleep. Her retreat to the solitude of the woods is very similar to her retreat within a world of dream and sleep. She ventures out, 'a furlong from the castle gate', to pray for the safety of her lover, but she also ventures into the somnial space of her mind, where, in versions of the poem drafted between 1797 and 1801, she moans and leaps as she dreams of her knight (*CKK* 5). Coleridge, as poet, also effects a double retreat: first into the world of imagination to write the poem, and second, into the fitful sleep of Christabel, with which he empathises. This sleep is encountered not merely in Christabel's sleeping life: she recognises features of it when she thinks she is awake. As Geraldine undresses, the narrative poet reveals how her

> silken robe, and inner vest,
> Dropt to her feet, and full in view,
> Behold! her bosom and half her side –
> A sight to dream of, not to tell! (*CKK* 18)

Perhaps the 'sight' of Geraldine is akin to Christabel's dreams of her beloved knight, dreams which make her 'moan and leap' and which cannot be freely articulated because they belong in a special somnial space. Such visions and dreams are inexorably unutterable. When the night has passed, and Christabel awakens and greets her father, she does not seem entirely sure that she has awoken, for the power of her dream-world is still so strong, as is the power of Geraldine: 'Christabel in dizzy trance, / Stumbling on the unsteady ground – / Shudder'd aloud, with a hissing sound.' The dizzy trance, and the earlier references to moaning and groaning in sleep, suggest that Christabel is no stranger to disturbed sleep: in fact, with 'open eyes' she is described as 'Asleep, and dreaming fearfully' (*CKK* 21). In this dizzy trance, Christabel is said to be bereft of her thoughts – 'her thoughts are gone' – in much the same way as, when she first awoke, she was in such a 'perplexity of mind' that she thought she had sinned. The remnants of her uneasy dream, and the ease with which the somnial space is apparently invoked in waking life by Geraldine, are significantly stronger in the earlier drafts of the poem. Her retreat into the forest and into fearful dreams closely parallels Coleridge's notion of a 'wild storehouse' of poems, a space which houses poetic materials.

Despite his letter to Poole, Coleridge was not always confident of his ability to gain access to those strange and often painful regions of the mind. Often, he did not want to gain access at all, for those regions were totally incompatible with his conscious morality. There are countless instances of the shocking realisation that there seem to be two different parts of the self, a division which is most potently manifested in and through the processes of dreaming and in dreams themselves. This realisation was particularly evident in times of deep despair, caused by his opium taking. In a letter to Matthew Coates, from December 1803, Coleridge complains of

the Horrors of my Sleep, and Night-screams (so loud & so frequent as to make me almost a Nuisance in my own house [)] seemed to carry beyond mere Body – counterfeiting, as it were, the Tortures of Guilt, and what we are told of the Punishments of a spiritual World – I am at length a Convalescent – but dreading such another Bout as much as I dare dread a Thing which has no immediate connection with my Conscience. (*CL* II 1020–1)

His genuine lack of knowledge as to why the 'Horrors' of his sleep visit him is counterbalanced by the implied realisation that those same horrors must be in some way connected to his conscience and to his own behaviours. Illness and the onslaught of yet more dreadful dreams are described as parallel fears. The want of a connection between what is dreamt and what is conscious to the self during waking life becomes indicative of a self which is perceived as fundamentally dislodged and disrupted: the experience of dreams, an experience which is intensified in nightmares, creates the potential for the paradoxically total fragmentation of the self. That Coleridge dreads and describes such a dream as 'a *Thing* which has no immediate connection with my Conscience' (my emphasis) immediately indicates the extent to which the dream can divide the mind into two entirely different regions with entirely different moralities: those 'Tortures of Guilt, and what we are told of the

Punishments of the spiritual World' are dichotomously opposed to
those 'pleasurable' visions (*CN* I 1718), and yet both belong to the
physical and psychic space of the mind. The use of the word 'Thing'
does, however, suggest that Coleridge was thinking of Baxter's
spirits, who are responsible for the horrors of sleep, rather than
anything connected with his own conscience.

What is perceived as belonging to the self is dramatically altered,
and it is through both a metaphoric and an ontological self-
fracturing that Coleridge's fears, guilts and terrors are projected on
to his dream forms, and re-projected back to him. This kind of
collapse between who feels what in a dream – the dreamer or the
'*Dreamatis* Personæ' – is part of the agonising dilemma of 'The Pains
of Sleep':

> Deeds to be hid which were not hid,
> Which all confused I could not know,
> Whether I suffered, or I did:
> For all seemed guilt, remorse or woe,
> My own or others, still the same,
> Life-stifling Fear, soul-stifling shame!   (*CKK* 63)

The qualifying 'seemed' in these lines was redrafted as 'For all was
Guilt, and Shame, and Woe': a redrafting which indicates his
conviction that there could be no doubt of the intensity and
character of the deeds and feelings in the dream (*PW* I 390).
Coleridge's dream creates an utter and apparently irreconcilable
confusion within his concept of 'I'; it creates within his mind a
slippery indecipherability between 'my own or others'. Who is the
criminal and who is the victim? Who should feel remorse? Who is
free from guilt and blame? There are no clear dividing lines in the
somnial space, and it is not solely a question of morals that becomes
problematic in dreams. It is also a question of identity.

Coleridge's mind, once self-praised as an entity which could be
entered and explored on both psychological and physical levels,
turns in on itself. In a draft of 'The Pains of Sleep', the poet writes
how it turns in on itself in an 'unmanly Vaunting' of its own
potentialities. The very identity and formative processes of the 'I' are
ruptured and undermined by dreams. This problem of a fundamental division in being is closely related to representations of the
body in Coleridge's writings on his dreams: often it is a dream, or
the remembrance of a dream, which draws painful attention to the

fragmented workings of the sick and diseased body while at the same time creating a division in the 'I'. This recognition of the potential of dreams to haunt and defy the reasoned workings of the conscious mind has been described by Lawrence Kramer as the greatest terror of the nightmare: because the self acts as a 'hostile other', it can become one of the dreamatis personæ.[12] After a nightmare in October 1810, Coleridge claims that he and the dreadful creatures he encounters are engaged in continual battle: 'Dreams, or Creatures of my Dreams, you may make me feel you as if you were keeping behind me/but you cannot speak to me – immediately I heard impressed on my outward ears, & with a perfect sense of *distance* answered – O yes! but I can – ' (*CN* III 3984).

The 'sense of distance' seems to indicate that the dreamer has physically isolated himself from the creatures and is on the verge of awakening. The feeling of helplessness and terror is played out within the dreamer's mind, with certain aspects of the hidden consciousness challenged and taunted by Coleridge's own sense that he is the creator of the dream. The defiant 'O yes! but I can', heard with the 'outward ears', marks a moment in which the dream creatures, hidden deep within the consciousness of the dreamer, are temporarily rebuffed. Coleridge attempts to control the dreamatis personæ. The schematisation of a battle – a physical confrontation – between dreamer and dream characters indicates the presence of a problematic identity. The dream creatures are seldom 'goodnatured' (N36, fo. 6), but can be ridiculous (*CN* II 2489, *CL* II 1028). They have the same '*feelings*' as the dreamer, but the looks and actions of the characters must be inferred by him (N35, fo. 37v).

The nature and capabilities of the 'I' in somnial spaces posed crucial, indeterminate philosophical questions for Coleridge. For years, he struggled with his opinions on the nature of 'I', and whether the mind which contained this 'I' was its own object or whether it was a subject. What the 'I' could be subjected to was yet another problematic, and at times frightening, speculation. The processes of poetic creativity and of dreaming frequently challenged his well-read opinions on the constitution of this 'I', particularly as he grew older and still continued to experience frightening dreams. In a notebook entry from November 1827 he praises his past theorisings on the nature of the mind and of the self-identity, the 'I' which generally accompanies the mind. However, dreams continue to obscure his theories:

The definition of mind by me [?long] adopted & still retained as a Subject that *is* it's own Object! – but for this reason it may with no less propriety be defined, an object involving its own Subject. But this is not the definition of the '*I*'. – this must be defined, a Subject recognising itself as a *Subject*. The 'I' therefore cannot be conceived as the *whole* mind; and tho' it is indeed the mind itself, of which the mind is conscious . . . yet it is not of necessity conscious of it *as* itself . . . Something more, therefore, seems to be required for the existence of an 'I' than in the universal idea. What is this? . . . I must examine – but I suspect, that the awful subjects of *Conscience*, on the one hand, and of the Personœ Sominis – *Dreamatis* Personæ, in which the Subject is recognised as an *Object*, depend for their solution on this distinction. The Conscience being the *real* antithesis of the I – and Dreams, the antithesis, in the absence of some higher power yet to be determined. (N35, fos. 48–48v)

The 'higher power' which could achieve some kind of reconciliation of antithesis is never given a fuller exposition by Coleridge. What is striking about this entry is his bold recognition that his relatively sound theory of the mind cannot withstand what he experiences in dreams. He posits the 'awful subjects of *Conscience*' against the 'Person Sominis', claiming that they are not identical entities. The essential problem that he cannot resolve depends on definitions of mind and consciousness. Such definitions are thrown into chaos by the 'awful subjects' of dreams, which are also often physically painful as well. Conscience becomes what Coleridge calls 'the real antithesis of the I', and dreams become the subjective 'antithesis'. Perhaps the 'higher power' that he mentions at the close of this entry is a power akin to, but not necessarily identifiable with, the creative imagination, a power capable of harmonising or at least controlling the conflicting forces and ideas within the mind itself. The terrifying experience of certain dreams confirms his philosophical opinion that the self, the 'I', cannot 'be conceived as the *whole* mind'.

In order for there to be any real definition of the 'I', at least for Coleridge, there must be recognition of the self as an identity. In his terms, the mind, the self, must be able to recognise 'itself as a *Subject*'. How is it possible for there to be an idea, a concept of the 'I', when differing aspects of that identity are in conflict, and contain such 'awful' things? How is it possible that the presence of dreams can be so disturbing that dreams become antithetical to the perceived self?

The questions themselves entail significant consequences, of some of which, in moments of honesty and awareness towards the end of his life, Coleridge was painfully aware. That dreams and the processes of dreaming threaten a coherent notion of the self was an idea of which he was always dimly conscious, and gradually came to accept in later life. The mind is perceived as split, not only in a positive sense so that there are magical and mysterious regions awaiting exploration, but also in a negative, destructive sense. Coleridge once identified this division of psyche and being in dreams as a consequence of those 'frequently ironical' images in dreams, 'as if the fortunes of the Ego diurnus appeared exceedingly droll and ridiculous to the Ego nocturnus' (*CN* III 4409). The self which exists during the day, the 'ego diurnus', can not only be 'droll' and 'ridiculous' to the self which emerges during the night, the 'ego nocturnus', but it can also be tormenting and insidious. The con-science of the dreamer is divided, too. There is a self, or conscience, of the day, and an opposing self of the night, and Coleridge suggests that there are perhaps 'two Consciences, the earthly and the spiritual' (*CN* III 4409). Each of these consciences and egos has its own unique characteristics, or 'personeities'. In another notebook entry he argues that the passions of the waking 'I', or ego, tend to be more 'subjective', while those of the somnial 'personeities' tend more towards the active (N36, fo. 6). These apparently irreconcilable antagonisms between the ego nocturnus and the ego diurnus are one of the fundamental 'qualities' of somnial space (*CN* IV 5360) – which, it seems, is irretrievably and irreconcilably divided.

Waking and sleeping qualities of the faculties of reason and understanding are one means of differentiating the waking and sleeping 'I'. In an unpublished notebook entry from 1827, Coleridge discusses the consequences of attempting to conceive of the 'I' as a stable entity across waking, reverie and sleeping existences:

from these dreams (and no week occurs in which I have not one or two, always originating in the kidneys, Bladder, or Intestinal Canal) I derive convincing confirmation of the diversity between Reason & Understanding. The latter we retain in dreams – it is 'I', Will, & the Understanding belongs to '*I* – . . . the *memory* is lost: for it is *objectivity* that differences Memory from Fancy – and Objectivity, the offspring of Reason, is by divine ordinance connected with the *Senses*. (N35, fos. 37–37v)

Only understanding is retained in dreams; reason is lost. Volition (or will) and understanding belong to the concept of the 'I'. What the self believes to be the self during waking hours, with the assistance of both reason and understanding, is not equitable with the experience of dreaming. Dreams provide compelling evidence of the disparities between reason and understanding, and by implication, compelling evidence of the assumed nature of the 'I' who dreams. Entering the somnial space has many implications, and Coleridge perceived that one of the most perplexing and often disturbing consequences was this 'diversity between Reason & Understanding'. He applies conditions to the stability of identity, of 'I': conditions which are seriously challenged by his frequent dreams. Furthermore, the roles of the physical senses and of organs in the whole dreaming, self-fracturing process cannot be underestimated: these important roles are explored in later chapters.

The severe philosophical and psychological consequences of this perception of a split self are boldly asserted in another unpublished notebook entry of October 1827, which appears to have been written immediately after a terrifying dream experience:

How am I to reconcile my theory of Ideas, as being the Heautognosis of the Soul, abstracted from its' subjective negations and *exclusive* εγω *quem* ille et olle non est. (I sacrifice syntax to clearness). By How, I say, am I to reconcile this theory of Ideas, as the Soul's knowlege of itself *objectively*, without reference to the individual *subject*, with the apparent fact of the precarious presence of Reason, exemplified in our dreams? – My theory agrees excellently with Milton's whence the Soul Reason receives; and Reason is her *Being*. But how does this agree with the humiliating experience in Sleep? (N35, fo. 22v)[13]

The answer to Coleridge's question is that his theory of the unity of the self, or of the primacy of reason, cannot agree with his experience of dreams and nightmares. What the soul consciously or objectively knows of itself is not as secure a knowledge as he would like it to be. In dreams, this knowledge, and reason itself, are precariously challenged by lawlessness and chaos: dreams then are no trivial matter. What the self, the mind, the soul, can know of itself is divided into an apparently accessible region – the region of the waking soul, which is governed by reason and objective ideas, both of which are its heautognosis (its essential constitution, its self-defining nature) – and a contrary inaccessible region, governed by a loss of volition, terror and uncertainty. This is why Coleridge time and time again, and particularly throughout the last ten years of his life, describes sleep as a 'humiliating experience'. Because reason is precariously balanced in the state of dreaming, so too is the very sense of self.

It is this kind of split consciousness and taunting of the mind's own powers that Coleridge experiences in his worst nightmares. Sleep becomes an 'evil' thing, far from the refreshing and revitalising thing it should be. Once seen as a 'wide blessing', it becomes 'distemper's worst calamity': a metamorphosis which depends on the somnial 'wide' space of the dream (*CKK* 63). And dreams can become so 'distempered' that life itself seems to be tottering on the edge of extinction (N44, fo. 52). The soul's or mind's conscious knowledge of itself is irreconcilable with what may lie in an under- or semi-consciousness. At their worst, dreams and sleep provide indisputable proof of the moral failings of the dreamer:

March 20, 1830
Should it please God – of his free Mercy to restore me for any measurable interval to bodily ease – and a competency of strength and general Sensation, so as to admit of a poetic Energy, I can think of no more affecting subject and materials for an lyrical Lamentation, than the comparison of the Night, and of the feelings with which it is welcomed or regretted, and of those with which the Watches (the Lying awake at intervals) of the Night, in <our past> Boyhood, Youth, early Manhood with *Health* – and in the decay of the Life and Body with Disease and Distemper . . . O most merciful God, by thy eternal Word my Creator, Redeemer and Judge, withdraw not thy Spirit from Me! (N43, fo. 3v)

More poignant than the recognition some years earlier that there is an ego diurnus and an ego nocturnus (*CN* III 4409), this cry in a time of extreme sickness, only four years before his death, reveals the extent to which his dreams have seriously challenged and destroyed many deep concepts of the self. These troubled somnial times are thought to be capable of yielding both subject and material for 'lyrical Lamentation', and Coleridge seems convinced that should he attain reasonable health for 'any measurable interval', then his 'poetic Energy' ill return. The connections between a refreshing sleep, a healthy body and a fruitful poetic output are strongly forged in this entry, as are the converse links between illness, disease and dreams. These links, explored in later chapters, indicate the complexity of his response to his somnial experiences.

Although Coleridge appears to lament the onset of night and the somnial tortures which might possibly ensue, he is careful to sneak in an admission that the advent of the somnial state is not always negative: he claims that night may be either 'welcomed or regretted'. There are times when the approach of night, and by implication, the chance to enter into the somnial world, are warmly welcomed. Coleridge believed that dreams could also indulge love fantasies (*CN* I 1718, *CN* IV 4537), exercising both the intellect and the imagination (*CN* I 1620, *CN* IV 5360, *N*35, fos. 35v–37). Sleep would also be welcome if it contained what Coleridge termed 'somnial erotica' (N36, fo. 6). Often, it was Sara Hutchinson who was the focus of his somnial fantasy life: he once exclaimed that his dreams were 'always connected in some way or other' with her (*CN* II 2055).[14] More particularly, he believed that they were not merely about or connected with Sara, but that 'whole dreams' were her (*CN* II 2061).

Some of those lyrical lamentations of somnial experiences were comical and sarcastic in tone, and anticipate Coleridge's recognition in the Notebook 43 entry of the feeling of watching and waiting for sleep:

> 'Tis hard on Bagshot Heath to try
> Unclos'd to keep the weary eye;
> But ah! Oblivion's nod to get
> In rattling coach is harder yet.
> Slumbrous God of half-shut eye! . . .
> Listen, listen to my prayer;
> And to thy votary dispense
> Thy soporific influence! . . .
> Bid many a dream from thy dominions
> Wave its various-painted pinions,
> Till ere the splendid visions close
> We snore quartettes in ecstasy of nose.
>
> ('Inside the Coach', *PW* I 26–7 lines 1–22)

The serious nature of the 'comparison of the Night, and of the feelings with which it is welcomed or regretted' (N32, fo. 3v), is given a light-hearted treatment in this 1791 poem. It is important to remember that Coleridge did not always subscribe to the belief that the ego nocturnus and the ego diurnus (*CN* III 4409) were irreconcilably opposed, particularly in his younger years. One of the most delicate metaphors for the relationship between the two egos is found in a poem first published in *The Morning Post* in September 1802, entitled 'The Picture; or the Lover's Resolution'. A 'love-lorn man' retreats to a secluded and idyllic spot to worship the 'spirit of unconscious life', close by the banks of a river, and gazes at the scene:

                                          he now
With steadfast gaze and unoffending eye,
Worships the watery idol, dreaming hopes
Delicious to the soul, but fleeting, vain,
E'en as that phantom-world on which he gazed,
But not unheeded gazed: for see, ah! see,
The sportive tyrant with her left hand plucks
The heads of tall flowers that behind her grow . . .
And suddenly, as one that toys with time
Scatters them on the pool! Then all the charm
Is broken – all that phantom world so far
Vanishes, and a thousand circlets spread,
And each mis-shape the other. Stay awhile,
Poor youth, who scarcely dar'st lift up thine eyes!
The stream will soon renew its smoothness, soon
The visions will return! And lo! he stays:
And soon the fragments dim of lovely forms
Come trembling back, unite, and now once more
The pool becomes a mirror.   (*PW* I 371–2 lines 81–100)

Coleridge quoted from this poem in his Preface to 'Kubla Khan', and it is equally useful as a comment upon the ways in which dreaming and waking selves concurrently exist and interact.[15] As a 'lyrical Lamentation' (N43, fo. 3v) it gently captures the mood of anticipation and reminiscence that defines certain types of dreaming and reverie states. The images and feelings of the dream, of the somnial space, are easily scattered, like the images on the water, but they can also return. The delightful 'phantom world' which seems to belong only to the 'steadfast gaze and unoffending eye' can nevertheless return once that gaze has been temporarily broken. This provides an illuminating metaphor for the relationship between the selves within the somnial space, and their often antithetical and frightening dramatis personæ.

CHAPTER THREE

The language of dreams

Coleridge was firmly convinced that dreams have a unique language: a language primarily expressed in 'Images and Sensations' (*CN* III 4409, *CM* III 376). He argued that the linguistic and psychological structure of language undergoes a transformation, or translation, in dreams. This language is one that ensures that the dream has a visual and somatic stress: to dream is to allow the eyes to 'make pictures when they are shut' ('A Day-dream', *PW* I 385), or to have the sense of 'such feelings' as both delight and 'perplex the soul' ('Sonnet; Composed on a Journey Homeward', *PW* I 153). Not only is a dream language one of images and sensations, it is also antithetical to the language used in waking life.

Coleridge believed that the dream language has 'various dialects', which are 'far less different from each other, than the various <day> Languages of Nations' (*CN* III 4409). One special day language was the one that he used to describe his dreams, particularly in his notebooks. His notebook writings, often set down in haste and confusion, attempt to be an accurate record of the dream experience. They are also selective accounts and analyses of particular dream experiences. This hermeneutic day-time dream language can be seen as another manifestation of a somnial language, complete with its own syntax, vocabulary and connotations.

Coleridge's belief that dream languages comprise primarily images and sensations, and that this feature of dreams is readily validated by his own experiences as well as by the 'Dream Books of different Countries & ages', implies that he was thinking of some kind of universal and symbolic dream language, across many different societies and centuries. Perhaps he was thinking of what would now be called an archetypal approach to dreams, although he records no detailed analysis of what archetypal symbols there may be or what they may mean. There is no comprehensive record of the kinds of 'Dream Books' Coleridge read, but it is highly probable that he was at least familiar with the major ancient dream manuals, such as Artemidorus' *Interpretation of Dreams*.[1] However, he is never entirely confident in interpreting possible universal signs and symbols, and he rarely ascribes universal meanings to his dreams.

For Coleridge, dream images are 'either direct, as when a Letter reminds me of itself, or symbolic – as Darkness for Calamity. Again, either anticipation or reminiscence' (*CN* III 4409). Thus, images can be relatively straightforward or they can be symbolic, or, as is often the case in dreams, a combination of both. These images are themselves part of a language of dreams, the specific nature of which is pictorial, imagistic. Dreams are most commonly remembered in images, both animate and inanimate: the image of a woman whose 'features were blended with darkness' (*CN* I 848), the image of a self-begetting Devil (*CN* II 2455), of Sara Hutchinson's beautiful naked breasts (*CN* IV 4537), of 'snakes, and Serpents, green, yellow & black, all covering the roads and rocky path' (*CN* IV 5360), or of an old man whose actions and features resembled those of a 'fantastic puppet' (N35, fo. 36).

The intermingling of direct and symbolic images is illustrated in a notebook entry of 1803, in which he scribbles down the details of a 'persecuting Dream' only minutes after awaking:

The Tale of the Dream began in two *Images* – in two Sons of a Nobleman, desperately fond of shooting – brought out by the Footman to resign their Property, & to be made believe that they had none / they were far too cunning for that / as they struggled & resisted their cruel Wrongers, & my Interest for them, I suppose, increased, I became they – the duality vanished – Boyer & Christ's Hospital became concerned – yet still the former Story was kept up – & I was conjuring him, as he met me in the Streets, to have pity on a Nobleman's Orphan. (*CN* I 1649)

Coleridge opens the entry not with the simple statement that the dream began with the 'two Sons of a Nobleman', but that it began with the 'two *Images*' of the sons. The images are given a class status with which the dream-Coleridge later identifies: the sons are not merely sons, but, more specifically, 'Sons of a Nobleman'. The initial image of two sons acquires a (personal) 'symbolic' dimension. Coleridge's own feelings of insecurity and abandonment are represented in the dream as the dream-Coleridge is presented as a 'Nobleman's Orphan'. That these initial images are so recognisable to the dreamer is inconsistent with the poet's observation, many years later, that the personages of dreams are spontaneous, and that during sleep, the dreamer is 'perfectly detached from the Dramatis Personæ – & they from you' (*CN* IV 5360).[2]

The images of dreams, either direct or symbolic, are also either in 'anticipation or reminiscence' (as in *CN* II 2418, for example). Perhaps it is this qualification which allows for the possibility that dreamer and dreamatis personæ are independent entities. These direct or symbolic images, which also have qualities of anticipation or reminiscence, may also be prophetic: they can anticipate specific images in waking life, or they may eventuate in waking life at a later time or place. Images that are reminiscent are those which have already been experienced in waking or in dreaming life (as with a dream that has been dreamt several times): a sense of déjà vu emerges.

The qualities of the dream language are beautifully expressed in 'Frost at Midnight'. This poem perfectly illustrates the ways in which anticipation and reminiscence work together with images from the schoolboy's reverie:

> But O! how oft,
> How oft, at school, with most believing mind,
> Presageful, have I gazed upon the bars,
> To watch that fluttering *stranger!* and as oft
> With unclosed lids, already had I dreamt
> Of my sweet birth-place, and the old church-tower,
> Whose bells, the poor man's only music, rang
> From morn to evening, all the hot Fair-day,
> So sweetly, that they stirred and haunted me
> With a wild pleasure, falling on mine ear
> Most like articulate sounds of things to come!
>
> (*PW* I 241, lines 23–33)

The intense gazing into the fire invokes a dream-state, in which the poet is described as dreaming with 'unclosed lids' of his 'sweet birth-place' and the memories associated with it. But the reverie also conjures up 'sounds of things to come', of anticipation. These sounds are visual as well as auditory, and are complementary to the thoughts evoked by reminiscing. The poet's memory slides easily between the present, the past and the future. All of his memories contain hopes for the future, the remembrance of the past, and an implied awareness of the present. Thus, the memory of being at school, with a 'most believing mind', is obviously located both in the past and in the present as the poet writes and remembers. But the memory also concerns the 'presageful' young boy who hopes that the stranger *will* portend the arrival of the absent friend. This description of waiting for the stranger and drifting into reverie is complicated by the recognition that the dream of past childhood contains 'sounds of things to come!'. The feelings and images of childhood are both reminiscent and anticipatory, and are readily seen in the poem's opening mood of 'extreme silentness' and calm.

Coleridge also suggests that those dream images that can be labelled symbolic may be 'either grounded on some analogy, as to see a friend passing over a broad & deep water = Death, or seemingly arbitrary, as in the signification of Colors, different animals &c. Frequently ironical' (*CN* III 4409). His dreams were often personal analogies, not only of himself, but also of his closest friends and family. At times, the images in the dreams become 'ironical'; at other times, they follow sexual feelings or fantasies.

In a letter to Southey of 1804 Coleridge describes several fantastic images, which together form the analogous, ironical and often symbolical language of dreams:

I dreamt among other wild melancholy Things, all steeped in a deep dejection but not wholly unmingled with pleasure, that I came up into one of our Xt Hospital Wards, & sitting by a bed was told that it was Davy in it, who in attempts to enlighten mankind had inflicted ghastly wounds on himself, & must henceforward live bed-ridden. The image before my Eyes instead of Davy was a wretched Dwarf with only three fingers; which however produced, as always in Dreams, no Surprize. I however burst at once into loud & vehement Weeping, which at length, but after a considerable continuance, awakened me. (*CL* II 1028)

The central image in this dream, which forms the basis for its interpretation and recording, is a transformed Davy. Although the image of Davy may function as a symbolic one, it is equally relevant for Coleridge's approach to his dreams that Davy has been physically, and painfully, transformed: he is a 'wretched Dwarf with only three fingers'. The image becomes obliquely analogous: does Coleridge fear that Davy will actually disfigure himself in the name of scientific discovery, or does he become a symbolic image of Coleridge, or of someone else? Why is it that the image of Davy becomes dwarfed in the dream? Is he a Christ-like figure, offering himself up in efforts to 'enlighten mankind'? In *Poetry Realized in Nature*, Trevor Levere suggests that this dream reflects Coleridge's anxiety that Davy would become vain and dissolute as a result of his scientific discoveries.[3]

However, in 1804, Davy had not yet made the discoveries which were
to secure his place in scientific history: the discovery and isolation of
the elements sodium and potassium.[4] Furthermore, three years after
this dream, Coleridge writes to Davy, praising him for his 'powers of
Intellect' – praise of the highest order in Coleridge's thinking, and an
opinion which he still held many years later (*CL* III 28). The
interpretative possibilities for this, and every other dream that
Coleridge records, are indesinent. The images of Davy have analogous, ironical and personal nuances. Perhaps the phrasing of
Coleridge's note is a clue to the complexity of the dream language,
with the poet qualifying his discussion of the symbolic element of
dream images as 'seemingly' arbitrary. All possibilities are equally
weighted, ensuring that the language of dreams is not only rich in its
own lexicon (or images) but also capable of a vibrant and dynamic
semantics (meanings and connotations).

   Some of the images which Coleridge believes form the basis of a
dream language are both implicitly and explicitly sexual, and several
scholars have commented on the psychoanalytical significance of
such dreams.[5] In the above dream of Davy, he describes his
emotional state as one in which all things were 'steeped in a deep
dejection but not wholly unmingled with pleasure'. Feelings of
sexual pleasure are often important features of Coleridge's dreams,
and these feelings also frequently become a strong element of the
language of dreams. Many of his dreams have been exclusively read
in this way. Another entry which has been singled out for sexual
interpretation dates from January 1804:

My Dream – History of Scotus, deranged as a youth / imagining himself in
the Land of Logic, lying on the Road & in the Road to the Kingdom of
Truth, falls into a criminal Intercourse with a Girl, who is in Love with
him, whom he considers as the Daughter of the King of the Land / –
impersonation & absolute *Incarnation* of the most Abstract – . Detected he
defends himself on this ground. O it was a wild dream, yet a deal of true
psychological Feeling at the bottom of it. (*CN* I 1824)

Some critics have read this dream as solely concerned with Coleridge's sexual fantasies.[6] Although the 'criminal Intercourse' mentioned here is indeed sexual, the interest of the dream is not
restricted to the sexual. For example, the implications of the Land of
Logic as being both 'on the Road & in the Road' are that logic
becomes an obstruction to truth, and that there are other possible
roads that may lead to the Kingdom of Truth. One such road may

eventuate with the help of the King's daughter, or it may arise through a kind of derangement.[7] The dream can be read in many ways, including a sexual one. This particular dream may also resonate with Coleridge's own captivation by the potential of logic, of Godwinian 'truth', and with the difficulties of following too rigidly a dream of reason and reason alone.[8] Perhaps this is also part of the 'true psychological Feeling' Coleridge senses at the 'bottom' of his dream. Able to recognise variations of this 'true psychological Feeling', he is nevertheless reluctant or perhaps unable to elaborate on his recognition of it. Much of the problem with interpreting this or any dream is the irreconcilable rift between the attempt to interpret it and the attempt to construct a theory about dreams. For Coleridge, this impasse was particularly acute. It is one reason why he argued that the language of dreams was symbolic, frequently ironical, often in anticipation of something that is not quite known, not quite resolved.

The sensations and images of the dream include the sexual, historical, personal, literary, ambiguous, tactile, visual: the 'criminal Intercourse' of the young Scotus (*CN* I 1824); the threatening 'huge bloated fat fellow' and evil children with huge sheaves of their reaped crop (N35, fo. 36). One of the most memorable dream personages is Robinson Crusoe, who

shot wild geese, swam, &c for his food, & . . . preserved from the wreck two or three Score fine penknives – amused himself with carrying the art of penmaking to perfection – and layed up in his caves such vast stores of the best possible Pens that he at last freighted a large empty Vessel driven to that desart Island with them / A vessel forced to throw all her bales & stores overboard – & having by an active mind salted down & dried a Vast quantity of Provision, he arrived in England worth – as it proved afterwards – 9, or 10,000£. (*CN* II 2489)

Coleridge's Crusoe is a very enterprising fellow, and is financially rewarded at the end of a perilous journey for his industriousness. Other characters in his dreams are not so fortunate, as evidenced by the image of a dwarfed and martyrised Davy (*CL* II 1028) and the struggles of the two noble orphans (*CN* I 1649). Another character whose meeting with the dream-Coleridge is memorable is found in the 'Scotch Corner in Hell, the only spot in all Devildom free from Brimstone': between two walls of this cosy corner in hell is a 'solitary Caledonian, writhing & frowning as in the vain hope of making the very frown-wrinkles of his forehead scratch each other' (*CL* III 369).

There were other writers at the beginning of the nineteenth century who were interested in the language of dreams. The German philosopher and physician, Gotthilf Heinrich von Schubert, published *Die Symbolik des Traumes* in 1814: a significant work on dream theory, it explores the potential for dreams as an indicator of a dynamic relationship with unconscious forces in the psyche. Schubert also devotes several sections in his work to the language of dreams. Inserted into Coleridge's copy of the 1821 edition are four leaves, containing notes which disagree with sections of Schubert's thesis and his illustrative use of dreams in *Die Symbolik*.[9]

Schubert argues that once asleep, the mind no longer thinks in a verbal language, but rather in a 'picture language' (or *Traumbild-sprache*). This language is capable of combining many concepts and images into one picture, and forms part of a universal symbol language. In the opening pages of his work, Schubert argues, as does Coleridge, that the language used during the day is different from that used in the night, or during dreams. Where Coleridge quite passionately disagrees with Schubert is in the latter's claim that the soul, or self, is only able to speak its 'idiosyncratic language' when freed from the confines of the body – and the soul is freed from the body only in death or dreaming. Coleridge claims that Schubert is fundamentally mistaken in this belief, using as part of his argument the 'astounding rapidity and complexity' of the succession of images in the 'somnial state'.[10] In another annotation, to Wilhelm Tennemann's *Geschichte der Philosophie*, written around the same time as the Schubert annotation, Coleridge argues that the soul cannot be '*made free*' during sleep because 'the suspension of the Free-will is a main constituent of Sleep'.[11] He wonders how it is possible for the soul to be 'free'd from the Body when the passiveness of the Soul to the Body is the principal character of Sleep'.

The marginalia in both these works point to Coleridge's fundamental disagreement with the concept of Schubert's dream language. Coleridge saw the language of dreams as dependent upon the rapidity and complexity of dream images, for the language of the dream is itself one written in and defined by images. The ultimate rejection of Schubert's entire work is tersely summed up in the note Coleridge jots at the end of his marginal comment: 'Schubert's prophetic and artistic Dreams form a *distinct* kind – and ought not to have been confounded with those of proper Sleep.' His argument with Schubert stems from his belief that there are many different dream languages, due to the imagistic nature of such languages and the rich variety of types of dreams. And there were also some types that were identified by their lack of visual stimuli and strong presence of touch, such as nightmares.

Coleridge's concept of a dream language became increasingly detailed after 1818, perhaps the result of concurrent disciplined study of the grammar of other languages (*CM* III 829 especially). In the notebook entry from 1818 in which he first discusses the language of dreams in detail (*CN* III 4409), he refers to a 'deeper Dream'. The language of a deeper dream is 'imageless', yet 'Profound', as it contains strong feelings of 'Presentiment or Boding'. The image language of the dream seems to have disappeared, yet the properties of anticipation or reminiscence still remain. His remarks in *The Statesman's Manual* demonstrate this point, and he takes the varying degrees of awareness between sleeping and waking as confirmation of the potential for imageless, 'deeper' dreams to contain 'presentiment or boding' (*CN* III 4409):

the dreams, which we most often remember, are produced by the nascent sensations and inward motiunculae (the fluxions) of the waking state. Hence, too they are more capable of being remembered, because passing more gradually into our waking thoughts they are most likely to be associated with our first perceptions after sleep. . . . But there are few persons of tender feelings and reflecting habits, who have not, more or less often in the course of their lives, experienced dreams of a very different kind, and during the profoundest sleep that is compatible with after-recollection – States, of which it would be scarcely too bold to say we *dream the things themselves*; so exact, minute, and vivid beyond all power of ordinary memory is the portraiture, so marvellously perfect is our brief metempsychosis into the very *being*, as it were, of the person who seems to address us . . . it ought not to surprize us, if such dreams should sometimes be confirmed by the event, as though they had actually possessed a character of divination. (*LS* 80)

This deeper, 'super-dream' (Ὑπερονειροζ, *CN* III 4409) has no images, but is instead a profound feeling, a sense left on awakening that is 'vivid beyond all power of ordinary memory' and which seems to belong to the realm of 'divination' (*LS* 80). A dream which has this element of divination is one of 'the most majestic Instances' of the dream's language. Moses and other prophets illustrate the dream's prophetic power at its most dizzying heights (*CN* III 4409). Despite Coleridge's description of these deeper dreams as 'imageless', the sermon extract is clothed in a vocabulary of vision and images to make its point: 'minute', 'vivid' and 'portraiture'. The emphasis he wishes to place on the feeling, the inward recognition of a powerful dream, still becomes a part of the language of the dream: it becomes multilingual, and grammatically fluid.

Coleridge's qualification that such vivid and profoundly deep dreams 'should sometimes be confirmed by the event' is indicative that his notion of a profound dream does not automatically imply that such a dream is divine, but rather that it seems 'as though' it possesses the 'character' of divination. 'Characters' are themselves part of language, each forming individual units (morphemes, phonemes, letters) which can be combined to make larger semantic and grammatical units (words, sentences). The character of divination works at the level of an analogy for the language of a dream and the potentials for diversity within that language. A profound dream may have the potential to be prophetic but Coleridge does not argue that this quality will always be present. Several years after writing the above, he scribbled in the second volume of his copy of Tennemann's *Geschichte der Philosophie* that it was impossible for dreams to have this 'character' of divination. The power of 'inferring' the past or the future could not possibly belong to a mind that was asleep: such a power, if it existed, 'would belong to the waking intellect'.[12] Regardless of the validity of somnial prophecy, Coleridge's acknowledgement of vivid, profoundly deep images as constituting the language of dreams remained.

His claim that the language of dreams is one of images is in many respects an attempt to understand the nature of other images: those of poetry. His dream language is similar to the creative imagination: the images in a dream will melt, diffuse (*CN* I 1649), alter at will, coalesce (*CN* I 1250), fade and grow more vivid (*CN* I 1620). The dream images form units which together comprise the dream itself: these images are spontaneous, active, and possess an energy which is frequently terrifying (*CN* III 3984, *CL* V 83). They also often possess an intense and ineluctable physicality. The dream requires pleasurable and horrible images for its animation; words are 'partially' substituted for pictures, and those pictures within the dream are still able to retain some of their linguistic properties (N36 fo. 7v). The language of poetry, too, can be seen to act in this manner: the imagination, an 'image-forming or rather re-forming power' (*CN* III 4066), works with its images as they are created. Esemplastic powers are equally evidenced in dreams as in poetry, the product of the imagination (*BL* I 168–71, 295).

While sailing to Malta, Coleridge observed the shapes and appearance of the sails. His gazing at the sails is not unlike his gazing into the fire in 'Frost at Midnight': on both occasions, thoughts lead on to dreams and a recognition that the language of dreams is creative and fluid:

> Ships, & their Picturesqueness – / Have I noticed the approximation to Round and Rondure, in the Square & triangular Forms – & that pleasure which depends on the subtle Sense of Est quod non est? – Balance: Synthesis of Antithesis? – and secondly (& if I have not directly or by Implication anticipated it, of first-rate importance to me), that which in my last night's Dose I called the Polyolbiosis of each appearance from the recollections of so many others subtly combining with it / Sails bellying with Sails under reef ~~felt in modify appear~~ the Ideas of full Sail modifying the impression of the naked Masts, not on the eye but on the Mind, &c &c. – How much of the pleasure derived from the countenance of an old friend or woman long beloved – at least, continually gazed at, may we trace to this in Dreams – so very strangely do they instantly lead to Sara as the first waking Thought. (*CN* II 2061)

The references to the naked masts and Sara are reminders of the tendency to fantasy in his dreams. The poet's observations of the ship's sails also provide a 'subtle' pleasure, as they seem to transform themselves into what they are not ('Est quod non est'). The ship's square and triangular forms seem to be 'Round and Rondure', and this provides the subtle pleasure. The recognition of a process he names a 'Synthesis of Antithesis' immediately leads him to contemplate his dream of the previous night, in which he had noted the mingling of the familiar and the unfamiliar, that the 'feeling of a Person' can be at times 'quite distinct' from the 'Image of the Person' (*CN* II 2061). The ways in which the shapes of the sails and the dreamatis personæ behave are very similar. In fundamental ways, they both reveal esemplastic potentialities.

This ability of dreams to display an 'image-forming or rather re-forming power' relies on the premise that the language of the dream is one of images and of sensations. In a dream from 1802, Coleridge sees a 'whimsical transfer of familiar Names and the sense of Identity and Individuality to the most unlike Forms & Faces' (*CN* IV 5360). This 'whimsical transfer' is not disturbing, although it may occasionally prompt uneasy thoughts.[13] It is not passive, but rather partakes of the active and vital potentialities of a dream, revealing how images can be fused and actively melted into each other:

I dreamt of Dorothy, William & Mary – & that Dorothy was altered in every feature, a fat, thick-limbed & rather red-haired – in short, no resemblance to her at all – and I said, if I did not *know* you to be Dorothy, I never should *suppose* it . . . & again I dreamt of a woman of a gigantic Height, dim & indefinite & smokelike. (*CN* I 1250)

The person Coleridge knows to be Dorothy is clearly not the dream-Dorothy. Identity and physical features have been modified and transformed, but recognition is still possible. There is nothing particularly disturbing about the features of the dream, and Coleridge is quite in control of its retelling, recognising alterations and at ease with the display of modified personal features. Dreams recreate certain scenes and images, and present them as if they were in fact real, drawing upon both fact and fiction to create new dream images. Like images created in poetry, those in dreams have a special power 'in and of themselves' (*CL* IV 641) and readily display esemplastic ability.

Most of Coleridge's observations on his dreams are recorded in his personal notebooks. He once referred to his notebooks as his only true friends: they were not merely little pocketbooks in which he jotted down drafts of his lectures, or recipes, or account ledgers. They were his personal confidantes, and he shared many of his deepest, rawest thoughts and most complex ideas with them for around forty years, from the time of his first walking tour in Wales in 1794 to within only a few weeks of his death in 1834. The notebook form also shapes and circumvents Coleridge's language as he attempts to record his dreams.[14] In choosing to write his dreams in his notebooks, he is confronted with the articulation of what is often unpleasantly disturbing. In this sense, what he writes about his dreams is often only half-expressed: owing not only to the haste with which many dream accounts are written, but also to his desire to screen out their unpleasant features as he writes the dreams into the notebooks. He was never entirely successful in hiding the contents of his dreams, and there are many entries which do record his uneasiness and his awareness of the potential terror of dreams. There are also countless other notebook entries which are stark and honest in their exploration of often sensitive or embarrassing issues.

But his desire to record, scrutinise and comprehend his dreams as accurately as possible was often much stronger than his attempts to hide their contents.

What Coleridge records in his notebooks is often written immediately after waking from a dream. At other times he delays the act of writing for several hours, days, or even weeks. Those entries which have been written immediately after waking are characteristically telegrammatic, but rarely fragmentary. When he returned to some entries days or even years later, he often declared them incomprehensible even to himself. This sense of his own incomprehensibility, for whatever reason, was an intermittent feature of certain notebook entries (*CN* II 2367, 2368). But even those hastily scripted entries are inadequate representations of the dream itself. Coleridge's language struggles to reconcile the desire to record accurately what has been experienced with the desire to evade the significance of what has been dreamt.

There are two primary features of his language which I would like to examine: first, his frequent recourse to censoring and ciphering systems; and second, some specific features of the lexico-grammar of the dream entries. Coleridge created a coded language for various reasons, the most immediate being the uncomfortable sexual nature of his dreams and / or their connection with his opium habits. He often slips into Greek, Latin or German, not only because his vernacular vocabulary sometimes proved inadequate, but also because it was useful to have other linguistic guises for stark and unsettling personal subjects. For example, when he refers to a deeper dream, or Ὑπερονειρος (*CN* III 4409), he resorts to Greek not for subversive purposes, but rather for the articulation of a complex idea. The fluidity of language frustrated Coleridge on many occasions, and his use of Greek, or Latin or German is evidence of this frustration. Similarly, he often coined new words in a vigorous attempt to stretch language to its utmost and to provide a description of something which had no nomenclature: coinages such as 'Suffiction' (*CN* IV 4518) illustrate his determination to provide more accurate descriptions of his feelings or discoveries.

Ironically, for a reader of the notebooks, his use of coded, coined and foreign languages draws attention to the very things he wished to conceal or deny. The earliest use of a simple coded language in the notebooks appears in 1803. But when Coleridge returned from Malta, the need for secrecy from family and friends increased, and the coding system consequently became more complex. A more elaborate system was devised in 1807, and is often seen in the notebooks after that date. There are also numerous entries, often written within set time periods, which are entirely coded.[15] By 1808 the system had become much more complicated, and included symbol as wells as number codes.[16]

More often than not, dream entries simultaneously state and deny their own uneasiness:

I felt myself in pleasurable bodily feeling half-asleep and interruptively *conscious* of being sweetly half-asleep / and I felt strongly, how apart from all concupiscence (unless perhaps that dying away or ever-subsisting vibration of it in the Heart & Chest & eyes (as it *seems* to us) which is the symbolical language of purest Love in our present Embodiment / for if mind acts on body, the purest ~~feeling~~ Impulse can introduce itself to our consciousness no otherwise than by *speaking to us* in some bodily feeling) – (bēnĕvŏlīfĭceňce, or rather ⌣ – ⌣, – ⌣ – nevolificence) I felt strongly how apart from all impurity if I were sleeping with the Beloved these kind and pleasurable feelings would become associated with a Being *out of me*, & thereby in an almost incalculable train of consequences increase my active benevolence . . . O yes, Sara! I did feel how being with you I should be so very much a better man. . . . yea, that the Pressure of the Husband's Hand or swelling chest on the bosom of the beloved Wife shall appear as strictly and truly virtuous, as *Actively* virtuous, as the turning away in the heat of passion from the Daughter of Lust or Harlotry. . . . to feel pleasure made more pleasurable, in legs, knees, chests, arms, cheek – ~~this~~ all in deep quiet, a fountain with unwrinkled surface yet still the living motion at the bottom, that 'with soft and even pulse' keeps it full – & yet to know that this pleasure is so impleasured is making us more *good*, is preparing virtue and pleasure for many known and many unknown to us. . . . But I, Sara! But I am not worthy of you / I shall perish! – I have not goodness enough to hope enough / and tho' I neither game nor ever connect myself with Woman <even by a Thought,> yet my bodily infirmities conquer me, and the cowardice of pain, or rather of danger of Life, drives me to stimulants that cannot but finally destroy me. O me / let me return! – Awake! awake! – (*CN* II 2495)

The self-consciousness of this entry, with Coleridge describing himself as perceiving 'interruptively' his pleasurable bodily feeling, is quite unusual considering his, and other Englishmen's, 'foolish shamefacedness' and reticence (as in *CL* II 663). The pleasure he feels could be the result either of taking opium or of physical arousal. Yet the admission of this physical feeling is qualified by the attempt to render pleasure somehow more morally acceptable:

being with the beloved is meliorative, as active 'benevolificence' increases, and Coleridge exclaims that he 'should be so very much a better man'.[17] The acknowledgement of that 'pleasurable bodily feeling', at the moment of falling asleep and within the dream itself, must be transformed into an abstract concept in order to render it more morally acceptable. This is a circular process within which he is doomed to become entrapped. Even as he writes of the consciousness of his pleasure, an antithetical desire to validate and partially deny that pleasure is activated: sexual awareness becomes the 'purest' feeling or impulse which is then experienced as a 'bodily feeling', and this dynamic chain forms the foundation for an increased social benevolificence, or *'goodwilldoingness'* (*CN* II 2495). Pleasure itself, when experienced within the bounds of marital love, becomes a source for both vicariously learned and self-generated virtue. Pure and total physical pleasure, from the cheek to the knee, is more intense when concurrently experienced with a moral dimension. Yet Coleridge's circumstances do not allow for the realisation of this vision, and he is left instead with a guilt-ridden conscience and a frustrated sense of both benevolificence and pleasure.

The implicit uneasiness within this entry cannot be resolved. While acknowledging sexual pleasure in dreams, or rather the potential for sexual fulfilment, the poet simultaneously claims, 'I neither game nor ever connect myself with Woman <even by a Thought,> yet my bodily infirmities conquer me' (*CN* II 2495). Dreams become somnial spaces for psychological retreat from irresolvable and highly unpalatable inner conflicts. The plea 'Awake! awake!' which closes the entry reveals the simultaneous desire for and repulsion of the kinds of feelings and sensations experienced. Coleridge needs no cipher or code to convey the uncomfortable nature of his thoughts: his language betrays his deep uncertainties.

The other distinguishing feature of his cryptic dream language is that, quite often, his half-formulated notes to himself are laden with the seed of future ideas, seductively pointing in the direction he may have been heading. Some dream statements are written in blatant, stark language, with no need for code or denial, while others are only partial, their discoveries not yet realised:

Sunday Night – 4 Feb. 1810 – I eat a red Herring for Supper, & had a dreadful night in consequence. Before I fell asleep, I had a spectrum of the

fish's back bone which immediately & perceptibly formed itself by
lengthening & curving the cross bone threads into a sort of Scorpion – with
a sense of fright – which doubtless was the sensation which produced it –

J. Bœhmen's mind may be well illustrated from Dreams – there is
meaning, important meaning, in both; both the exponents are almost
accidental – such infinity of synonimes exist in the language of vision,
considered as the language or representatives of Sensations & Notions. (*CN*
III 3692)[18]

Coleridge has no doubt that the 'dreadful night' of bad dreams was
caused by the red herring, and he expresses this in simple language.
The account of how the spectrum of the fish's back-bone forms
itself is intriguing: he ascribes motive and movement entirely to the
spectrum rather than to his own perceptions or to the nature of the
dream itself. The spectrum 'immediately & perceptibly' forms itself
by 'lengthening & curving the cross bone threads into a sort of
Scorpion'. What appears to be an inanimate spectrum has suddenly,
and, in Coleridge's words, perceptibly, metamorphosed into a
dangerous scorpion. The qualifying 'with a sense of fright' is
literally redundant, and it is clear that he has added the qualification as he writes the dream rather than as an element of the dream
itself.

In spite of his apparent conviction that it was the red herring he
ate which caused his dream, once he begins to think about what has
happened, he resorts to cryptic notes to himself. These notes do not
entirely explain the event, but only suggest various possibilities and
variations.[19] Could the dream itself be a red herring, designed to
distract and divert the dreamer from more important or relevant
issues? Or is a comparison intended between dream person and
dreamer? Coleridge perhaps perceives a considerable similarity
between his own mind and that of Jacob Böhme, for his next
thought after his vision of the spectrum of the herring's back-bone is
of Böhme. The phonetic similarity between bone and Böhme may
help to explain the unusual association. While he admits that 'there
is meaning, important meaning' in the illustrating of Böhme's mind
from his dream, he does not elaborate on the subject. The connections between his pre-dream vision of the fish's back-bone and the
revelations of Böhme's mind are described as 'almost accidental',
due to the infinite possibilities within the 'language of vision'.
Dreams oscillate on more than one centre of meaning and potential
interpretation, sliding between differing potential narratives.

Coleridge's point concerning Böhme is developed more fully in a marginal note:

Jacob Behmen, *the Philosopher*, surprizes us . . . For Behmen was indeed a Visionary in two very different senses of that word. Frequently does he mistake the dreams of his own over-excited Nerves, the phantoms and witcheries from the cauldron of his own seething Fancy, for parts or symbols of a universal Process; but frequently likewise does he give incontestible proofs, that he possessed in very truth 'the Vision and the Faculty divine!' (*CM* I 558)

The problem with Böhme, according to Coleridge, is a problem with the 'representatives of Sensations & Notions' (*CN* III 3692), in which he confuses, or rather 'mistakes', his dreams as part of a 'universal process' when they are perhaps 'accidental' (*CN* III 3692), a result of sensations which cause specific dreams. In his own dreams, Coleridge may suffer from a similar mistake. On the other hand, the connections between Coleridge and Böhme suggested in this entry may simply be irrelevant. To dream of the red herring may itself be a diversion from another feature of the dream; perhaps the point Coleridge raises about the 'language of vision', as a language of sensations and notions, is the more salient point of the entry. Again, the inherent difficulties in reconciling dream criticism with dream theory obscure and prevent fixing a definite meaning upon the dream and its features.

Coleridge's dream language is both a feature of his approach to dreams and a linguistic feature of his dream entries, as illustrated in a notebook entry from December 1803. For ease of reference, the entry is here reproduced in full:

Wednesd. Morn. 3 °clock, Dec. 13, 1803. Bad dreams / How often *of a sort* / at the university – a mixture of Xts Hospital Church / escapes there – lose myself / trust to two People, one Maim'd, one unknown / insulted by a fat sturdy Boy of about 14, like a Bacchus / who dabs a flannel in my face, (or rather soft hair brown Shawl stuff) (was this a flannel Night-cap?) he attacks me / I call to my Friends – they come & join in the Hustle against me – out rushes a university Harlot, who insists on my going with her / offer her a shilling – seem to get away a moment / when she overtakes me again / I am not to go to another while she is '*biting*' – these were her words / – this will not satisfy her / I sit down on a broad open plain of rubbish with rails & a street beyond / & call out – whole Troops of people in sight – now [?cannot] awake. – Wind & the τα αιδοῖα πενιλια & somewhat painful / – but what wonderful wanderings thro' the Hall, with bad Portraits of the Emperor of Russia, the Hall belonging to the E. – the wanderings thro'

Streets, the noticing the Complex side of a noble building, & saying to my
Guides – 'it will be long before I shall find my way here – I must endeavor
to remember this' / the turning up a Lane with wall & magnificent Trees
(like a quiet Park-garden wall). In the early part of the Dream, Boyer, & two
young Students, & R. Allen: Legrice & I quizzing / N.B. arrogant sense of
intellectual superiority under circumstances of depression, but no envy / –
'*Obsonant*'[†] The Harlot in white with her open Bosom certainly was the
Cambridge Girl, <Sal Hall> – One thing noticeable in an after Dream / a
little weak contemptible wretch offering his Services, & I (as before afraid
to refuse them) literally & distinctly remembered a former Dream, in which
I had suffered most severely, this wretch leaping on me, & grasping my
Scrotum / – I therefore most politely assured him of the 3 guineas, but I
meant only to get rid of him / – Again too the slight pain in my side
produced a fellow knuckling me there / – My determination to awake, I
dream that I got out of bed, & volition in dream to *scream*, which I actually
to[o] did, from that volition / & the strange visual Distortions of all the bed
Cloaths, some lying as on a ~~form~~ frame toward the fire / some one way,
some another / all which, I in my dream explained as the effects of an my
eyes being half-opened, & still affected by Sleep / in an half upright posture
struggling, as I thought, against involuntary sinking back into Sleep, &
consequent suffocation / twas then I screamed, by will / & immediately
after really awoke /
[†] one of the words used by the young [?Fowos / Foward]. (*CN* I 1726)

As with many dream accounts, ellipsis permeates the style of this
entry. The ellipses are varied, and include the frequent omission of
the signifying 'I'. In the opening section of the entry, the 'I' is
conspicuously absent. There is no 'I' attached to the 'bad dreams';
rather, it is stated that there are 'Bad dreams / How often of a sort'.
This dream entry is also a good example of how the language of
dreams is a language of both images and sensations: the visual and
physical details, including the dreamer's body, are emphasised much
more than any causal or cognitive features.

There are at least three different dreams in the above entry: first,
the dream of Christ's Hospital and his school companions Charles
Legrice and Robert Allen; second, the remembrance of a former
dream of a 'little weak contemptible wretch'; and third, a dream in
which Coleridge complains of his most severe suffering, and of his
scrotum being grasped by a 'wretch'. The vocabulary, syntax and
grammatical processes of all three dream segments are quintessentially linked with and formed by the dominant theme of the two
educational institutions, Christ's Hospital and Cambridge. For Coleridge, the distinctive personal features of these institutions are

commerce, sexuality, illness and pain. The combination of education, sexuality and commerce discourses obscures Coleridge the dreamer of these dreams, as well as Coleridge the pursued figure within the various structures of the dreams.

The matter-of-fact opening is an easily glossed-over feature of this entry. 'Wednesd. Morn. 3 °clock, Dec. 13, 1803': the precise date and time are an attempt to bring the dreamer and the writer back to some sense of security and ease after the physical distress and psychological disturbance created by the dream. The dating technique employed by Coleridge as he commences his writing functions as a temporary bridge between the world of the real and familiar, and the bizarre, frightening world of the dream. This immediate need to impose certainty and control upon the forthcoming dream account is typical of the notebook dream entries. Implicit in this desire for control through the act of writing is an anxious relation between representation and vision, between the dream itself and the reality that returns to the dreamer after the dream has vanished.[20] In most dream entries he is determined to record the dates, times, and often the locations, of his dreams and his dream narratives. On a chilly Friday night on 28 November 1800, he awakes from a 'frightful Dream' (*CN* I 848); on 26 April 1826, a Wednesday night, a 'little before three', he discusses his dreams and nightmares after awaking from one of his 'most grievous and alarming <Scream> Dreams' (*CN* IV 5360).

Coleridge's efforts to be precise with the dates and times of his notebook entries do not offer the depth of reassurance that he sought. The entries, as that of December 1803 exemplifies, are confused, rushed, ambiguous and inconclusive. The clear and definite setting of the entry is offset by the truncated and hesitant dream account that follows: 'Bad dreams / How often *of a sort* / at the university'. The use of the solidus conveys haste in composition, a breathlessness as well as a reluctance to elaborate on the nature of the 'bad' sorts of dreams. The solidus is not merely used to separate ideas, but to prevent some of them from further elucidation. As a physical mark upon the page, it blocks further potentially stressful self-exploration. The ideas and the images of the dream are rapidly repeated in the writer's mind as he begins to write, and it is significant that Coleridge feels obliged to use the solidus more intrusively at the beginning and the end of the entry. The sentences in the body of the entry tend to be fuller, even if they still retain a sense of urgency: 'what wonderful wanderings thro' the Hall, with bad Portraits of the Emperor of Russia, the Hall belonging to the E.'. Towards the end of the entry, when writing must cease and the dream narration must be left behind, the sentences are more dependent upon the solidus: 'some one way, some another / . . . twas then I screamed, by will / & immediately after really awoke / '.

The attempt to return to stability is only half successful. The dream narration meanders through a series of events and actions, and is hesitant in dealing with feelings. For every word denoting a feeling, there are almost four times as many conveying action. Whereas Coleridge and his dreamatis personæ (N35, fo. 48v) 'trust', feel 'depressed', 'afraid' or 'assured', they are often more likely to be *doing* something: the propensity for action is indicated through his lexical choices – 'escapes', 'biting', '*dabs* a flannel in my face', '*call* to my friends', 'out *rushes* a University Harlot who *insists on my going* with her', 'I *sit* down', 'wanderings', 'this wretch *leaping* on me', '*grasping* my Scrotum', 'I *screamed*'.

Actions which inflict, maim and harm dominate this dream. The prevalence and rapidity of action and observed behaviours leave the writer no time to linger over the unpleasant, frightful potentialities of the dream. It is enough to record the insulting 'fat sturdy Boy' and his Bacchus-like qualities and then to move quickly on to the appeal to his friends for help. Perhaps it is the potential for a 'release of mass emotion' that is enough to silence Coleridge. The sensation of bodily pain is undoubtedly present ('the slight pain in my side', the 'somewhat painful' gastric winds), but the true terror and discomfort of the dream lies more with the remembrance of school-days. His school-day experiences and feelings of being insulted, lost, chased, humiliated, captured, suffocated and pursued, form, are a dominating feature of, this dream entry.

Coleridge's unease with the retelling of his dream is evidenced through his use of qualifiers, the most striking example occurring at the close of the entry. Not entirely convinced that he is awake and free from the terrors of pursuing figures, he writes that it was only after he screamed that he '*really* awoke' (my emphasis). This kind of qualifying occurs several times as he attempts to give the dream some degree of solidity and realism through, and in the act of, recounting and recording it. These qualifying devices are also employed by Coleridge to give himself the illusion of more control over the action of the dream. But both these efforts are doomed to fail. The dream-Coleridge says to the guides, 'I *shall* find my way here' states that he '*must* endeavor to remember'. The use of 'shall' and 'must' illustrates his use of the qualifier as a means to control the dream as it is remembered and experienced, but also the narration as it is written. That the complicated pathway is in fact remembered back into waking and writing life is proof of the success of the 'endeavor'. Later in the dream, the narrative voice, the 'I' of the dream, does not merely remember a former dream, but 'literally and distinctly' remembers, in a similar fashion to the dream character who 'most politely' assures an assailant of three guineas, and who suffers 'most severely'. The entry is itself a qualified dream narration: a 'bad' dream.

The cause of this extreme uneasiness the half-conscious strugglings, the screaming, and the terror of an 'involuntary sinking back into Sleep' – is described as characteristic of all 'bad' dreams and can be traced back to Christ's Hospital. Coleridge suggests in other notebook entries that most of his bad dreams take their inspiration from his 'uneasy' days at Christ's (*CN* I 1176; *CN* II 2539). In *Biographia Literaria*, he claims that the memories of Boyer's severe disciplinary actions 'not seldom furnish the dreams, by which the half-blind fancy would fain interpret to the mind the painful sensations of distempered sleep' (*BL* I 11). Not only is it the people of Christ's Hospital who haunt Coleridge's memory: even the 'solitary gloom' of the cloisters has a part to play in dreams ('Quae Nocent Docent', *PW* I 8 line 12).

Coleridge was not the only one to notice the powerful effects of school-days and of childhood experiences generally in the formation of disturbing dreams in adult life. Other Romantic writers also remarked upon it.[21] De Quincey was particularly aware of the power and significance of childhood memories and experiences to weave themselves into his dreams.[22] In 'Suspira de Profundis', he asserts that the 'deep deep tragedies of infancy' are immortally impressed upon the brain, and re-emerge in 'convulsions of dreaming or delirium' (*Confessions* 146). Even the 'minutest incidents of childhood' are often revived in dreams, and with horrifying consequences (*Confessions* 69).

For Coleridge, the torments of childhood are mixed with those of early manhood. He cites the combination of Christ's Hospital and Cambridge as the cause of the 'bad' aspect of the dream in the opening lines of the *CN* I 1726 entry. Part of the uneasiness and painfulness of the remembrances of Christ's is due to illness (*CL* 1 348, *CL* 1 388–9),[23] and, later, to awakening sexuality. Once he is at Cambridge, illness and sexuality join forces with the problem of increasing financial difficulties to dominate and terrorise him.

Coleridge's language is dominated by metaphors of illness, and acts of both physical and psychological pain. The observation becomes even more pertinent when coupled with the question of who it is that does the hurting, who is suffering. More often than not, the dream-Coleridge suffers, and is not in control of his body, his actions, his desires or feelings (see especially N35, fo. 35v). This is indicative of the extent to which the poet often felt that his dreams possessed him, and that he had no control over their narrative or structure. One of the first dream characters mentioned is 'Maim'd'. The next, the 'fat sturdy Boy of about 14' (the age suggests that the dream-Coleridge is also around the same age, back at Christ's Hospital), 'attacks' and insults him. No physical injuries are described, save that there was a 'Hustle'. The next character, a 'university Harlot', is quite insistent, and there seems to be some kind of uneasy pursuit, for our hero seems 'to get away a moment / when she overtakes me again / I am not to go to another while she is "*biting*"'. Biting occurs in other dreams Coleridge recorded, and became a painful motif in them. In 1827, he describes the rather savage and very realistic feel of the bite of a dog in another dream (N35, fo. 36).[24] The harlot from the entry of December 1803 does not seem to have inflicted as much injury as the 'villainous little dog' is to do in 1827. What they share is their tendency to lunge at and bite the dream-Coleridge. The potential for sexually transmitted diseases is another reason why biting assumes such prominence in his dreams.[25]

Coleridge's slippage into Greek as the action within the dream becomes threatening and nightmarish only draws attention to the pain he feels as he sleeps and dreams his dream: 'τα αιδοῖα πενιλια'. That he experiences this feeling is suggested by the framing solidi, which provide an abrupt break in the dream narrative. In this case, Coleridge's Greek is significantly incorrect. He has not used a Greek word, but rather he has transliterated a Latin word into Greek, τά αἰδοῖα, from *pensilis*, meaning 'hanging, pendent genitals'. It is possible that the university harlot actually bites the vulnerable genitals of the dream-Coleridge. This explains why the dominant feeling of this section of the dream is 'somewhat painful'. But the ambiguous wording and structure make it equally possible that the 'wind & the τα αιδοῖα πενιλια' refer not to the dream-Coleridge, but to the dreamer himself. Wind in the stomach, more than likely caused by the effects of opium, and the unavoidable feeling of painful genitals, are somatic intrusions into the dream account added as Coleridge pens the entry, perhaps as he dreamt it too. The staccato phrasing supports the notion that at this crucial moment in the dream's narrative (the distress is intense as the harlot is biting and the dream-Coleridge cannot get away), Coleridge suddenly becomes aware of his sexual body. This intrusion of the sleeping body into the dream is described as 'somewhat painful', but is mediated by the beautiful scenery that is visualised as part of the architecture of the dream, the 'wonderful wanderings thro' the Hall'. His choice of words, especially his transliterated Greek, points to the complicated and painful nature of his dream, and the inexorable connections between dreamer's body and dream personæ.

The dream-Coleridge and Coleridge seem to escape their assailants, although neither are able to awake. The descriptions of the hall and its environs are quite beautiful, but such pleasant feelings are doomed to be short-lived because of the intrusion of yet another dream (cf *CN* I 1725), an earlier one in which the dream-Coleridge suffers 'most severely', he recalls, with a 'wretch' leaping on him and grasping his scrotum. A tussle ensues, and again a 'fellow' knuckles Coleridge, and probably continues to beat him, for he begins to scream and resolves to awake himself from this torment. The struggle to awake and leave behind the plethora of potential dream assailants seems to act as a catalyst for an intense feeling of suffocation and further screaming. After all this leaping, grasping, biting, suffering, knuckling and struggling, the dream ends.

These violent features are typical of Coleridge's dreams, for he is often being pursued, by both human and non-human figures, and sometimes by the Devil, and it is almost always he who suffers, he who is victimised (*CN* III 4046; *CL* III 369; *CL* v 83). These features create a very dramatic element, and reinforce the analogy between dreams and drama in Coleridge's experiences. He loses control over his body and its responses to pain when he enters a dream: urination is no longer controlled by the dreamer, but by a maliciously predatory figure (N35, fo. 37); pain is more likely to be experienced when asleep, often with a greater intensity (N41, fo. 53v). There is an

overwhelming awareness of the dream-Coleridge's passivity, as
wretches and fellows leap upon him, grasping his scrotum and
knuckling him painfully in the side. Both Coleridge and dream-
Coleridge experience the pain, and this power relationship is one
that does not alter in any dream entry. Even on the one occasion
when the dream-Coleridge describes himself as being physically
bigger, and presumably stronger, than surrounding characters, he
remains gentle, unaggressive (N36, fo. 4v).

Only in one dream is the dream-Coleridge said to inflict harm
upon another character: in an effort to help a 'solitary Caledonian'
who is vainly trying to make the 'very frown wrinkles of his forehead
scratch each other', Coleridge begins to flog him with a 'large
Branch of prickly Holly' (*CL* III 369). But the instant he begins the
flogging, he is thrown into the flaming oven. This is not to suggest
that there are not other creatures who suffer in Coleridge's dreams,
but those who suffer do not do so as a direct result of his action.
When he describes a dream in which he stumbles upon Davy, who
has 'ghastly wounds', it is discovered that the wounds were 'inflicted'
by Davy upon himself, in 'attempts to enlighten mankind' (*CL* II
1028). As both dreamer and dream character, Coleridge is destined
to experience pain rather than to inflict it.

To try and rid himself of the advances of the university harlot
from the *CN* I 1726 dream, the dream-Coleridge offers her one
shilling. After a pursuit through a beautiful but threatening landscape, a 'little weak contemptible wretch' offers his services. In order
for services to be offered, some kind of exchange must be enacted,
and again the services are refused by the dream-Coleridge. Relations
between the dreamatis personæ in this dream are implicitly governed
by notions of exchange and physical recompense for previous
financial favours. The description of the wretch immediately
reminds Coleridge, as he sits and writes down the dream, of an
earlier dream in which another 'wretch' leapt on him, grasped his
scrotum, and demanded money. The two wretches are alike in that
they both pursue the dream-Coleridge to regain their loans. Again,
the 'I' of the dream runs into trouble delivering the money, and is
capable only of courteously assuring his assailant in order to prevent
physical injury: 'I . . . most politely assured him of the 3 guineas, but
I meant only to get rid of him.'

The world of barter and monetary exchange is obviously a source
of concern, for an interruption in the flow of this exchange results in

knuckling, grasping and groping. That Coleridge 'literally & distinctly' remembers the exact amount of money owed and that there was no real intention to honour the payment, also hints at the importance of monetary matters within the general air of unease and distress in this dream entry.[26] The physical abuse associated with the delivery of a relatively small sum of three guineas stands in stark contrast to the opulence of the Emperor's palace, and the 'Lane with magnificent Trees'.

Matters of a sexual nature are strongly associated with money: the two women in this dream are both prostitutes. The first, the 'university Harlot', is not only insistent, but also persistent, and refuses the offer of one shilling. She is perhaps possessive and determined too, commanding that the fleeing dream-Coleridge not 'go to another while she is "*biting*"'. The second woman in the dream is 'the Harlot in white with her open Bosom'. The description of her breasts as not only 'open' but also as 'white' brings a flash of colour into the otherwise colourless landscape of the dream. Coleridge himself does not escape notice of a sexual kind: his scrotum not only becomes the primary site for injury and pain (note the capitalisation of both scrotum and bosom in this entry), but also becomes the rather tender bargaining point for the return of three guineas.

The uneasy, inarticulate and quite ambiguous link between this dream's financial, educational and sexual discourses is the 'I'. This 'I' is inconstant, passive, frightened, mysterious. Only towards the end of the entry does it emerge as more assertive and confident: 'I in my dream explained as the effects of . . . my eyes being half-opened . . . twas then I screamed, by will.' Understanding and control seem to be more centred in the 'I' here than at any other stage of the dream. The 'I' is positioned at the grammatical and physical beginning of the clause: 'I in my dream', rather than the more passive construction of 'in my dream, I . . . '. The understanding that the distorted bedding materials are not a result or even a cause of another 'wretch' being about to attack is important, for it means that both dream-Coleridge and Coleridge realise there is a waking world bordering on the somnial world. That the 'visual Distortions of all the bed Cloaths' are explained and believed to be a result of their position in relation to the fire and an awakening consciousness ensures that the 'I' who explains and who screams is at least taking some initiatives in a dream in which the 'I' is continually passive.

Throughout the dream narration, the 'I' occupies a number of different positions: it is in relationship with the other dream characters, and with itself, as well as with the writer and interpreter of the dream. The position of the 'I' is a fluid one, as it attempts to understand and to avoid the events around it (this fluidity is also part of the language of the dream). At the beginning of the entry, the presence of the 'I' is implied rather than stated. Even when 'myself' is mentioned, it is primarily to state that the self in dreams is lost: 'Bad dreams / How often *of a sort* / at the university – a mixture of Xts Hospital Church / escapes there – lose myself.' To be lost is to be displaced. The self is displaced to a less prominent place within the dream, even though the action still centres on this 'I'. Throughout the dream, the 'I' is acted upon rather than acting for itself. The 'I' character is tormented, pursued, attacked and affronted by wretches and open-breasted women. When it does emerge for itself, it is a passive figure, told what to do and where to go: 'I am not to go . . .', 'I sit', 'I had suffered', 'I therefore most politely. . .'. The 'me' is also a much beleaguered figure: a flannel is dabbed in 'my face', 'he attacks me', 'a university Harlot, who insists on my going with her', 'she overtakes me', 'this wretch leaping on me', 'grasping my Scrotum', 'a fellow knuckling me'.

Coleridge noted this passivity of the 'I': 'In dreams one is much less, in the most tranquil dreams, a spectator only – one seems always about to do, or suffering or thinking, or talking – & I do not recollect that state of feeling so common when awake of thinking on one subject, & looking at another, or at a whole prospect' (*CN* II 2302). Again, the language of dreams differentiates thoughts and feelings when awake from thoughts and feelings in dreams, even in the 'most tranquil' of dreams. Although in such dreams 'one is much less . . . a spectator', there still is an element of passivity. The dream characters do not act in the present: they are 'always about to do, or suffering or thinking'. The denotation of continuous action traps the dreamatis personæ into something that is both anticipatory and reminiscent. Coleridge notes the crucial differences in acting and actions, according to the type of dream that is dreamt.

In dreams the fragile and emerging strength of the 'I' is fleetingly portrayed. Returning to the *CN* I 1726 entry, the problems with the 'I' figure are highlighted through Coleridge's choice of vocabulary. In the phrasing in the middle of the entry – 'I shall find my way here – I must endeavor to remember this' – there is a suggestion that the 'I' is determined and strong in purpose. The determination to find the way and to remember is not confined to the need to remember the way through the wandering streets. The dream itself must also be navigated and remembered: the 'I' who is assaulted and lost needs to find a way through the dream's landscape and through the mind of its creator so that it can be remembered and later written down, even if only in a partial or fragmentary form.

As the dream continues, the position of the 'I' becomes increasingly ambivalent. Although the dream entry appears to be overladen with details, observations and facts, there are so many holes and ellipses in the narration that very little can be stated about the dream's factual details. The reader is forced to read between the lines and infer what may or may not have happened at any particular moment. The loss of the 'I' and the loss of more detailed information, in spite of the illusion of detail, are complementary characteristics of this entry. A series of fragmentary images and sensations is presented, with little to connect them. Part of the illusion of detail relates to the convoluted construction of Coleridge's sentences. Subject and object, 'I' and 'them', are blurred as grammatical constructions deeply buried within each other: a mirroring effect of the ways in which subject and object, dream theory and dream practice are also inherently blurred. For example, it is difficult to determine how each sentence, broken by the use of both solidus and dash, is related to another, and what the nature of the connections between cause and effect may be. And even if those relationships and causal connections could be determined, they may still prove to be irrelevant.[27]

The already tenuous relation between language and meaning is more hazardous when a dream is interpreted. This is partly because the language of dream exists in a somnial space (*CN* IV 5360). The difficulty in translating from the somnial language to the language of every day is apparent in many dream entries. In the above extract from *CN* I 1726, the realistic intrusion of the act of dreaming in the apprehensive admission that the dreamer 'cannot awake' is inexplicable, and almost irrelevant. Such indeterminacies and impossibilities are idiosyncratic of the dream itself, and its language. Coleridge maintains the ambivalence and intrigue of the dream language in the language he uses to record, interpret and understand his dreams. The language of dreams is one of images, often symbolic or ambivalent, and this particular dream entry is especially coded in images. Primarily because such a language is perpetually indeterminate, to the point of oracularity, there is little chance of the written dream account being as detailed or as clear, qualitatively or quantitatively, as Coleridge (or perhaps any reader) would like.

Caught up and often obscured in the garbled transfer from waking to sleeping, from literary worlds to dream language to dream writing, is the 'I' figure. Some actions and feelings are dislocated from an originating animate or human source. The action of turning into a lane, for instance, is nominalised at the expense of any notion of 'I': 'the turning up a Lane with wall & magnificent Trees'. This grammatical fragility and vulnerability of the 'I' corresponds to the psychological and physical vulnerability of both the dreamer (Coleridge) and the character (Coleridge): the former is vulnerable as he sleeps and dreams a terrifying dream; the latter as he is attacked, hunted, grabbed and assaulted throughout the course of the dream/s.

The dream entry selected here for analysis is one of many of Coleridge's dream writings which pivot on a discourse of pain. One of the fundamental features of such a discourse is the destruction and extreme internal dislocation of the 'I'.[28] Both dream character and dreamer articulate themselves and their bodies primarily through a language of pain. The dissolution of the 'I' when the body or the mind is in pain is inevitable for several reasons. First, the experience of pain automatically isolates the person who feels the pain from all others. No one else can experience or understand the pain of another. To be in pain or to have a painful sensation is to be enclosed within a private world in which that pain is the dominant reality. To be in pain while dreaming is an act of triple enclosure: dreams occur within the somnial space, and not only are the dreams of another person essentially inaccessible to others, but any pain experienced within that dream will automatically be inaccessible, and often denied its potency or dominance.

Coleridge often focussed introspectively on his bodily pain to the exclusion of all else. This feature constitutes a second reason for the dissolution of the 'I': physical pain has the power to 'destroy language' because pain monopolises language.[29] Physical pain was a feature of many of his dreams as well as of his life in general. Pain becomes the only subject that language can access; it dominates thought processes while also ridiculing and disrupting many bodily processes; it 'drags' all thoughts back to the 'unfortunate Self' who suffers (*CL* III 73). Once the usual avenues of language production have been severed in this manner, it is possible for the 'I' to disappear entirely, to fade in and out unpredictably. Pain splits the 'I' from others, but also splits 'I' from self. Such a disruption is evident when Coleridge attempts to record his dreams. If the language of dreams is one of images, then it must also be remembered that it is one of 'sensations' (*CN* III 4409). A 'sensuous nature' provides a 'Lexicon raisonné of Words', an essential vocabulary and structure for a dream language (*CN* III 4409). Painful sensations, which form the interpretative and symbolic language of a dream, are as much a part of Coleridge's dreams as the rarer pleasant and at times sexual sensations. But it is intense and nagging pain which becomes so 'external' to the self that on one occasion he declares that the subjective 'I' 'cannot exist' alongside such pain (N46, fo. 35v). Because the dream-Coleridge is consistently attacked, bitten, grabbed and pursued (as in *CN* I 1726), it is very difficult for the 'I' to emerge, as either a character or as a grammatical unit.

The dream language – the language in which a dream is written as well as the special language of dreams – is coloured by the predominance of pain and sensation. The language of dreams, based in images, has the potential to be both reminiscent and anticipatory. These features are discernible in many of Coleridge's dreams, irrespective of their type and intensity.

CHAPTER FOUR

Genera and species of dreams

When Keats met Coleridge in 1819, along Millbank Lane near Highgate, the younger poet jotted down snippets of the encounter:

I walked with him a[t] his alderman-after dinner pace for near two miles I suppose. In those two Miles he broached a thousand things – let me see if I can give you a list – Nightingales, Poetry – on Poetical sensation – Metaphysics – Different genera and species of Dreams – Nightmare – a dream accompanied ~~with~~ by a sense of touch – single and double touch – A dream related – First and second consciousness – the difference explained between will and Volition – [1]

Coleridge's awareness of different 'genera and species of Dreams' is amply evidenced through Keats' rendition of his encounter with him. Throughout his life, Coleridge sought to understand and analyse the differing types of reveries, dream-like states, and those moments between sleeping and waking in which the 'vestibule of Consciousness' is displayed (*CL* 1 445). He also subtitled two of his most intriguing poems a 'Poet's Reverie' and a 'Vision in a Dream', carefully choosing the descriptors of reverie and dream. These different moods and awarenesses could be seen as degrees or species of dreaming life, ranging from the perception that poetry was a type of dream – a 'rationalized dream' (*CN* 11 2086) – to reveries of delight and fantasy, and to the terrifying nightmares he frequently endured.

Coleridge's interest in and efforts to distinguish between various levels of consciousness have previously been noted.[2] Many of his notebook entries, letters, philosophical and religious writings explore the influence of different states of consciousness on various levels of mental activity, ranging from the poetic to the artistic to the deeply personal and even to the ridiculous. There are many entries in which he notes a peculiar mood, in which his perceptual faculties are not fully in his control, or in which the objects before his vision are seen

in very unusual ways. One of the earliest such observations was
written when Coleridge visited the Hutchinson family farm in 1799:
'Print of the Blackwall Ox, of Darlington – so spot-sprigged/Print,
how interesting – viewed in all moods, unconsciously distinctly,
semiconsciously, with vacant, with swimming eyes – a thing of
nature thro' the perpetual action of the Feelings!' (*CN* 1 576). The
picture before the eyes is not static: when viewed in all kinds of
moods it acquires remarkable properties. Four years later, the
experience of viewing the print was still fresh in Coleridge's
memory:

Print of the Darlington Ox, sprigged with Spots. – Viewed in all moods,
consciously, unconsc. – with vacant, with swimming eyes – made a Thing
of Nature by the repeated action of the Feelings. O Heaven when I think
how perishable Things, how imperishable Thoughts seem to be! – For what
is Forgetfulness?[†] Renew the state of affection or bodily Feeling, same or
similar – sometimes dimly similar/and instantly the trains of forgotten
Thought rise from their living catacombs! – Old men, & Infancy/and
Opium, probably by its narcotic effect on the whole seminal organization,
in a large Dose, or after long use, produces the same effect on the *visual, &
passive* memory/.

[†] so far was written in my b.pocket[book] Nov. 25th 1799 – Monday
Afternoon, the Sun shining in upon the Print, in beautiful Lights. (*CN* 1
1575)

He firstly recognises that there are distinctly different effects of
perceiving a particular work of art in various 'moods', and also that
the artefact can become a 'Thing of Nature' through the agency of
feelings. A 'Thing of Nature' contains within itself or is able to
invoke all those differing moods and states of consciousness, for
Coleridge often spoke of natural things as combining opposites into
a beautiful artefact. This represents the 'reconciliation of opposite or
discordant qualities' which was also one of the principal features of
the poetic imagination (*BL* 11 16). The 'repeated action of the
Feelings', the 'state of affection or bodily Feeling', and memories
themselves, are reconciled in both the conscious and unconscious
viewing of the print. The bringing together of opposite, or 'incompatible' thoughts constitutes an uniquely identifiable *state of mind*,
which Coleridge terms a 'bull' (*BL* 1 72–3).

Not only is it that a psychological faculty is capable of producing
and comprehending these various moods of perception, it is also
possible to achieve a very similar effect through an external and

physiological source, as when a 'large Dose' of opium is taken. Opium affects the visual and the passive memory, and these in turn contribute to yet another 'mood' in which to view the print. Coleridge's grammar in entry 576 is ambiguous: does he imply here that the optimum time for viewing the print in its most 'distinct' mode is when this can be done 'unconsciously'? The travelling down the depths of the somnial space into hazy levels of consciousness, that he describes as a mood of vacancy and swimmingness, seems to increase, not decrease, the appreciation and individuality of the object in view (cf 'Frost at Midnight', *PW* i 241 line 38 and 'This Lime-Tree Bower my Prison', *PW* i 180 lines 39–40). It is the combination of all these different moods – conscious, unconscious, that semi-conscious, demi-conscious, 'semi-demi-conscious' (*CN* ii 2073) – with repeated emotional activity, that creates a 'Thing of Nature'. The principle which unifies all these moods and which surfaces repeatedly in Coleridge's dream writings and aesthetics is that of association: via the 'trains of forgotten Thought' the various responses to the print collaborate and are gradually recognised as meaningful. In this sense, he articulates here ideas very similar to those expounded by Erasmus Darwin in *The Botanic Garden*. But, in these two entries, while Coleridge is able to appreciate the influence of 'trains of forgotten Thought', he is careful not to advocate an entirely passive model of the mind.

His recognition that opium allows access to 'trains of forgotten Thought' because of its effect on the physiological 'seminal organization' of memory posits memory as both passive and active, visual and verbal. Many of Coleridge's dreams illustrate the ways in which memory is given a unique and specialised role in the dreaming process. Memory creates a collage of events in daily life. Memories merge, and assume correspondences based on feelings, as in this dream account from November 1804: 'Of my Dream of going into a Field with men on horseback all in blue which made me, then a Child of 7 years old, burst into Tears in a corner of the Parlour at Ottery – the corresponding reality bursting on me near Reading in the 15th of Light Dragoons' (*CN* ii 2290). The ambiguity of this entry testifies to the complexities and potency of those 'forgotten' trains of thought. One reading of it is that the earlier dream, of the seven-year-old child, anticipates the later experience in the Dragoons. Or perhaps Coleridge records two dreams as one experience, with similar qualities, although recollected many years later. Or is it that those childhood feelings of terror, anger and uncontrollable anxiety are repeated in a 'corresponding reality' in his Dragoon days? The dream's use and representation of memory are visual and tactile, passive and active, but also indeterminate and random. Coleridge's dream could be a simple account of two past events, yet there are elements in it still active as he writes his entry in November 1804: the use of the past tense, the realisation that the two events become similar in the context of the dream. The memory is visual, with the stark description of the 'men in horseback all in blue', and also tactile, with reality 'bursting' in on the dream protagonist and dreamer, and the 'bursting' into tears. The memory of a reality intruding, or 'bursting', upon the child sitting in the Ottery parlour and the 'corresponding reality' of the Dragoons are intimately associated with both a dream state and a day-dreaming state.

Memory becomes a unique species of dream in and for itself. The active process of remembering creates a state of mind in which it is possible to create and selectively recreate the past. To remember is to suspend temporarily Cartesian concepts of time. As time is suspended in somnial space, memories and ideas from different times are easily fused. The importance of memory in dreams is illustrated when Coleridge attempts to explain a particular type of dream, which seems to be a type of reverie, dependent as it is on a feeling of sleepiness and slipping in and out of wakefulness. His interest in the following dream entry pivots on the realisation that dreams have their own internal structure and relevance, their own 'connections':

Wednesday Night – Dreamt that I was saying, or reading, or that it was said to me, 'Varrius thus prophecied Vinegar at his Door by damned frigid Tremblings' – just after which I awoke – I fell to sleep again, having in the previous Doze meditated on the possibility of making Dreams <regular,> and just as I was had passed on the other side of the confine of Dozing I afforded this specimen/I should have thought it Vossius rather than Varrius – tho' Varrius being a great poet, the idea would have been more suitable to him/only that all his writings were *unfortunately lost in the Arrow.* Again I awoke. N.B. The Arrow Captn Vincent's Frigate, taken by the French, with our Malta Letters and Dispatches having been previously thrown overboard, in Feb. 1805. – This illustrates the connections of Dreams – (*CN* II 2542)

Kathleen Coburn's note explains that the two names which Coleridge confuses here are those of Marcus Terentius Varro (116–27 BC), the Roman man of letters, and Gerhard Johann Vossius (1577–1649), a German classicist and theologian (*CN* II 2542n). This particular type of dream not only reveals to Coleridge the frequent 'connections of dreams' with waking life, but also illustrates the ability of the mind to drift meaningfully and freely into meditation, dozing, dosing, sleeping and dreaming. The mind is aware of making these meaningful drifts and connections. Such dreams are examples of the implicit yet obscured links between waking and dreaming life, although he later conceded that they were not always present in other types of dreams. There is also the suggestion that some dreams are able to be willed, with Coleridge meditating 'on the possibility of making Dreams <regular>'. Dreams can somehow be *made*: more specifically, they can be made to be 'regular'. The will, in such cases, becomes more active than it is normally thought to be in dreams.

The role of the will in Coleridge's distinctions between dreams and reverie, reverie and day-dreams, visions and dreams, is clearly elucidated in a notebook entry from March 1808. His attention to tactile awarenesses and the active meditative power of the mind convinces him that he has discovered a 'fact' about the peculiar state of mind in which some types of vision occur:

I was thinking of something introversively and gazed meantime on the wall, over a chest of Drawers, close to the Wall & close by the Bed's head, so that between the Bed & the Wall there was not so much as a foot; & between the Chest of Drawers and the Wall not more than three Inches. On the Chest of Drawers was a Lookingglass – *touching* it on the left (*facing* the C. of Drawers) the Curtains of the Bed at its *pillow*-part/on the right, within a foot & a half a window. . . The wall was papered . . . as I gazed the marks on the paper grew not only *larger*, but far more *vivid*, all increased & the distance between the bed & wall, & Chest of Drawers & Wall became such that a pair of Friends might walk arm in arm in the Interstice. – As I gazed at this, I again voluntarily threw myself into introversive Reflections, & again produced the same Enlargement of Shapes & Distances and the same increase of vividness – but all seemed to be seen thro' a very thin glaceous mist – thro' an interposed Mass of Jelly of the most exquisite subtlety & transparency. But my reason for noting this is – the fact, in my second & voluntary production of this Vision I retained it as long as I like, nay, *bent over* with my body, & looked down into the wide Interspace between the Bed & Chest of Drawers, & the papered Wall, without destroying the Delusion . . . The power of acting on a *delusion*, according to the Delusion, without dissolving it. (*CN* III 3280)

Coleridge's comments reveal how the potential to will a vision is realised: via the 'second & voluntary production' of the vision, which is achieved by retaining it for 'as long as' he likes. Because of the strength of the will, there is 'power' to act on an admitted delusion, without dissolving it. As was often the case with Coleridge, this entry reveals his considerable attention to the details of his surroundings, but without the comfort that such minute observation usually brings. The chest of drawers, the wall, the curtains and bed are all precisely located. Yet the act of gazing, coupled with an introversive reflection, creates an entirely different scene. The vision itself is not entirely unconscious or unsolicited: he claims that he 'voluntarily threw' himself into it, and that his will was partially able to control what was seen. This ability of half-creating and half-succumbing to a visual delusion is a stunning illustration of the mind's powers in suspension between waking and sleeping. Coleridge's phrasing in this entry also reveals his determination to possess and control dreams in his own somnial space as much as possible, through his action of voluntarily throwing himself into 'introversive Reflections'.

The poem, 'Frost at Midnight', reveals that he used in poetry the phrasing and ideas of differing consciousnesses expressed in his early notebook entries. The notion of a blurred, swimming sense, of the various moods of the mind, of the creative and active powers of memory, and of the influence of those feelings of perception and reception of things inanimate and animate, is given a poetic embodiment:

> But O! how oft,
> How oft, at school, with most believing mind,
> Presageful, have I gazed upon the bars,
> To watch that fluttering *stranger!* and as oft
> With unclosed lids, already had I dreamt
> Of my sweet birth-place, and the old church-tower...
> ... So gazed I, till the soothing things, I dreamt,
> Lulled me to sleep, and sleep prolonged my dreams!
> And so I brooded all the following morn,
> Awed by the stern preceptor's face, mine eye
> Fixed with mock study on my swimming book.

(PW I 241 lines 23–38)

The rhythm of this section of the poem is very similar to that of a reverie. The initial repetition of 'how oft!, / How oft' is a sign that the 'I' is about to drift off into reverie, with the possibility that sleep will soon follow. In 'Frost at Midnight', Coleridge blurs the boundaries between what seems and what may actually be: a 'thin blue flame' (line 13) that still quivers, yet quivers not; the conviction that the stranger's face *will* be seen when eyes are lifted from the page (lines 40–1). Actions are subdued, preparing the reader to enter and descend into the opaque world of consciousness: to be 'presageful', to gaze (line 25), to watch something that flutters (line 26), to dream (line 27), to be 'lulled . . . to sleep' (line 35), to brood (line 36), to have a book before you that swims. All that occurs within the domains of gazing, lulling, dreaming and being soothed is unclear and only partially understood. The repetition of the easeful 'l' and 's' sounds culminating in the drawn-out, dazed quality of that last line, 'fixed with mock study on my swimming book', paradoxically clarifies the obscurity of the whole description. And although that description is one of being 'fixed', the only fixing seems to be one which is mutable. The 'swimming eyes' which viewed the Darlington Ox print are also described as 'vacant' (*CN* I 1575), and the suggestion in Coleridge's poetic reconstruction of his school-days is that the vacant mood becomes one of 'mock study' in the classroom (see also 'A Fragment Found in a Lecture-Room', *PW* I 35). A mood of idleness, of productive day-dreaming, is portrayed with exquisite delicacy.

These different moods, these differing ways of seeing and receiving information from the outside world, form a continuum in which dreams and poetry are never very far apart. Coleridge's recognition that the mind slips in and out of dreaming and waking, and a whole assortment of moods in between, is one that he explores both in his poetic writings and in his efforts to understand dreams.

'Frost at Midnight' is also suggestive of a state of consciousness in-between waking and dreaming. The poet claims that the 'soothing things' that he dreamt 'lulled' him to sleep, but that sleep 'prolonged my dreams'. The mood described, of gazing and entering into deep thoughts, creates its own type of dream, and sleep becomes an extension of that dreaming state. The usual divisions between waking and sleeping, so beautifully captured in the poem, are forgotten in this particular state. The subtlety of Coleridge's phrasing is almost hidden in the rhythm of the poem, as he explains how he gazed and gazed at the 'soothing things' until they lulled him to sleep.

Located somewhere between a dream and a reverie, or perhaps somewhere closer to the delusion experienced in a 'scream dream' nightmare (*CN* IV 5360), are many unusual and often inexplicable semi-conscious, or semi-dreaming states. There were many instances in medical, literary, scientific and popular literatures of visions, feverish dreams and spiritual sights. That Coleridge considered dreaming, apparitions and witchcraft to be complementary studies is clear from his determination to devote a substantial, unified study and lecture to such topics (*F* II 117, 145; *Lectures* II 196). Francis Hutchinson's *An Historical Essay Concerning Witchcraft* (1718) (see *CN* III 4395), Cotton Mather's *The Wonders of the Invisible World* (1693), John Ferriar's *An Essay Towards a Theory of Apparitions* (1813), and other works were read by Coleridge in preparation for his lecture series of January to March 1818. Equally useful would have been John Aubrey's *Miscellanies* (1721), John Cotta's *The Triall of Witch-craft, Shewing the True and Right Methode of the Discovery: with a Confutation of Erroneous Wayes* (1616), and John Stearne's *A Confirmation and Discovery of Witch-craft* (1648).[3] What he selected from these works for his own elucidation and exposition is not only the historical and social interest of such cases, but also the psychological interest of the phenomena of witchcraft and apparitions. In *An Essay Towards a Theory of Apparitions* Ferriar considers the influence of physiology on visions and apparitions, and wonders:

whether the improved state of physiology affords any glimpse of light on this subject, and whether such extraordinary and terrific impressions cannot be explained, from the known laws of the animal œconomy, independent of supernatural causes . . . a partial effect of the brain may exist, which renders the patient liable to such imaginary impressions, either of light or sound, without disordering his judgment or memory.[4]

The author concludes that spectral visions need to be closely studied by both the philosopher and the physician, and that the relationships between the brain, the external senses and the visions must be taken into consideration. Years of study of his own experiences as well as those of others led Coleridge to sympathise very closely with Ferriar's position.

Ferriar was not the only writer who began to explore the influence of the nervous system upon the occurrence of visions and ghosts. Coleridge would have encountered similar views in his readings of the *Journal of Natural Philosophy, Chemistry and the Arts*. In November 1803, a celebrated essay appeared on the 'Appearance of Spectres or Phantoms Occasioned by Disease, with Psychological Remarks'.

Coleridge owned this journal, and would no doubt have borrowed ideas from it in the formulation of his own views on spectres, ghosts and various other apparitions.[5] In the essay, the German sceptic philosopher Christoph Friedrich Nicolai reports his extraordinary visions, in which he saw, heard and spoke with acquaintances who had died. After leeches were applied to his anus, and the apparitions disappeared, he came to believe that they were a result of his fatigued, diseased state, combined with his natural tendency towards a lively and 'pictorial imagination'. Nicolai concludes that the visions 'originated in my internal consciousness alone; in a consciousness which was also disordered'.[6]

Reading this compelling essay, and the later works of Ferriar and others, Coleridge may well have incorporated similar ideas into his own thoughts on the subject. The ways in which he approached the phenomenon of apparitions can be seen to suggest that they were yet another 'species' of dream-related experience. This approach, particularly for the last twenty years of his life, reflected his rejection of empirical psychology and mechanical science in their efforts to explain the appearance of ghosts, spectres and apparitions (*TT* I 52–3). Rather than adopt the view that ghosts and visions were solely the result of trains of association and thought, he eagerly explored their psychological manifestations and causes. He often claimed that he had many experiences akin to apparition-seeing, but that he did not believe in the 'existence of Ghosts &c' because he had 'seen too many of them', a remark both unintelligible and profound (see *CN* II 2583, *LS* 81n). Does Coleridge here imply that he does believe in ghosts and that his own experience proves his belief? Or is he mocking the existence of ghosts *per se*? His non sequitur allows him simultaneously to claim and disclaim the existence of ghosts, thereby removing the difficult question of whether the irrational and inexplicable phenomenon belongs outside of the mind, or deep within it.[7] Such paradoxical statements did not prevent him from commenting on many of the popular ghost stories he read, and his conclusions on the validity of those stories were frequently just as inconclusive.

In an 1819 annotation to Johann Jung's *Theorie der Geister-Kunde* (1809), he comments upon a particular case in which a young journeyman, who had died three weeks earlier, returns to visit his master. Coleridge's judgement regarding the master's vision draws on his ideas as to the nature of differing states of consciousness, and on his thinking about the spectrum of dreaming and waking experiences. He argues:

There often take place fits of Slumber so brief and momentary as to escape the Slumberer's own consciousness. In these cases the Images and Sounds from the Brain blend with those from the Outward Senses, their distance being determined by their comparative vividness – just as reflected and transmitted Light, where a window fronts the fire-place. We see the Fire among the Bushes in the Garden, for instance – (supposing the window to overlook a Garden) and nearer and nearer as it grows darker & darker. Now the impossibility of proving, that this Johannes was not a Dream or Brain-creature of this kind, amounts to a proof that it *was/* (*CM* III 212)

Once again, in that closing sentence, Coleridge has his cake and eats it too, arguing that the impossibility of proving the vision 'amounts to a proof' that it *was* one. His explanation of Johannes' vision demands that a brief, sudden sleep has occurred. But this sleep has been entered into unawares; it is a fit of 'Slumber so brief and momentary as to escape the Slumberer's own consciousness'.[8] Coleridge describes the state of mind in which we think we see ghosts as a specific species of dream. In this peculiar state of consciousness, somewhere between sleeping and waking, images and sounds from within the brain are 'blended' with images and sounds in the environment. It becomes extremely difficult, if not impossible, to distinguish an image from within the brain from an image outside it. Ghosts and visions are examples of unique types of dreams (*CM* III 198), which can be further explained by reference to the effects of both a disturbed or fatigued mind and a diseased body (*TT* I 16, 52–3).

Coleridge's classification of a state of mind in which a brief and momentary 'fit of Slumber' occurs finds an interesting parallel in Wordsworth's Lucy poems as well as in his own Preface to 'Kubla Khan'. In the poem 'Strange Fits of Passion I have Known', Wordsworth presents a scenario which nearly exactly matches the kind of 'fit' that Coleridge describes in his *Geister-Kunde* annotation. The trudging of the horse's hooves, and the hypnotic effect of gazing at the moon, plunge the lover into a 'strange' fit of 'passion', in which 'sweet dreams' are encountered. He dreams, although his eyes are open. But the 'sweet' dream is not of 'Nature's gentlest boon', but rather of the 'wayward' thought that Lucy might be dead.[9] In this brief lapse into a somnial state, the intrepid lover seems to be both conscious and unconscious of being asleep. Coleridge's explanation

of such states of mind was that the 'Images and Sounds from the
Brain blend with those from the Outward Senses' (*CM* III 212). In
Wordsworth's poem, it seems that the lover's own 'fond and
wayward thoughts', combined with the descending moon and the
horse's trudging steps, create apparent 'sweet dreams' which instead
lead to thoughts of death. And in his Preface to 'Kubla Khan',
Coleridge claims that he fell victim to a peculiar sleep in which
'images rose up before him as *things*, with a parallel production of the
correspondent expressions, without any sensation or consciousness of
effort' (*CKK* 52). While he admits that he had fallen into a 'profound
sleep', he qualifies this sleep as a state in which images from within
his mind suddenly appeared as things, with 'parallel' expressions.

Coleridge believed this unique species of dream could account for
a number of apparently inexplicable phenomena. In the second
essay of *The Friend* (1809), he explains Luther's sighting of the Devil,
and his hurling of the ink-pot, in terms of a lapse into a sudden
sleep. He argues that Luther's sedentary lifestyle, his ailing health,
the 'great irritability of his nervous system' and his theological
training combined to influence and produce an 'unconscious half
sleep', or more specifically, a rapid alternation of 'the sleeping with
the half-waking state' (*F* I 139–40). Coleridge describes these unconscious half-sleeps as 'the true witching time', the very season in
which 'spirits hold their wont to walk' (*F* I 140).[10] Taking into
consideration the concurrence of all these conditions, and the
existence of unconscious half-sleeping states, he concludes:

Nothing improbable, that in some one of those momentary slumbers, into
which the suspension of all Thought in the perplexity of intense thinking so
often passes; Luther should have had a full view of the Room in which he
was sitting, of his writing Table and all the Implements of Study, as they
really existed, and at the same time a brain-image of the Devil, vivid
enough to have acquired apparent *Outness*, and a distance regulated by the
proportion of its distinctness to that of the subjects really impressed on the
outward senses. (*F* I 140)

As in the *Geister-Kunde* annotation, Coleridge explains Luther's
vision as a confusion between which sights and sounds originate in
the brain and which are seen in a 'momentary' slumber. The 'fits of
Slumber' are half-waking, half-sleeping states, examples of an
'unconscious half sleep' (*F* I 139). Often, 'intense thinking' inexorably
leads into one of these unusual slumbers, and the persistence of one
thought induces Luther's vision of the Devil. Thoughts and realities

are condensed and conflated; Luther falls into a 'trance of slumber' whereby, 'all at once' in his dream, he 'sees the Arch-fiend coming forth on the wall of the room, from the very spot perhaps, on which his eyes had been fixed vacantly during the perplexed moments of his former meditation' (*F* 1 142). Had Luther understood the 'nature and symptoms of Indigestion', or the 'detail of Subjective Seeing and Hearing, and the existence of mid-states of the Brain between Sleeping and Waking', he would have been, Coleridge believed, a 'greater Philosopher' (*CM* iii 770). He is firm in his belief that what Luther mistakes for a vision is in fact an '*Ocular Spectrum*'.[11] He explains such visions and experiences in highly subjective terms, attributing their cause to psychological processes rather than to supernatural visitations.

The unusual state of mind which partakes of both dreaming and waking may have been rare, but it was not inconceivable or entirely elusive. Luther was not the only man to succumb to a belief in the objectivity of an essentially subjective phenomenon.[12] One evening in January 1823, Coleridge spoke of the impossibility of 'really' seeing 'with the bodily eye what was impalpable, unless it were a shadow': subjective and objective are confused to such an extent that it can be at times very difficult to separate the two (*TT* 1 16–19). Jacob Böhme and Emanuel Swedenborg also fell victim to sudden onslaughts of dreaming and sleeping, and an accompanying confusion between subjective and objective phenomena (*CM* 1 558, *CM* iii 991, *SWF* ii 927–32). In the writing of his *Heaven and Hell* (1758) Swedenborg unwittingly experienced a unique dreaming state. Coleridge suggests that Swedenborg truly believed in the spiritual apparitions he saw because he may have been the 'subject of a very rare but not (it is said) altogether *unique*, conjunction of thate somniative faculty (. . . by which the products of the Understanding . . . are rendered instantaneously into forms of Sense) with the voluntary and other powers of the waking state' (*CM* iii 991). The so-called 'conjunction' of the somniative faculty with certain waking faculties creates a situation in which Swedenborg is forced to assert and believe that he saw a 'supernatural Illumination' (*CM* iii 991). Considering the possibility that such a hypothetical explanation might be true, Coleridge concludes that

by some hitherto unexplained affection of Swedenborg's Brain and nervous System he from the year 1743 thought and reasoned thro' the medium and

instrumentally~ity~ of a series of appropriate and symbolic visual and auditual
Images spontaneously rising before him, and these so clear and so distinct
as at length to ~become~ overpower his first suspicions of their *subjective*
nature and to become *objective* for him – i.e. in *his own* belief of their kind
and origin – still the Thoughts, the Reasonings, the Grounds, the
Deductions, the Facts illustrative or in proof, and the Conclusions, remain
the same! (*CM* III 991–2)

What Coleridge extracts from his hypothesis is both the *validity* of
Swedenborg's facts and conclusions and the *incorrect reasoning* under
which those conclusions were formed. Because Swedenborg was in a
unique dreaming state, and because there were certain faculties
within his mind that were still functioning as though he were fully
awake, he was unable to distinguish what he saw from what he
thought he saw: images both clear and distinct from his own mind
are eventually seen as objective. What Coleridge points out is that
those clear and distinct images are more likely to be subjective, and
are the result of that 'very rare conjunction of the somniative faculty
. . . with the voluntary and other powers of the waking state'.
Swedenborg's theology arose out of an experience which, in Coleridge's thinking, was a unique but identifiable dreaming state.[13]

As a poet whose primary concerns in the *Lyrical Ballads* were to be
'directed to persons and characters supernatural' (*BL* II 6), Coleridge
shows an interest in witchcraft and apparitions that becomes even
more intriguing.[14] A comment he made about *Christabel* is revealing
of his thoughts on ghosts and apparitions. In October 1804, in a
cryptic note written three years after the poem, he makes a
tantalising reference to Geraldine's character: 'Saturday Morning
. . . a most tremendous Rain storm with Lightning & Thunder, one
Clap of which burst directly over . . . Vivid flashes in mid day, the
terror without the beauty. – A ghost by day time/Geraldine' (*CN* II
2207). Years later, on 1 July 1833, he claimed that the reason why he
had not yet finished *Christabel* was not because he did not know how
to finish it, but rather because he could not 'carry on with equal
success the execution of the idea – the most difficult . . . that can be
attempted to Romantic Poetry – . . . witchery by daylight' (*TT* I
409–10). Although this comment has often been seen as another
attempt to rationalise why he had not completed the poem, it is also
highly likely that Coleridge's reasoning is quite correct. For over
thirty years, he attempted to understand the often cited/sighted
occurrences of ghosts, witchcraft activities and visions. If he had not

yet ascertained in his own mind the exact explanation for such phenomena, he could not finish his poem.

His description of Geraldine as a 'ghost by day time' sheds light on his thinking on dreams and visions, and the ways in which an understanding of witchcraft could further elucidate the mysteries of dreams. His comment also reveals the important connections he perceived between the studies of witchcraft and those on dreaming (*F* II 117, *Lectures* II 196). From the time that Geraldine encounters Christabel by the 'broad breasted old oak tree', and particularly those times surrounding awakening and sleeping, it seems that it is indeed the 'true witching time'. The similarities between dreaming, sleeping, spirits and witchery are suggested in an early review of the *Christabel* volume, by John Morgan, although Coleridge is thought to have suggested certain ideas in it. Commenting on the powerful descriptions of Geraldine's first meeting with Christabel, the reviewer argues that a poetic difficulty arises after the two women have awoken the following morning:

We have hitherto seen the mysterious Geraldine shrouded in night; shown either by the uncertain light of a clouded moon, or by the glimmer of a dim and oscillating lamp; – at a time too when all nature around her was still, and at rest. The poet has now to introduce this supernatural being in the light, and joyousness of day.[15]

Geraldine's position as a 'ghost by day time' (*CN* II 2207) seems to be indicated by the effect she has on Christabel. When Christabel awakes, she greets Geraldine with 'such perplexity of mind' that she can barely determine who it is that greets her, or why she feels so troubled:

> And Christabel awoke and spied
> The same who lay down by her side –
> O rather say, the same whom she
> Rais'd up beneath the old oak tree!
> Nay, fairer yet! and yet more fair!
> For she belike hath drunken deep
> Of all the blessedness of sleep!
> And while she spake, her looks, her air
> Such gentle thankfulness declare,
> That (so it seem'd) her girded vests
> Grew tight beneath her heaving breasts.
> 'Sure I have sinn'd!' said Christabel,
> 'Now heaven be prais'd if all be well!' (*CKK* 29–30)

It seems that the 'fair Geraldine' whom Christabel found 'beneath the old oak tree' is not entirely the same as the Geraldine who 'lay down' by Christabel's side. The blessedness of sleep seems to have affected the two women in remarkably different ways. The qualifying 'O rather say . . .' demands that Geraldine's identity be seriously questioned. The apparent transformation from the night-time Geraldine to the Geraldine of the morning, as well as her behaviour and ambiguous appearance, may be explained if she is 'a ghost by day time'. Christabel's own thoughts and fears, perceptions and ideas, may form Geraldine's character[16] in the same ways that Luther's brain formed the offending Devil, in Coleridge's explanation of the incident as cited in *The Friend*. What Christabel sees and what she thinks she sees are questioned through the use of the parentheses: '(so it seem'd) her girded vests / Grew tight beneath her heaving breasts'. Whether this is the poet-narrator or Christabel's hesitation is not as important as the suggestion that what is seen is not perhaps an objective but a subjective phenomenon. If Geraldine is a ghost, and more particularly, a ghost who 'nothing' doubts the power of her spell (*CKK* 29), then it would follow that what Christabel sees and feels is more akin to a 'fit of slumber', caused by a conflation of subjective and objective states.

The possibility that Geraldine may be a 'ghost by day time' may help to explain the unusual psychological relationship between Christabel and Geraldine, as well as that between Sir Leoline and Geraldine. Coleridge had earlier commented on the power of tears, when coupled with a state of extreme emotion, to alter the ways in which external objects are perceived (*CN* II 2583). The Baron is described as having 'tears . . . on his face' as he 'fondly' embraces Geraldine (*CKK* 34), and perhaps the power of his tears radically alters his perceptions. This power of alteration is clearly seen in the relations between the human figures in the poem, and their dreams and visions. Geraldine's undressing is a sight for Christabel to 'dream of, not to tell!' (*CKK* 18). Christabel has been silenced in a somnial world; her visions cannot be transferred to waking life. This silencing forms part of Geraldine's powers as a 'ghost by day time' (*CN* II 2207), but it is also an integral feature of dreaming itself. Earlier in the poem Christabel had dreams of her absent knight: disturbing dreams which made her moan and prompted her to go stealthily into the 'midnight wood' (*CKK* 5). Both of Christabel's dreams – of Geraldine and of her beloved – are inexpressible. Both the language of the dream and the language in which to express the experience of a dream are unutterable. Christabel's vision of Geraldine occurs before the two women lie down together. The 'sight to dream of' must then be a specific type of dream, perhaps a dream that is dreamt when the eyes are already open. The conflation between what is seen, what is thought to be seen (a possible 'fit of slumber') and Geraldine's witch-like qualities all combine to create a curious and egregious species of dream. Coleridge also argued that 'terror and the heated imagination will, even in the daytime, create all sorts of features, shapes, and colours out of a simple object possessing none of them in reality' (*TT* ii 47): a description which aptly fits the action of *Christabel* at this climatic point in the poem.

The history of the publication of *Christabel* also contributes to the ghostly aspects of the poem. Byron's involvement in encouraging Coleridge to publish the poem is well known, and his influence should not be underestimated. The publication of *Christabel* in 1816 occurred at a time when Coleridge's reputation as a poet was at a low point, but also at a time when other English poets were increasingly enchanted by the mysteries of sleep, dreams, visions, apparitions and mesmerism. At the end of June 1816, Byron, his physician John Polidori, Percy Bysshe and Mary Shelley, and Clair Clairmont gathered at Lake Geneva. The results of a competition they held to determine who could write and narrate the best supernatural story have become Romantic folklore. What Polidori records in his diary on one particular evening in June is perhaps less well documented for the ways in which he provocatively links *Christabel* with the dream and spirit preoccupations of all those present:

Twelve o'clock really began to talk ghostly. L[ord] B[yron] repeated some verses of Coleridge's Christabel, of the witch's breast; when silence ensued, and Shelley, suddenly shrieking and putting his hands to his head, ran out of the room with a candle. Threw water on his face, and after gave him ether. He was looking at Mrs Shelley, and suddenly thought of a woman he had heard of who had eyes instead of nipples, which, taking hold of his mind, horrified him.[17]

Much discussion has centred on the possible sources for Shelley's hallucination,[18] but what is of equal intrigue in terms of the influence of Coleridge on the gathering is the description of Geraldine as a witch. Whether it was Polidori or Byron, or perhaps Shelley, who labelled her a 'witch' is not clear: what is evident is that she is remembered as possessing powers akin to those of a witch, through her ability to bewitch Christabel and others in Christabel's home. The plethora of different moods and the exploration of the possibilities between waking and sleeping in *Christabel* provide rich examples of Coleridge's ideas on the different species and genera of dreams, especially those dreams which were in some way connected with or partook of the phenomena of witchcraft. Furthermore, at the time of *Christabel*'s publication in 1816, interest in another scientific and psychological phenomenon which had somnial overtones was reigniting across Europe: animal magnetism.

John Beer has commented on the attraction of animal magnetism, or mesmerism, for Coleridge.[19] It opened up for him a rich and diverse area, in which he could easily explore the different species and genera of dreams. In a marginal note to John Webster's *Witch-craft* (1677), he speaks of 'magnetic sleep'. Magnetic sleep is, for Coleridge, a unique category of consciousness, similar to the stupor of the nightmare. While having properties in common with deep dream sleep, magnetic sleep is not entirely the same as that state of consciousness:

During the magnetic sleep, the reaction of the Will ceases and with it the power of reason and understanding, and man becomes, as to the organism of the senses, a mere passive instrument for the manipulation of influences, commonly of no very high, and sometimes of a malignant nature. Hence this can be no sequla or continuance between this and the wakeful state, because the one depends upon the reaction of the mind and self-consciousness, and the other <is grounded> upon the [?entire] substance of both.[20]

The suspension of the powers of volition, reason, and understanding occurs in magnetic sleep, as with normal sleep.[21] But in the case of magnetic sleep, there is 'no continuance between this and the wakeful state'. That is, there is no 'mind', and no 'self-conscious-ness', but sometimes there are moments when the sleeping and dreaming mind is capable of being and remembering itself. In another marginal comment Coleridge refers to magnetic sleep as a 'morbid sleep' in which the 'organs of sense remain in stupor' (*CM* III 371). During this state, 'the reaction of the Will ceases and with it the power of reason and understanding', to such an extent that the person magnetised becomes 'a mere passive instrument for the manipulation of influences'. These influences are often of a 'malig-nant nature'.[22]

Familiar with the principles of animal magnetism as early as 1795, Coleridge built up over the years an impressive library of works by the magnetists, but it was not until 1815 that this interest became an intellectual challenge (*TT* I 96; *Lectures 1795* 327–8; *PLect* 104). There was a general resurgence of interest following the publication in 1813 of J. P. Deleuze's *Histoire critique du magnétisme animal* and, more significantly for Coleridge, in 1815 of Karl Kluge's *Versuch einer Darstellung des animalischen Magnetismus*. Not only did Coleridge read many of the major works on the subject, he also met and befriended some of the authors and leading scientific men publicly involved in the magnetism debate, including Ludwig Tieck.[23]

What attracted Coleridge to magnetism, and what kept reigniting his interest in it, was its ability to counter theories of scientific materialism. Magnetism advocated the power of unseen forces in the cure of diseases and offered explanations for many phenomena which could not adequately be explained in terms of physical laws. It posited the influence of psychological powers, particularly those of the imagination, and possessed a mysterious aspect which could not be matched by theories of association (*CN* I 920). Coleridge's interest in animal magnetism was a cautious and slightly sceptical one.[24] Although initially he did not believe any of the claims made by the magnetists, he later came to believe that it could usefully explain away many of the biblical miracles, and various superstitions;[25] it could also account for apparently inexplicable states of consciousness, especially those akin to dreaming. His opinions changed, but his curiosity never waned. In 1809, for instance, he ridiculed the curative potential of magnetism (*Lectures 1795* 327–8), but in 1818 he reconsidered his objections (*F* I 59, II 51). In 1821 he was sufficiently in favour of magnetism to draft the beginnings of an essay on the subject (*SWF* II 911–14), perhaps as a result of his search for alternative methods of healing (*CM* III 1067). It was in 1817 that he was able to conclude that 'the Idea is legitimate and philosophical' (*CN* IV 4908), despite the fact that only twelve months earlier he had denounced at least one form of magnetism as a fraud.[26] Occasionally, his scepticism re-emerged, as can be seen in his comment in March 1830 that he was 'in a state of philosophical doubt as to animal magnetism' (*TT* II 96). In general, it seems that he continually questioned certain aspects of magnetism while still being fascinated by it, with his interest periodically reignited as magnetism moved through distinct developmental phases throughout his lifetime.

The man generally associated with the discovery of animal magnetism was Anton Mesmer, who later emerged as a charlatan figure in the controversy surrounding the new science. There were numerous followers of Mesmer's doctrines, many of whom did not wholeheartedly agree with his ideas or his methodologies, and created their own brand of mesmerism.[27] Coleridge was aware of the differing schools of thought within the field (*CM* iii 396–7), and especially of the ideas of Mesmer himself. In 1778, Mesmer proclaimed his discovery of a fluid which penetrates and surrounds all bodies. In a dissertation of 1799 he set out twenty-seven propositions in support of his new doctrine, including that there exists a 'mutual influence between the Heavenly Bodies, the Earth and Animate Bodies', that there is a 'universally distributed and continuous fluid' which is the 'means of this influence' and that animal bodies can be brought under the influence of heavenly bodies. This action, termed 'animal magnetism', can be used to cure nervous disorders 'directly and other disorders indirectly'.[28] The fluid can be directed to act on other objects, human and non-human. This strange and untestable force also has an antithesis: there is not only an animal magnetic force, but also an anti-magnetic force, which, according to Mesmer, has all the properties of the magnetic forces except that it produces opposite effects. In an era dominated by Isaac Newton, who hypothesised that there were universal and invisible laws which governed the universe, Mesmer's claim that there is an invisible force acting between and through bodies was not implausible.[29] One of Coleridge's arguments in support of magnetism was that whereas it was received in many scientific circles with a 'scornful and pertinacious' air, the equally invisible force called electricity was 'eagerly' received (*CM* iii 373; *SWF* i 499, 590).

One of Mesmer's followers described mesmerism as a science which 'embraces the physical and the metaphysical', which gives a 'knowledge of the phenomena which are evoked by the action of spirit upon matter, and their reaction'.[30] Animal magnetism could be used medically, and it is with this claim that Mesmer made and lost his fortune. He believed that health was a state of harmony between the individual microcosm and the celestial macrocosm.[31] Disease resulted from the presence of obstacles within the body preventing the free and healthy flow of animal fluid. Certain individuals could control and stem the flow of the fluid's action by mesmerising or massaging the body's poles, which would then remove the obstruction. Certain techniques were conducive to the channelling, storage and conveyance of this fluid between persons. The removal of the obstacle was termed a 'crisis', and often took the form of convulsions, but sometimes less violent reactions were obtained.[32] The result of the onset of the crisis was the restoration of health. Part of this process involved the patient being put into a trance, or into what Coleridge described as a magnetic torpor, a magnetic sleep.[33]

Potentially, magnetic sleep had numerous properties beyond those found in 'proper' sleep and dreams. For instance, Coleridge believed that a morbid sleep could be utilised for medicinal purposes, thereby explaining many of the apparently inexplicable phenomena of animal magnetism as cures for a diverse range of both minor and major ailments. His general interest in the subject prompted him to investigate further the potential of one of the crucial elements of magnetism itself, the hypnotic or somnambulistic trance, or 'sleep', which all patients experienced.

The magnetism session relied heavily on the production of this magnetic sleep or torpor, which could be induced in two ways. The mesmerist could direct the movement of the pervasive fluid with his hands and fingers, or sometimes with an iron rod, over and around the affected bodily organs or parts. Or sometimes huge tubs were used, around which the sick sat, sometimes up to one hundred at a sitting: inside the tubs Mesmer placed water which he had mesmerised, or iron filings. Patients were attached to the tub with rods and ropes, forming a kind of mesmeric circuit.[34] The tub could dispense the valuable fluid through its ropes or rods, and when the fluid reached the patient, a 'crisis' was induced. Once the fluid had passed from magnetist to patient, he or she experienced differing degrees of mesmerism. The most common and profound response was the mesmeric sleep, in which the patient was said to be in a 'deep' trance, a 'sleep' so intense that 'all consciousness, sensation, and volition are suspended' and only the 'involuntary nervous action' remains.[35] It was in this state that diseases could be relieved, and surgical procedures performed without pain.[36]

Coleridge was not the only one to be fascinated by the potential for magnetism as a cure for diseases, and as an illustration of a unique species of dream. In 1815, Polidori published his dissertation on somnambulism, *De Oneirodynia, Disputatio Medica Inauguralis, Quaedam de Morbo, Oneirodymia, Complectens*; in 1833 Thomas De

Quincey penned his opinions on animal magnetism in an anonymous article in *Tait's Edinburgh Magazine*. Years earlier, in 1807,
Robert Southey had introduced many English readers to the
wonders of animal magnetism in his *Letters from England*.[37] Percy
Bysshe Shelley was also aware of the phenomena and underwent
mesmeric therapy in Pisa in December 1820 to relieve painful
spasms caused by kidney stones.[38] It was the concurrence of many
factors within the mesmeric session that fascinated Coleridge and
enabled him to see it as a unique kind of sleep, a 'magnetic' sleep.
While he did not believe in the existence of a magnetic fluid, he did
believe in the existence and efficacy of that special sleep (*CM* III 383,
386). He was also ready to give magnetism a fair hearing in the light
of the French Royal Commission's 1784 conclusion that its effects
and cures were the results of the imagination. Coleridge saw the
Commission's findings as testimony to the 'intellectual' (*CM* III 371)
validity of magnetism, evidence of the 'producing and beholding'
powers of the imagination (*CM* III 376). His interest in the subject
was a result not only of his enquiries into the potential powers of the
imagination, but also a result of his interest in the many degrees and
stages of wakefulness and dreaming (see *SWF* I 588). In an annotation to Kluge, Coleridge argued that 'under certain conditions one
human Being may so act on the body as well as on the mind of
another as to produce a morbid Sleep, from which the Brain awakes
while the organs of sense remain in stupor. I speak exclusively of the
intellectual phænomena of An. Mag' (*CM* III 371). This magnetically
produced stupor is different in kind, intellectually different, from any
other stupor or dream or delirium state. Coleridge at times doubted
the medical properties that were proclaimed for mesmerism (*CM* III
375, yet see also *CN* IV 4908) but he never lost interest or belief in
magnetic torpor as unique, as a state of consciousness caused by the
influence of one person over another.

Magnetic sleep also revealed to him the fundamental aspect of all
genera of dreams: the splitting of the somnial space in what was
often an irreconcilable divide. One of Mesmer's students, Armand
Marie Jacques de Chasten, marquis de Puységur, observed that after
he magnetised one of his patients, the patient fell fast asleep in his
arms, but was able to converse on a variety of topics. The patient
later had no knowledge of what had happened. Puységur listed the
features of this magnetic sleep as a sleep-waking kind of consciousness; a 'rapport' or special connection with the magnetiser; suggest-

ibility; and amnesia, in the waking state of events in the magnetised state. Patients are induced into a special state of consciousness which is neither sleeping nor waking. But, as Puységur discovered in his patients, the inability to recall events or conversations while magnetised persisted long after the patient had awoken from the session. This led him to conclude that the demarcation between the magnetic sleeping state and full consciousness was so great that the two states must be regarded as two different existences: he later developed this into a notion of a 'divided consciousness'.[39]

Not only would Coleridge have been attracted to this splitting of somnial and waking consciousnesses, he would also have been fascinated by this special state of consciousness which forms the perfect medium for one person to be profoundly influenced by another (*PLect* 105). This potential intrigued him, especially as it was an influence that could be effected during an abnormal and profoundly altered state of consciousness. He found that there was 'no impossibility in the human Will . . . extending its influence beyond the visible outline of the Willer's own body; or . . . in the metastasis of the sentient power from one part of the Nervous System to . . . another' (*CN* IV 4908). Nor did he deny that there existed 'in certain states and under certain suspensions of the Activity of the bodily Organs' the potential for a higher, more profound sense to operate (*CN* IV 4908). What the practice of mesmerism presented to Coleridge was this: in certain altered states of consciousness, not only could a sick person be restored to health but certain parts and organs of the body could act upon and interact with others; the deep torporific state also permitted the extension of one human will over another (as in *CN* IV 4908).

The power by which this influence arises is a result of at least two forces: first, the undeniable friction between the nervous system and the skin, and second, the power of the imagination. This second power could be seen at work within the patient's own body and mind, in addition to the mind of the magnetist. In an essay written around 1821, Coleridge argues that the incidents of animal magnetism sessions may be explained according to

the present System of Physiology without recourse to any new powers, agents, or modes of nervous or vital Action . . . first, regular Friction, and the state produced thereby in the cutaneous nerves especially, and then the increased sensibility of the nervous system generally, by direct or sympathetic Communication with the Skin . . . Secondly, the tendencies

. . . of sentimental Love and Sexual inquietude diffused and metastatus, awakened by the Cutaneous Action . . . 3^{rdly} Association, in its widest sense. 4^{thly} and lastly: Imagination, which in this instance must be extended to the Power, by which . . . a Patient's Mind produces changes in . . . his own body, without any intentional act of the Will – as a Blush for instance, contagious Yawning, Night-Mair, Fever Phantoms, Palpitation of the Heart <from Fear> in short, what not? (*SWF* II 912–13)[40]

Coleridge firmly places the theories and practice of magnetism in the context of contemporary medical and philosophical thinking. The moments when the patient is in the trance are the moments when his imagination is capable of producing certain effects upon the body, sympathies which are tangible and observable. The excitation of this power is at once the strongest and the weakest point of the anti-magnetist's reasoning. Not only is there within the magnetic sleep the potential for the magnetist to act upon the patient, without his conscious will, but the potential also exists for the patient's own mind to act upon the body according to magnetic principles (*SWF* II 114). What magnetism offered for Coleridge was a means of perceiving potentially reciprocal influences between the imagination and the body, in either a healthy or an unhealthy state. He perceives and uses the imagination as an explanation for scientific and medical phenomena while at the same time perceiving it to be a pivotal agent in the cause of dreams.

The many possible psychological, physical, theological and medical consequences of a patient entering into a torpor or trance continually fascinated Coleridge. In a notebook entry of November 1827, he does not question the possibility that a magnetic trance might be induced, but rather wonders what possibilities arise as a result of that trance existing in the first place. He begins his questioning with a reference to Kluge's *Versuch*:

It would not be altogether a waste of Time, to go thru' the phœnomena of Zoomagnetism as . . . collected by Kluge, with such additional Facts as later Magnetists have made known, and to determine the conclusions, that would necessarily or legitimately follow from the admission of their truth and subjective reality. For instance, assuming the truth of the case attested by Hienholt <that the patient had not deceived him>, and that neither he nor his Patient had deceived himself, [?or/if/of] the female Clairvoyant who in her own [. . .] sleep or rather Desensuation recollected accurately every thing that had taken place both within herself, and all that had been done and said by others, during her fainting fits, in which she lay to all appearance utterly senseless, and all of which she was entirely unconscious in her coming to life again. Could this fact, if a *Fact*, . . . admit of any other solution, but that of the Soul, = principium individualities, or substantial person capable <if not> of existing separately from the body, yet of perceiving, remembering, and thinking independently of the bodily organs of Sense, Memory & Thought – i.e. [?from] the Senses? . . . And *then* would it not follow that the Body is a moveable Dungeon with windows, and Sound-hobs – & that we might well exclaim with the great Apostles, who shall deliver me from *the Body of this Death*? (N36, fos. 3v–4)

In April 1819 Coleridge felt (perhaps only briefly) that he no longer needed 'additional proof' of the facts of animal magnetism (*CN* IV 4512), and in this later notebook entry it is clear that his main emphasis is not so much on the truth of the reality of the magnetist's powers, but rather on the 'conclusions' that 'necessarily' and 'legitimately follow' from the act. Coleridge suggests that during the session reported by Hienholt, the patient experienced a 'Desensuation', a type of magnetic sleep in which she could accurately report not only all that had been said and done by others, but also what had occurred within her own bodily organs. The ability during this clairvoyant phase of magnetism to see within the body struck Coleridge as another illustration of dreaming (*CM* III 717), explicable according to the notion that the soul may be able to exist separately from the body, while still being capable of remembering, perceiving and thinking independently. The idea that the soul can exist independently of the body in a type of dream conflicts with many of his other commentaries on dreams as they related to his body. But he also once stated that magnetic patients could enjoy 'the most delightful dreams [coupled] with a highly pleasurable state of Being' (N36, fo. 59). A species of dream which did not offer such potential pleasure was the nightmare.

CHAPTER FIVE

'Nightmairs'

For most of his adult life, Coleridge was plagued by a 'dreadful labyrinth of strangling, hell-pretending Dreams' (*CN* IV 5375). There were also '<Scream-> Dreams' (*CN* IV 5360), dreams which forced him to awake to a sense of 'gouty suffocation' (*CN* I 1833), and 'Dreams of Terror' (*CN* II 1998) which were accompanied by painful emotional and physical sensations (*CN* II 2838). He collectively referred to all such dreams as the 'Afflictions of Sleep' (*CN* IV 5360). However, the discomfort and anguish associated with nightmares did not prevent him from attempting to understand the many ways in which they could be distinguished from other species and genera of dreams.

In a letter to Poole of November 1796, Coleridge attempts to explain Charles Lloyd's illness. Lloyd had been staying as his pupil in Bristol for some weeks before the fits began:

Charles Lloyd has been very ill, and his distemper (which may with equal propriety be named either Somnambulism, or frightful Reverie, or *Epilepsy from accumulated feelings*) is alarming. He falls all at once into a kind of Night-mair: and all the Realities round him mingle with, and form a part of, the strange Dream. All his voluntary powers are suspended; but he perceives every thing & hears every thing, and whatever he perceives & hears he perverts into the substance of his delirious Vision. He has had two principal fits, and the last has left a feebleness behind & occasional flightiness. Dr Beddoes has been called in. – (*CL* I 257)

Coleridge positions himself as an authority on the subject of 'Somnambulism, or frightful Reverie, or Epilepsy . . . a kind of Night-mair'. He quickly distinguishes Lloyd's condition as not merely a 'Night-mair', but more specifically as a 'kind of Night-mair'. The reference to Dr Beddoes confirms the dangerous medical nature of Lloyd's illness, a kind of 'Epilepsy from accumulated feelings'. That Beddoes was called in also reveals this eminent physician's interest in cases such as Lloyd's, an interest which he later elaborated in his popular *Hygeia* (1802–3). In that book Beddoes observes the differences between 'reasoning dreams' and waking dreams, and mentions the dangers of delirious dreams, associated with nervous complaints.[1] Beddoes and Coleridge undoubtedly had many discussions about Lloyd's complaint, and about dreaming in general. The distinction Coleridge offers between what his pupil was suffering and the standard definition of dreams in contemporary literature is an important feature of his enquiry into dreaming and dream psychology. He labels Lloyd's experience as a 'strange Dream' on the grounds that his 'voluntary powers are suspended', but then backtracks by adding that Lloyd is still capable of perceiving and hearing 'every thing'. He is reluctant, however, to describe his condition as a nightmare state, qualifying his behaviour as 'a kind' of nightmare.

Coleridge's qualification implies that he had other notions of nightmare, even as early as 1796. In 1808 he maintained that there were distinguishing features of the nightmare, and that there were some dreams which had some of its qualities but could not be termed nightmares as such:

It is a general, but, as it appears to me, a mistaken Opinion, that in our *ordinary* Dreams we judge the Objects to be real. I say, our *ordinary* Dreams: because ~~in~~ as to the Night-mair the opinion is ~~in~~ to a considerable extent just. But the Night-mair is not a mere Dream, but takes place when the waking State of the Brain is re-commencing, and most often during a rapid alternation, a *twinkling* as it were, of sleeping and waking . . . the mind, I say, in this case deceived by ~~her~~ past experience attributes the painful sensation received to a correspondent ~~cause~~ Agent – An assassin, for instance, stabbing at the Side, or a Goblin sitting on the Breast, &c – . . . Add to that the Impressions of the Bed, Curtains, Room &c received by the Eyes in the half-moments of their opening blend with, & add vividness & appropriate distance to, the Dream-Image <which returns> when they close again: and thus ~~the~~ we unite the Actual Perceptions, or their Immediate Reliques, with the phantoms of the inward Sense – and thus so confound the half-waking, half-sleeping Reasoning Power, that we actually do pass a positive judgement in for the reality of what we see & hear: tho' often accompanied by doubt and self-questioning, which . . . as I have myself experienced will at times become ~~so~~ strong <enough> even before we ~~are~~ awake, ~~that we become convinced~~ to convince us, that it is what it is – the Night-Mair. (*Lectures* I 135–6)

For Coleridge, the 'Night-mair' was a special dream, more akin to reverie than to 'ordinary' dreams; and there were also dreams which were extraordinary, which occurred in the 'twinkling' time between sleeping and waking. Judgement is passed in the half-waking, half-sleeping state of the nightmare. When it contains painful sensations, the half-waking, half-sleeping mind is deceived and attributes those painful sensations to a 'correspondent' agent: the dream assassin or dream goblin. The physical surroundings are crucial in the definition of this kind of dream: the impressions of the bed, curtains and room; the eye's vision of those objects; and the confusing, half-waking, half-sleeping 'Reasoning Power'. A nightmare is not merely the mingling of realities as experienced by Lloyd, but rather the equivalent of being 'whirled about without a center . . . no gravity – a vortex without a center' (*CN* III 3999). This conveys a sense of a wild, uncontrollable and powerful force unleashed in psyche and body. It is a disorientating and possessing, engulfing power, giving the impression of great speed and haste: a 'night-mare sense of fleeing' ('Limbo', *PW* I 430 line 13). Nightmares are not 'mere' dreams, but occur when the 'waking State of the Brain is re-commencing, and most often during a rapid alternation, a *twinkling* as it were, of sleeping and waking'.

This 'twinkling' between sleeping and waking differs from the 'sudden fit of slumber' experienced by Swedenborg and Luther (*CM* III 212):

Night-mair is, I think, always – even when it occurs in the midst of Sleep, and not as it more commonly does after a waking Interval, a state not of Sleep but of Stupor of the outward organs of Sense, not in words indeed but yet in fact distinguishable from the suspended power of the senses in true Sleep; while the volitions of *Reason* i.e. comparing &c, are awake, tho' disturbed. This stupor seems occasioned by some painful sensation, of unknown locality, most often, I believe, in the lower Gut, tho' not seldom in the Stomach. (*CN* III 4046)

As in his efforts to explain the occurrence of ghosts and visions, Coleridge turns to an examination of the distinctions between outward and inner 'organs' of sense, between objective and subjective, to explain the true nature of the 'Night-mair'. The relative powers of reason and volition and the influence of the stomach's pain are also distinctively altered in this state. His use of 'night-mair' as opposed to 'nightmare' is significant. In *Biographia Literaria*, he explains why he uses the unusual 'mair' suffix (*BL* II 70). He distinguishes between 'mair', meaning a (usually female) goblin or a monster (from the Old English 'mare'), and 'mare', which is derived from the Old English 'mere', a female horse. Coleridge chastised Shakespeare's use of the word 'night-mare' in *King Lear*, claiming that the playwright, for 'his own *all-justifying* purpose', incorrectly introduced the word 'Night-mare'. Coleridge's understanding of a night-mair was that it was a goblin or a monster, a creature that visited the dreamer and imposed the horrible dream — it was certainly not a female horse.

Perhaps he also wished to differentiate his own perception of it from one of the most popular and quite sensational images of the night-mair in the late eighteenth century, Fuseli's 'Nightmare' painting.[2] In his paintings, Fuseli utilises both a goblin and a horse in the terrifying and erotic visitation which he calls a 'nightmare': the goblin sits upon the helpless woman's breast, while a horse's head leers from the darkness. Fuseli and his paintings were known to Coleridge.[3] Coleridge's choice of 'night-mair' in preference to 'nightmare' is as much an illustration of his attempt to understand the many different types of dreams he experienced as of his determination to set himself apart from accepted ways of thinking about those types of dreams. With few exceptions, he continued to use the 'mair' ending when he spoke of his frightening dreams: a choice which implicitly conveys his belief in their suffocating, monstrous qualities.[4] Because he particularly wished to differentiate his usage from the connotations surrounding the use of 'nightmare', I also adopt his 'mair' ending for the purposes of this chapter.

Coleridge's nightmairs were specific frightful dreams, usually accompanied by powerful psychological and physical feelings. In the nightmair, the dreamer is

> run-down and stared at,
> By hideous shapes that cannot be remembered;
> Now seeing nothing and imagining nothing;
> But only being afraid — stifled with fear!
> While every goodly or familiar form
> Had a strange power of spreading terror.   (*PW* II 861)

The nightmair is a powerful illustration of the nothingness, the essential emptiness of somnial experience: the hideous shapes *cannot* be remembered, nothing can be seen, nothing can be imagined. The only feeling or reality in this state is the overwhelming sense of fear, overwhelming to the extent that fear actually stifles the dreamer. The terror and torment that characterise the nightmair are actually caused by 'hideous shapes that cannot be remembered'. The sense of suffocation – 'stifled with fear!' – further conveys the sense and feeling of the goblin or monster as inhibiting the dreamer's breathing. These creatures haunt and possess the somnial space.

Thomas De Quincey also found his terrifying dreams to be populated with 'dreadful faces' and tumultuous occurrences (*Confessions* 79). Both his 'Suspira de Profundis' and *Confessions* are littered with threatening figures and shapes, a 'gloomy grandeur' which he claimed overhung his dreams 'at all stages of opium' (*Confessions* 92). Undoubtedly, Coleridge's opium ingestion also contributed to the terror of many of his nightmairs. But neither man shrank from the terror that his dreams produced; rather, each turned towards an analysis of his most horrifying somnial moments.[5] Coleridge's exploration of his darkest and most fearful dreams centred heavily on trying to determine exactly how such dreams differed from the many other species and genera he experienced.

For Coleridge, the nightmair is not really a state of sleep at all, but rather a state of 'stupor of the outward organs of Sense' which is also distinguished by stupor of the inner faculties. These organs of sense are stupefied during a nightmair, whereas they are suspended in normal sleep, and rendered incapable of receiving sensory information. Similarly, in nightmairs, the reason is thoroughly disturbed, while in normal sleep it is merely suspended. Coleridge offers an explanation as to why the organs of sense may be in a state of stupor: it is due to 'some painful sensation, of unknown locality, most often . . . in the lower Gut, tho' not seldom in the Stomach'. His distinction between the 'outward organs of Sense' involved in the nightmair and the 'power of the senses in true Sleep' suggests that the forces of the nightmair have a stronger physiological base than normal sleep.

Stupor, however, is not to be mistaken for sleep which is refreshing and beneficial: the stupor and consequent sleep occasioned by a large dose of mercuric acid, or what Coleridge terms other 'morphias', is 'different in kind' from refreshing sleep (N50, fo. 7v). The onslaught of a narcotic sleep is sleep 'only as consequent on the stupor of the outward senses', not to be mistaken for the more replenishing kind (N50, fo. 7v). Truly restful sleep he often saw as a 'gentle thing', yet it was difficult to attain (*LB* 21 line 284). Nor should the presence of stupor necessarily imply that a nightmair is being experienced, for there are other important types of stupor of which Coleridge was aware (for example, that associated with animal magnetism). The stupor of the nightmair must then be seen as part of a dream-continuum of varying levels of stupor, disturbed reason and intestinal pain.

In the case of the nightmair, the intensity of the pain, most commonly originating in the lower stomach, shifts attention from certain realities or ideas, and permits the nightmairish terror to enter into the dream. All psychic and physical attention is then centred upon the intensity of the pain, nullifying the presence of other realities. This presence of pain, which he calls a 'derangement', is one distinguishing feature of the nightmair as Coleridge experienced it:

when ever this derangement occasions an interruption in the circulation, aided perhaps by pressure, awkward position, &c, the part deadened – as the hand, or his arm, or the foot & leg, on this side, transmits ~~single~~ double Touch as ~~double~~ single Touch: to which the Imagination therefore, the true inward Creatrix, instantly out of the chaos of the elements <or shattered fragments> of Memory puts together some form to fit it – which derives an over-powering sense of Reality from the circumstance, that the power of Reason being in good measure awake, most generally presents to us all the accompanying images ~~exactly as we~~ very nearly as they existed the moment before, when we fell out of anxious wakefulness into this *Reverie* – ex. gr. the bed, the curtains, the Room, & its furniture, the knowlege of who lies in the next room &c – (*CN* III 4046)

Several factors emerge as grounds for distinguishing a true nightmair: the entire circulation system is interrupted, memory is called upon to create some sense of the chaos, the power of reason is 'in good measure awake' yet not fully empowered, there is pressure on certain organs, it or parts of the body may be in an awkward position, and there is a corresponding awareness that the senses have been deadened. This derangement transfers, or translates, specific sensations to specific regions of the brain and the body upon which the imagination, the 'true inward Creatrix', then acts. Coleridge coins these sensations either 'single' or 'double' touch.

What he meant by these two terms evolved over a considerable period. Little has been written on his complex use of them, although their importance has been noted by some critics.[6] If single and double touch are seen to be related to a special mode of volition only,[7] then Coleridge's use of the terms in discussions of his nightmairs seems incomprehensible. It also seems that his speculations on single and double touch went beyond, but still were included in, the confines of animal magnetism.[8]

Coleridge was not the first or the only person to explore the possibilities of single and double sense phenomena, but his investigations are particularly coloured by his profound and often complex meditations on dreaming and dreams. The importance of a concept of single and double sensation is indicated in an 1828 notebook entry, in which he plans to 'make an analysis of the functions of the five Senses, with sensation or single perception as the ground and Material' (N37, fo. 3v). Single and double touch seem to be inexorably connected for him with organs and the flesh, but most specifically with experiences of sexuality and the sexual organs. It is not only touch which can be delineated into single and double manifestations: vision also has this capacity, and it is quite possible that both vision and touch are at work in the derangement of the circulation in nightmairs.

The first mention Coleridge makes of single and double sense awareness occurs in September 1798, while he was in Ratzeburg, Germany:[9] 'Tuesday, Sept. 25th – Dined at the Table-d'hot / Wine Soup with currants in it . . . – That night sate up till 4 in the morning, & versified 200 lines / went to bed, could not sleep – saw a curious instance of single & double vision – / –' (*CN* 1 343). Kathleen Coburn makes no note of his 'curious instance of single & double vision', her silence suggesting that perhaps she thought it another illustration of opium-related sensory experience. Coleridge carefully records in his notebook the circumstances preceding the 'curious instance', an indication of his fascination with what has happened and his determination to understand it. He is also very careful to distinguish between normal vision, normal touch and his 'double' visions in later notebook entries.[10] What he terms 'single' touch or 'single' vision most nearly approximates to a definition of those senses: touch or vision in their elemental forms. He was fascinated by the functions and qualities of the differing senses, writing constant memos to himself to analyse the senses more carefully, to determine how they could be understood philosophically, physiologically, aesthetically and subjectively (N37, fos. 3v-6v).[11] In an entry of 1828 he thoughtfully distinguishes between levels of sensory awareness, placing 'sensation or single perception as the ground and Material' of the five senses (N37, fo. 3v). Single vision, for instance, is loosely parallel to the sensation of seeing, the 'material' act of seeing, whereby images are received on the retina and the information sent to the brain. When this perceptual act is considered as part of

complex relational processes within the material act of seeing –
questions of magnitude, space, and consciousness of the other senses
– Coleridge describes the vision as 'double'.

The specific connections of body and perception are characteristic
of normal vision and touch, but are seen more specifically in double
and single vision or touch:

> Mrs C. told me, Monday Night, May 9th, that since she had had the
> Influenza, & her Skin had been evidently affected by the State of her
> stomach, that the Baby lying on her arm <often> seemed two Babies – she
> not <absolutely> asleep – both on the same side – & that she often seemed
> to have two Breasts on the same side. – (*CN* I 1188)

Coleridge here explores the connections between skin and other
organs, between organs and perception processes such as vision and
touch: connections readily seen when sleep is not 'absolutely'
experienced. The role of the body and of sickness becomes crucial in
the recognition of the unusual sensations accompanying instances of
double touch or vision. His description of Sara's experience approximates to one of double rather than single touch. In another
notebook entry, he finally articulates the implied connections
between this and other entries about double touch:

> Of the intimate connection of Volition, and of the Feeling & Consciousness
> of Volition, on the state of the Skin, I have noticed long ago in a former
> Pocket-book, occasioned by the curious phænomenon experienced the
> Xtmas of 1801 at Mr Howel's . . . my Skin deadened, the effect of violent
> Diarrhœa / My Speculations thence on double Touch – the generation of
> the Sense of Reality & Life out of us, from the Impersonation effected by a
> certain phantasm of double Touch &c &c &c, and thence my Hope of
> making out a radical distinction between this Volition & Free Will or
> Arbitrement, & the detection of the Sophistry of the Necessitarians / as
> having arisen from confounding the two. – Sea sickness, the Eye on the
> Stomach, the Stomach on the Eye / – Eye + Stomach + Skin – Scratching
> & ever after in certain affections of the Skin, milder than those which
> provoke Scratching a restlessness for double Touch / Dalliance, & at its
> height, necessity of Fruition. – Fruition the intensest single Touch, &c &c
> &c. (*CN* I 1827)

Double touch, but also the sense of touch in general, are intimately
connected with volition. The 'state of the skin' holds remarkable
correspondences with the will, which in turn can influence the
formation of dreams and nightmairs. It is, after all, the absence, or
the diminished presence, of volition which Coleridge uses as a

partial definition of the onslaught of a nightmair. In *Notes* he refers to 'the sensation of volition which I have found reason to include under the heading of single and double touch' (*Notes* 331), the absence of the sensation of volition contributing significantly to the terror of the nightmair. This terror of a lack of volition, an intimate part of the the nightmair experience, is created by the 'generation of the Sense of Reality & Life out of us'. 'Double' vision, or, in the case of the above entry, double touch, involves connecting varying levels and notions of sensual experience with each other, all of which become concentrated in one sensual experience. The psychological, intellectual act of volition, coupled with both the feeling and the consciousness of having volition, is intimately connected to the state of the skin, which becomes, in its turn, an agency of double touch, both through vision and through a sense of temperature. In the notebook entry cited above, double touch is described as a series of interconnected sequences: 'Sea sickness, the Eye on the Stomach, the Stomach on the Eye / – Eye + Stomach + Skin'. Vision and touch are joined via the presence, sight and feeling of the stomach. Because the relationship between double touch and the other senses is an intimate and complex one, the eye and the sense of the skin must work together to produce a special 'double' sense of touch. This sense of touch is reliant not merely upon the eye, but upon a consciousness of volition, on the connections between volition and the skin itself, and on what Coleridge terms a 'certain phantasm of double touch', an itch that is characterised by its 'restlessness' as well as its need for 'fruition'.

He later describes the connections between different senses in the creation of double touch as being dependent on varying degrees of heat. In an unpublished marginal note to Karl Wolfart's *Mesmerismus* (1814) Coleridge reconfirms his qualified belief in the phenomena of animal magnetism, declaring 'I think it possible, that An. Magnetism will be found connected with a *Warmth-sense*: & will confirm my long long ago theory of Volition as a mode of *double Touch*.'[12] Volition, because of its 'intimate connection' with the state and perception of the skin, becomes a mode of touch, of physical perception, but more especially an example of 'double touch'. In this way, double touch is the 'aid' to the other cognitive faculties, and particularly to the senses of 'Sight and Hearing' (*CN* II 2405).

By 1805, Coleridge's fascination with the relationship between the external and internal organs of perception had become relevant to his attempt to explain the nature of nightmairs. In a long and complicated notebook entry, he attempts to clarify the exact relationship between the sense organs and external objects. In the articulation of his ideas, he is led directly into a consideration of the nature of single and double touch. He begins with a query as to the possibility that certain organs, when accompanied by passionate feelings, can become the sites of 'particular feelings'. The ideas are so rushed and complex that he needs to make footnotes to himself in an effort to remember all that seems relevant:

Touch – double touch / [1] Touch with the sense of immediate power [2]with retentive power – [3]retentive power extinguishing the sense of touch, or making it mere feeling – & the gradations preceding these is extinction / [4]retentive power simply, as when I hold a thing with my Teeth / [5]with feelings of Touch in one part of the machinery, both in the other, as when I press a bit of sugar with my Tongue against my Palate / [6]with feeling & even touch but not enjoyment specific stim*ulari* (esse sub stimulo) as when I hold a quill or bit of fruit by my lips – 1. emm. vi / Riley. inacts of Es*sex*. 2. The Lips, or the thumb and forefinger in a slight pressure. 3. The Hand grasping firmly an inanimate Body – that is the one extreme of this third Class – the other would be a Lover's Hand grasping the soft white hand of his mistress / Here the retentive power and nisus modify but not extinguish the Touch – it tells the story still & the mind listens to it. – (*CN* II 2399)[13]

Coleridge's first point is merely a note to himself – 'touch – double touch' – so that his accompanying note, when read in isolation, is not self-explanatory. The sexual nature of the connections between feelings of touch in particular is playfully subdued in the pun on virile and 'acts of Es*sex*', but immediately harmonises with the indisputably sexual nature of the nightmair as he experienced it. His toying with the word 'Essex' also acquires a sexual overtone as derived from the Latin *esse*, 'to be': in sexual acts, there is being. The pun functions on a bilingual level, and suggests that it is both in being, and in acts of sex, that double and single touch can be experienced. Immediately before his first comment, Coleridge wonders whether the aroused (female) nipple can become the 'seat of particular feeling' (*CN* II 2399). The transition from an aroused nipple to double touch to 'inacts of Es*sex*' further suggests the cognitive links in his mind between organs and passion, between organs and their differing susceptibilities to single or double touch.

The implications of this entry for Coleridge's enquiry into different types of dreams become clearer when it is remembered that he

refers to the existence of double touch in order to explain the role of
the imagination in the formation of the nightmair (*CN* III 4046). The
argument in the above entry (2399), and his general approach to
perception and the use of the senses, are fundamentally related to his
quest for a 'mode of consciousness and philosophic concept which
would accommodate both the self and the reality outside the self'.[14]
The need to ground his self-identity in external objects becomes very
dependent on the senses, especially touch and vision, *feeling* in all its
modes. Indeed, he often uses the word 'feeling' to include the
combination of emotion and touch. Organic perceptions and feelings are capable of excluding and opposing each other, and when
organic perceptions become 'more organic', feelings become 'less
passionate'. Touch can be transformed into feeling, and is capable of
many differing gradations of experience. Coleridge believes it is
possible to achieve a condition in which these states are realised: the
world of feeling and the world of perception are insufficient, for at
best they can independently accord with a dim, universal idea, and
at worst, they are indications of madness (*CN* I 1822). As Raimonda
Modiano argues, the ideal put forward by this entry seems to be a
state in which the 'vital Feelings', those 'parts which assimilate or
transform the external into the personal' (*CN* I 1822), do not suppress
the 'Organic Perceptions'. It is a state in which emotion, while
curing touch of its rougher physicality, does not deprive the self of a
'tangible connection with the external world'.[15]

Coleridge's second and subsequent points in the *CN* II 2399 entry
further reveal the importance of an awareness of single and double
touch in his discussion of nightmairs. One form of touch is that
which is experienced 'with the sense of immediate power', as when
lips brush or in the gentle touch of thumb with forefinger. Touch
with immediate power is differentiated from touch with 'retentive
power', as illustrated in the type whereby a hand firmly grasps an
'inanimate Body', or when a lover's hand grasps the 'soft white hand
of his mistress'. Different degrees and types of touch need to be
noted, because to Coleridge's mind they produce different dreams.
The 2399 entry attempts to classify the many levels of awareness
associated with touch, including the absence of awareness: 'the
imperfection of the organs by which we *seem* to unite ourselves with
external things' (my emphasis).

Perhaps the strongest indication of the intensity of Coleridge's
interest in double touch and double vision, and how this relates to

an awareness of the nature of dreaming and nightmairs, stems from the days he spent in London between November 1801 and January 1802, writing for the *Morning Post*, attending Humphry Davy's lectures, and in the company of Thomas Wedgwood. In 'An Enquiry into the Origin of our Notion of Distance', Wedgwood discusses the problems of George Berkeley's notion of vision and distance. Berkeley argued that our awareness of distance and magnitude is solely traceable to the eye, or to 'outness'. Wedgwood summarises Berkeley:

We form tolerably correct estimates of what we call the real distances and magnitudes of objects not very remote from us, and we substitute them so instantaneously for the apparent ones that the mind is unconscious of the change, and mankind in general consider real magnitude and distance from ourselves as direct and primary perceptions of sight. By this great change, which it is impossible for any man who has grown up to maturity, with the use of his senses, fully to conceive, vision becomes so important and comprehensive an inlet to knowledge . . . Distance and magnitude, according to his [Berkeley's] perceptions, acquired by the sense of touch. [16]

Wedgwood and Coleridge disagree with Berkeley's concept of 'outness' and his belief that the acquisition of magnitude comes via the agency of vision. Experience proves, argues Wedgwood, that vision alone cannot guarantee reliable spatial knowledge. In supporting his ideas he refers to the

common experiment of a body seeming double when felt in the angle of the tips of the first and second fingers crossed. A person is blindfolded, and desired to attend to the impression of touch from a body so placed; the bandage being removed, he is directed to look at his fingers, while the object is placed as before. He will say, that the first time he felt two bodies at a distance from each other, and that now he feels only one . . . As the sensations of touch from the same impressing body must have been the same in both cases, the supposed difference in them must have been owing to some circumstance of vision: in the first case, the experimenter was deceived by a visual idea; in the second he was rightly informed by a visual impression. In the same manner we may conclude that the notions of magnitude and figure suggested to us by the contact of solid bodies in the dark are derived from the visual idea of the portions of our skin which are touched by the solid bodies. [17]

Wedgwood's ideas formed the starting point for the more complex treatment Coleridge was to give to single and double touch. Both men would have conversed on the problems of touch, vision and magnitude. Their experimental starting points would have been similar, that things appear to be and feel as if they were 'double', but Coleridge uses the idea as an integral feature in his discussion of the nightmair.

Coleridge believed that when touch becomes so subjective that it is, or appears to be, distanced from reality, it causes nightmairs and ghoulish dreams:

As if the finger which I saw with eyes Had, as it were, another finger invisible – Touching me with a ghostly touch, even while I feared the real Touch from it. What if in certain cases Touch acted by itself, co-present with vision, yet not coalescing – then I should see the finger at a distance, and yet the two senses cannot co-exist without a sense of causation / the *touch* must be the effect of that Finger, I see, yet it's not yet near to me, <and therefore it is not it; & yet it is it. Why,> it is it in an imaginary preduplication. . . . How few would read this Note – nay, *any one?* / and not think the writer mad or drunk! (*CN* II 3215)

The 'what if in certain cases Touch acted by itself' speculation is answered in other notebook entries and letters: touch which is perceived to act by itself, 'co-present with vision yet not coalescing', is the touch specific to the nightmair, a touch which gives 'the *idea* and *sensation* of actual grasp or touch contrary to *my* will, & in apparent consequence of the malignant will of the external Form'. The touch of the nightmair is an '*abstract touch*', abstracted from consciousness (*CN* II 2468); it is an unreal yet real touch, and Coleridge's simile – 'as if' – gives a further indication of the real and unreal terrors of the nightmair – which are due not to the ordinary sensations of touch but rather to the co-presence of touch with vision, with the conflation of the 'Eye on the Stomach, the Stomach on the Eye' (*CN* I 1827). The 'invisible' finger is just as terrifying as the finger that is seen and felt. Double touch is a '*sensation* of volition' (*BL* I 293), and the altered state of volition in nightmairs allows for stomach and eye to interact, but also for actual grasps of dream-creatures to be felt. In the nightmair, which is partially characterised by this special sense of touch, double touch is the 'generation of the Sense of Reality & Life out of us' (*CN* II 1827; also, *Omniana* 181–5).

To conclude that an apparently immutable, cryptic sense such as touch can be so modified as to have discourse with the imaginary, with things invisible actually felt as though they were corporeally present, was to run the risk of being considered 'mad or drunk'. Even Coleridge's fears are relevant: madness and drunkenness are two other states in which the cognitive faculties are altered. Dreaming opened up the disturbingly similar world of madness, with dream-creatures ready and eager to assault and possess the dreamer. But he was far from believing that dreaming and madness were identical. He maintained that delirium, whether experienced as a result of organic disease or in the course of mental derangement, was different from nightmairs and other genera of dreams. What differentiated them was the type of touch that was experienced (N36, fo. 6v).

The psychological component of the act of perception, touch or vision, plays an important role in the course of the nightmair's etymology. Nightmairs are visions of 'fear', but they are visions with 'touch and pain' (*CKK* 34). In an unpublished notebook entry dated 24 December 1830, Coleridge discusses specific chapters in contemporary anatomy texts. Going on to distinguish between feeling and touch, and the differences between these two modes when encountered in a nightmair, he writes: '*Feeling* being the proper [?Antiaction] of *Touch* / as subjective to objective, interminate to indeterminate, sensitive to perceptive, <as> Hearing to Listening. In the mere *Feeling* the knowlege derived is an influence by an act of Mind . . . / as in night-mair, and often in a less degree in other dreams' (N49, fo. 22v). Feeling is passive; it is the 'antiaction', or the opposite of touch, which is active. Knowledge derived from the passive mode of feeling is influenced by an act of mind. In animals, knowledge is not a result of the mind or of feelings relative to touch; rather, all is reduced to a 'mechanico-chemical Process'. In nightmairs, feeling seems to be influenced by an act of mind which imagines an actual grasp or touch contrary to the dreamer's will. The role of touch and feeling is in many respects the strongest and most powerful feature of a nightmair.

When we return to Coleridge's comment in *CN* III 4046 that the stupor of the nightmair is caused by a derangement of the circulation, we see how the role of single and double touch becomes crucial. His confusions are of relevance in his explanation:

when ever this derangement occasions an interruption in the circulation, aided perhaps by pressure, awkward position, &c, the part deadened – as the hand, or his arm, or the foot & leg, on this side, transmits ~~single~~ double Touch as ~~double~~ single Touch: to which the Imagination therefore, the true inward Creatrix, instantly out of the chaos of the elements <or shattered fragments> of Memory puts together some form to fit it – (*CN* III 4046)

He confuses the roles of single and double touch in the disruption of the circulatory system. But the 'true inward Creatrix', the imagination, seems capable of coping with the disarray, both of the organs and of the poet's grammar. The 'shattered fragments' and chaos of the memory are calmed by the imagination. Also assigned to the imagination is the ability to form, to translate or to correct the chaos of the stupor, and the 'interruption of the circulation' caused by the nightmair. In addition, the imagination clearly has an important physical role to play in the struggle against nightmairs. The action of the imagination makes up for the absence of a sense of 'Reality', that connection with the internal and external organs of the senses which Coleridge mentions in other notebook entries (*CN* II 2399). Once the imagination and reason are 'in good measure awake', the nightmair can be challenged:

the power of Reason being in good measure awake, most generally presents to us all the accompanying images ~~exactly as we~~ very nearly as they existed the moment before, when we fell out of anxious wakefulness into this *Reverie* – ex. gr. the bed, the curtains, the Room, & its furniture, the knowlege of who lies in the next room &c. (*CN* III 4046)

The return to some form of control, after disruptions both psychological and physiological, marks the end of the 'reverie', of the nightmair. Awareness of external objects and events returns, and the stupor of the nightmair is contained. Coleridge calls this return a 'delivery':

Last night before awaking or rather delivery from the night-mair, in which a claw-like talon-mailed Hand grasped hold of me, interposed between the curtains, I ~~haved~~ just before with my foot felt some thing seeming to move against it (– for in my foot it commenced) – I detected it, I say, by my excessive Terror, and dreadful Trembling of my whole body, Trunk & Limbs – & by my piercing out-cries – Good Heaven! (reasoned I) were this real, I never should or could be, in such agony of Terror – . (*CN* III 4046)

Once again, the importance of touch is highlighted as both a cause of, and an escape from, the terrors of the nightmair. The latter are terrible by their physical nature: the grasp of a 'claw-like talon-mailed Hand' is the grasp from the depths of the nightmair, removed from the usual organs of perception and now entirely subjective; the awareness of the foot, of the 'dreadful Trembling of my whole body', marks the beginning of the return to wakefulness. Coleridge's uncertainty as to the reality of his experience 'Good Heaven! (*reasoned I*) were this real, I never should or could be, in such agony' stands as further testimony to the very specific psychological and physical nature of the nightmair reverie. I emphasise the 'reasoned I' because the interjection of the 'I' and the highest of all faculties, reason, is an attempt to diminish the terror and 'dreadful Trembling'. Coleridge's doubt as to the reality of his experience is much darker and more problematic than Keats' similar question at the end of 'Ode to a Nightingale': 'Fled is that vision / Do I wake or sleep?'[18] Keats' question may have its origins in that same conversation (or monologue) which I quoted at the opening of the previous chapter, the now famous one between him and Coleridge of 1819. Coleridge's attempt to impose a sense of order and control ultimately fails, as the weak and rational parenthesised 'reasoned I' commands little power in the aftermath of the nightmair's 'excessive Terror'. Yet the nightmair is also characterised by very physical sensations, a 'dreadful Trembling' of the entire body, an intense 'agony of Terror' caused by the apparent grasp and touch of a 'talon-mailed Hand'. The defining characteristic of the nightmair is not so much that the faculties of reason and will are partially *absent* as that of the undeniable *presence* of the tactile, corporeal world. Touch, double touch, the grasp of a fiend's claw, feeling and sensation: the undeniable presence of these features provides both the terror and the realisation of the nightmair's power.

Sensations of touch, sight, hearing and taste play a major role in Coleridge's discussion of the nightmair, and from the very earliest of his enquiries into somnial states, in his attempts to distinguish nightmairs from other types, or species, of dreams. In a letter to his wife, of March 1803, he pushes for more details as to the dreams she has described: 'Of what kind are the Dreams? I mean, are they accompanied with distinct bodily feelings – *whizzings up* into the head, fear of strangulation – &c – or simply great Fear from fearful Forms and Combinations – or both at once? – ' (*CL* II 940). His curiosity whetted, Coleridge is compelled to question Sara as to the type of dream she has been experiencing: he asks if the dreams are 'accompanied with distinct bodily feelings' or if they invoke 'great fear', or perhaps display 'both at once'. Perhaps he was trying to ascertain if she, too, suffered from the same kinds of dreams as himself. His questions indicate the importance he placed upon their physical features, and his careful distinctions between dreams and nightmairs, dreams of the day, dreams of the night and even '*day-mairs*' (*CL* I 242, *CN* III 4046).[19]

For Coleridge, the nightmair cannot belong to the realm of simple dreaming:

Night-mair is not properly *a Dream;* but a species of Reverie, akin to Somnambul~~an~~ceism, during which the Understanding & Moral Sense are awake tho' more or less confused, and over the Terrors of which the Reason can exert no influence ~~that~~ because it is not true Terror: i.e. apprehension of Danger, but a sensation as much as the Tooth-ache, a Cramp – I.e. the Terror does not *arise* out of ~~the~~ a painful Sensation, but is itself a specific sensation = terror corporeus sive materialis. – To explain & classify these strange sensations, the organic material Analogons (Ideas materiales <intermedias,> as the Cartesians say) of Fear, Hope, Rage, Shame, & (strongest of all) Remorse, forms at present the most difficult & at the same time most interesting Problem of Psychology, and intimately connected with prudential morals (= the science of morals in its relation, not the ground & Law of Duty, but to the ~~known~~ empirical hindrances & fumbulations in the realizing of the Law by the human Being) – . The solution of this Problem would, perhaps, throw great doubt on this present dogma, that the Forms & Feelings of Sleep are always the reflections & confused Echoes of our waking Thoughts, & Experiences. – (*CN* III 4046)

Once again, the confusion of the moral sense is highlighted in the nightmair, just as it had been in Coleridge's description of Lloyd's illness (*CL* I 257). Both understanding and the moral sensibilities are awake, but they are 'more or less confused'. Reason, the most exalted of all mental faculties, is almost powerless in the face of this confusion, not because there is a true 'apprehension of danger', but rather because the terror which is experienced during the nightmair is itself a sensation. Reason has no power over sensation, particularly a sensation which Coleridge describes as 'painful . . . specific', a terror which is corporeal, or material – 'corporeus sive materialis'. The terror is not, cannot be, only psychological. It must be completely beyond the domain of the powerful reason, a terror necessarily belonging to 'corporeus sive materialis'. The connections between sensation, double touch and the nightmair are causal.

The sensations encountered during a nightmair are indeed 'strange'; and they have 'organic material Analogons'. Seeing these sensations as 'intimately connected with prudential morals', Coleridge seriously questions the 'dogma' which maintains that 'the Forms & Feelings of Sleep are always the reflections & confused Echoes of our waking Thoughts, & Experiences'. It is possible that he was putting a part of his own dogma under interrogation, for in *The Statesman's Manual* he claims that the dreams most often remembered are those 'produced by the nascent sensations and inward motiunculae (the fluxions) of the waking state' (*LS* 80). In denying the connection between dream-sensations and 'prudential morals', he must affirm the importance of 'organic material', simultaneously throwing out a challenge to psychologists of the day (for instance, *CN* III 4046). In questioning the idea that feelings and forms in sleep are the 'reflections and confused Echoes' of waking life, he also conveniently evades the problem of why it was that he dreamt such horrible things and why he often awoke feeling the burden of sin. This evasiveness arose from a moral revulsion towards the self as well as a genuine desire to suggest other possible explanations of the cause of nightmairs and dreams.

In a much later notebook entry, from 1829, Coleridge quite smugly concludes his own theory on the causal relations between touch and the nightmair. Pondering the event of flying in dreams, he comments that dreams of flying are usually accompanied by a pain across the lower abdomen. The question as to why this should occur is posed and answered:

What is it? Imperfect awakening of the Volition, with sense of the nascent activity of the voluntary muscles – In short, Motion without *Touch* but with sense of *efforts* all corrupt in a [?continuing] series (awaking & [?relaxing] Volition) seems to solve the [?problem] . . . However, you never fly in a night-mair – for then the Sensation of *Touch* or of being touched is called up. (N41, fo. 1)

The contradistinguishing feature of dream and nightmair rests on the calling-up of the sensation of being touched. Touch, or the sensation of being touched, transforms the dream into a species of nightmair. Volition again plays a dominant role, with Coleridge arguing that both the originating stomach pain and the dream of flying are the result of an imperfectly awakened volitionary sense. Volition affects the action of the voluntary muscles, but, of course, in a nightmair, voluntary control over certain bodily actions is suspended. Volition is more impaired during the nightmair than in more usual states of dreaming or sleeping. Once again, he explains a difference between 'suspended' powers and powers in a 'stupor' (*CN* III 4046). The motion or action of flying without a sense of touch is a type of dream. The instant when volition is sufficiently disturbed to give the impression of touch, is the moment when the dream gives way to nightmair. Nightmairs are themselves distinguished according to the degree of touch felt or experienced; the terror of a nightmair is, more than anything else, seen by Coleridge as a 'bodily sensation', 'called up' by images or even by the absence of any image (*CN* III 3322). In another unpublished notebook, he comments that 'Somnial erotica' also partake of the 'Nature of the Night-mair' through the associated 'Sense of Touch' that is called up (N36, fo. 6v). Any dream, whether apparently benign or malignant, can be classified according to the degree to which it 'bordered on waking' and what kind of touch accompanied it.

Coleridge's dilemma over the nightmair takes on a more sinister aspect in so far as 'organic material', that is sensations, may be 'intimately connected with . . . morals' (*CN* III 4046). He tries to make his observations more palatable to his own sensibilities by 'throwing doubt' on the idea that the 'Forms & Feelings of Sleep are always the reflections & confused Echoes of our waking Thoughts, & Experiences'. Motivated by the need to disguise his own perceived moral shortcomings, he must question a 'dogma' that sees the dreamatis personæ as originating within the thoughts and inconsistencies of the waking psyche. This is as much the horror of the nightmair as the ugly demons which attack the sleeping victim: the 'Forms & Feelings of Sleep are *always* the reflections & confused Echoes of our waking Thoughts, & Experiences' (*CN* III 4046, my emphasis). For Coleridge, the nightmair exhibited uneasy proof of the connections between waking and sleeping lives, and the moral questions which arose as a result of a discrepancy between those two, at times disparate, lives: the 'ego diurnus' and the 'ego nocturnus' (*CN* III 4409). Sometimes, however, the nightmair could also prove the discrepancy between sleeping and waking experiences, to the extent that the dreamer could seriously wonder from what deep somnial recess of the mind such a dreadful dream could emerge. In such cases, the importance of the physical sensation, experienced so intensely that the reason can 'exert no influence' (*CN* III 4046), becomes crucial. The nightmair truly embodies the pains of sleep, as a sensation that is experienced as physical, and as a pain that cannot therefore belong to the 'Moral sense'. The terror of the nightmair also resides in the fact that it occurs on the fringes between waking and sleeping, between honest moral awareness and slippery delusion.

For Coleridge, nightmairs were amongst the most terrifying and physically immediate types of dreams. In some critical discussions of his poetry, mention is made of his nightmair experiences. Coleridge's own subtitling of the 1800 edition of *The Rime of the Ancient Mariner* as a 'A Poet's Reverie' encourages such readings: a nightmair is, after all, a species of reverie. Edward Bostetter utilises the ideas of a nightmairish world to elucidate certain aspects of *The Rime of the Ancient Mariner*.[20] He refutes both Robert Penn Warren and John Livingston Lowes[21] on the grounds that, although they recognise the dream quality of *The Rime of the Ancient Mariner*, they dismiss or minimise the meaning of the poem's dream qualities. Bostetter suggests that the clue to the significance of the poem may lie in Coleridge's subtitle.[22] Bostetter argues that what Coleridge meant by the term 'reverie' was a 'waking dream', in which the mind was aware and the faculties of reason not completely in control of the imagination. Although the subtitle 'A Poet's Reverie' was removed in the 1817 edition of the poem,[23] a year after Coleridge had published two other poems with dream titles and strong dream motifs, his understanding of a reverie can shed some light on the mariner's nightmairish horrors. Coleridge's nightmairs were deeply grounded in theories of volition as a mode of touch, in the general importance of the body's capacity to be touched and to touch, as well as in the recognition that nightmairs are very specific degrees of dreaming experience which were often characterised by an alarming sensation of emptiness and nothingness. A nightmair world may well be one in which 'stupor' rather than 'sleep' dominates, but this nightmair stupor is occasioned by 'painful sensation' (*CN* III 4046). The faculties of reason are altered, yet so too are the body's functions.

The mariner seems to partake of Charles Lloyd's medical condition: he 'perceives every thing & hears every thing, and whatever he perceives & hears he perverts into the substance of his delirious Vision' (*CL* I 257). The mariner is unable to distinguish between subjective and objective sights and sounds: a distinction which, if weak, Coleridge strongly believed could account for the existence of many visions and otherwise supernatural phenomena. Much of the mariner's experience can be seen as this integration of all things seen and heard into a 'delirious Vision': the dead bodies, with 'each right-arm burnt like a torch', with 'stony eye-balls' (*LB* 29 lines 495–6); the moon pops up into the sky, but then 'no where did abide' (lines 254–6); and the mariner himself is described as an 'it', that 'hath a fiendish look' (line 571). But the mariner's experiences are intensely physical while also being void of properties usually ascribed to physical entities: the stifling, suffocating stillness of the ship as it is 'stuck' upon the ocean, with neither 'breath ne motion' (line 112); the burden of the albatross around his neck (lines 137–8); the desperate act of biting his arm to suck his blood to give his mouth moisture (line 152); the feeling of his eyeballs as beating pulses under his eyelids (lines 240–1).

There were not only dreams, varying levels of day-dreaming and nightmair, but countless other possible divisions in the consciousness. In a notebook entry from 1827 Coleridge wrote: 'Every dream has its *scheme*/and is very different from Delirium – more different, I suspect, than can be fairly explained by comparing the Delirium to a confusion of simple types' (N36, fo. 6). After years of careful analysis, Coleridge declares that each dream, including his nightmairs, is unique, and has its own 'scheme' of characters, events, causes and narrative. There could be as many possible 'schemes', or species and genera, of dreams as there are dream-plots or dream-characters. A further illustration of the types of 'scheme' of different dreams is seen in an unpublished marginal note to Schubert's *Die Symbolik des Traumes*. Coleridge claims that Schubert's dreams are not to be confused with 'proper' ones.[24] The dreams Schubert selects for discussion in *Die Symbolik* are not 'proper' because they are 'prophetic and artistic'. Artistic dreams 'form a *distinct* kind' of dream, as do prophetic dreams. These latter types of dream are in a class all of their own. Schubert's dreams are, in fact, 'far more akin to Madness', for in both cases of madness and artistic dreams the brain is not in balance with other bodily organs. Other organs are deemed to be asleep, yet the brain is artistically active, diffusing itself in making artistic dreams. It is also likely that Coleridge wished to distance himself from the possibility that his own dreams were a sign of madness. Artistic and prophetic dreams are two 'species' of dreams that he seeks to differentiate from delirium. Dreams and delirium cannot be likened to each other, for in dreams there seems to be a unique purpose to the confusion encountered. An entry from Notebook 36 claims that the unique language of the dream is primarily characterised by a 'translation', or 'conversion', of pain into mental passions within the dream itself. Physical pain is a crucial defining factor of the dream, but it is a pain different from that encountered within the nightmair.

Nightmairs in particular, but also other species or genera of dreams, opened up many serious moral as well as intellectual questions for Coleridge. The deep dilemmas he faced in a notebook entry such as *CN* iii 4046, in which he claims that the 'organic material Analogons' of 'Fear, Hope, Rage, Shame' and remorse are 'intimately connected with prudential morals', forced him to contemplate possible explanations for the origin of his dreams. Were they always the 'reflections & confused Echoes' of waking thoughts and experiences (*CN* iii 4046)? Were nightmairs and other dreams products of bodily sensations? His nightmairs were indeed distinctly physical experiences, but what other roles did the body and the imagination play in dreams? Or were all species and genera of dreams, pleasant and unpleasant, caused by creatures who took temporary possession of the dreamer?

CHAPTER SIX

The mysterious problem of dreams

After many years of studying his dreams and nightmares, Coleridge claimed that 'no explanation of Dreams or attempt to explain them' had 'in the least degree' satisfied his judgement or 'appeared to solve any part of the mysterious Problem' (*CN* IV 5360). In 1827 he declared that all he had read on dreams and dreaming was 'utter shallowness and impertinency' (*CL* VI 715). This perceived absence of any cogent or comprehensive theory that could account for the different and bizarre qualities of dreams presented him with no other option than to suggest his own possible solutions.

The question of the origin of dreams was one which intrigued Coleridge for most of his life. Throughout his notebooks, letters and critical writings it is possible to discern three general dream-origin arguments, all of which arise from his vast reading of dream and medical literatures coupled with his own experiences: first, that dreams are caused by gods intervening in the lives of men; second, that they are a result of the action of malignant spirits; and third, that the dreamer's bodily position and state of health both causes and influences dreams. This third possibility presented him with a greater dilemma than the simple question as to why it was that dreams were dreamt. The poet's body dominates all his speculations about dreams and dreaming: a body frequently diseased, racked with pain, and often violently opposed to his intellectual and moral life. Just as pain is a feature of the dream's language and the language of the dream, so too does pain become a feature of Coleridge's explanation of the origin of the many species and genera of dreams he experienced.

His interest in a prophetic reading of dreams has close parallels with his belief that the language of dreams is one of anticipation and reminiscence (*CN* III 4409). He surmised that if the language of dreams was anticipatory, or prophetic, then perhaps its origin could also be prophetic. The idea that dreams formed a direct link with gods was one that Coleridge would have encountered in his readings of classical writers, including Aristotle, Galen and Cicero, as well as in his study of the Bible, especially the Book of Daniel.[1] Cicero's *De Divinatione* forms the basis for one of the earliest references to a prophetic reading of dreams in the notebooks. Cicero and Quintus query whether the gods can intervene in the lives of humans through dreams and prophetic visions. In Book I of *De Divinatione*, Quintus presents evidence from dreams for his pro-divination arguments. In Book II, Cicero replies:

A diviner was consulted by a man who had dreamed that he saw an egg hanging from the bed-cords of the bed in his sleeping-room – the story is from Chrysippus *On Dreams* – and the diviner answered, 'A treasure is buried under your bed.' The man dug, found a quantity of gold surrounded with silver and sent the diviner as much of the silver as he thought fit. The diviner then inquired, 'Do I get none of the yolk?' For, in his view, the yolk meant gold, the white of the egg, silver. Now, did no one else ever dream of an egg? What a lot of poor devils there are, deserving of divine assistance, who never were instructed by a dream how to find a treasure! Furthermore, why was this man given so obscure an intimation as that contained in the fancied resemblance between an egg and a treasure, instead of being as plainly directed as Simonides was when he was bidden not to go on board the ship? My conclusion is that obscure messages by means of dreams are utterly inconsistent with the dignity of gods.[2]

Cicero's conclusion that obscure messages in dreams could not possibly be consistent with the dignity of the gods exemplifies the ridicule that he heaps upon Quintus' arguments. Cicero sarcastically attacks his brother's claims, asking 'what do the gods mean by sending us in our dreams visions which we cannot understand ourselves and which we cannot find anybody to interpret for us . . . Besides, what purpose is served by dark and enigmatic dreams?'[3] He pleads with Quintus to ensure that his own simple dreams are not 'set at nought by superstition and perversity'.[4] The ambiguous nature of dream images and symbols leaves open the possibility that dreams might not have divine origins.

An early dream reference in Coleridge's notebooks concerns Cicero's discussion with Quintus. Coleridge's pithy entry simply reads: 'If you dream of an egg hanging at your bed's Head by a string ~~it is a~~ signifies finding hidden Treasure' (*CN* I 1027). However, the entry may well have been written with ironic undertones, reflecting the poet's ambivalence towards the divine theory of dreams. Cicero's counter-argument to Quintus also leaves open the possibility that those dream messages that are not obscure may support the argument that gods *do* intervene and often create dreams. Perhaps such simple messages prove both the dignity of gods and the intermediatory quality of dreams. Whereas Cicero claims that the obscure messages cannot be seen as evidence of divine existence or of divine intervention in the lives of humans, Coleridge was more open-minded as to the origins of his own dreams and was willing to consider the possibility that dreams might have divine sources.

The notebook entry concerning Cicero's *De Divinatione* was written in the period November 1801–January 1802, a time when Coleridge's ill-health produced several nights of terrifying dreams (*CL* II 772). The possibility that some of these were prophetic was one of several ideas he entertained. In recreating the circumstances of his father's death in one of the autobiographical letters to Thomas Poole he writes:

my Father went to Plymouth with my Brother Francis . . . He arrived at Exeter . . . and was pressed to take a bed there by the Harts – but he refused – and to avoid their intreaties he told them – that he had never been superstitious – but that the night before he had a dream which had made a deep impression. He dreamt that Death had appeared to him, as he is commonly painted, & touched him with his Dart. Well he returned home . . . At length, he went to bed, very well, & in high Spirits. – A short time after he had lain down he complained of a pain in his bowels, which he was subject to . . . In a minute my mother heard a noise in his throat – and spoke to him – but he did not answer – and she spoke repeatedly in vain. Her *shriek* awaked me – & I said, 'Papa is dead.' (*CL* I 355)

Coleridge quite freely mythologises some aspects of this story, perhaps painting a more sympathetic and sensitive picture of his young self than was actually the case. But his account of his father's death reveals that he believed in the prophetic powers of the dream. Although his father claimed that he 'had never been superstitious' (as we would expect of a clergyman), Coleridge's account of his death confirms the powerful and mysterious prophetic powers of dreams. He often returned to this childhood incident as a prefiguration of his own fate: one of his greatest anxieties about sleeping was that he too would die in his sleep, thereby 'imitating' his father (*CN* IV 5360). The incident came to be fictionalised as a fundamental part

of his self-concept. He often associated his dreams with an originating 'pain' in the bowels, and frequently awoke shrieking and
screaming from his dreams (*CN* i 1619, *CN* iv 5360). That this
partially fictionalised episode from his childhood is conveyed with
the aid of a prophetic dream is itself a significant association: dreams
and the act of imaginative (self)recreation are strongly linked in
Coleridge's mind.

Acts of clairvoyance, visions and spiritual revelations were all well-
documented occurrences in Coleridge's lifetime, and often such
accounts included discussions of the dream as a prophetic agency.
Sleep and dreams were readily seen as the vehicles for divine
inspiration and expression in such works as John Aubrey's popular
Miscellanies, Rachel Baker's *Remarkable Sermons*, and even the *Spectator*
ran a few articles on visions, and dreams much to Coleridge's
delight.[5] The story of Rachel Baker would have been of special
interest to him.[6] Born in 1794 in America and barely educated, when
she was awake Baker was a quiet, introspective girl. But when in a
state between sleeping and waking, she uttered the most eloquent
and, according to Dr Douglas', 'extraordinary' spiritual sermons.[7]
These attracted considerable notice and acclaim, and at the age of
fifteen she successfully toured America. The combination of an
unusual religious occurrence with speculative discussions on
dreaming would undoubtedly have appealed to Coleridge. And
Baker's history would have made compelling reading, as it includes a
number of interesting essays on dreams and visions by authors such
as Dugald Stewart, Dr Samuel Mitchell, Dr Benjamin Rush and
Joseph Priestley. Mitchell attended many of Baker's somnial sermons
and attempted to provide a theoretical framework for what he had
witnessed. He termed all her strange states a 'somnium', a state in
which certain bodily and mental actions are performed without
direction of the will and without recollection afterwards.[8] What
attracted Coleridge even more to Baker's history was the potential
that, while she was in this dreaming state, she held direct communion with the divine being whose sermons she delivered.

Coleridge's awareness of the dream's prophetic and supernatural
possibilities is understandable, especially given the currency and
popularity of such views. That dreams could be read prophetically
was one of his earliest opinions on the subject of their origin (*CN* i
432). In a letter to Mary Evans in 1793 he writes: 'I hope Mrs Barlow
is well – I have dreamt about her so often lately, that tho' not much

inclined to superstition, I am afraid that something must have been the matter with her' (*CL* 1 51). This apparently innocuous, playful statement firmly places the dream within a prophetic framework of interpretation: the dream comes to hold certain messages and omens for the dreamer, provided that the correct interpretation is made about the symbols and events in it. The dream needs to be interpreted, and some interpretations demand a prophetic explanation. Because Coleridge had lately been having dreams of Mrs Barlow – or so he says – he suggests that 'something must have been the matter' with her, or else he would not have dreamt about her so often. He tries to defend his position by adding the disclaimer that he is 'not much inclined to superstition', but he really cannot help himself: the admission of a 'superstitious' explanation, as in the account of his father's dream, is a tempting half-satirical, half-serious explanation.

Coleridge's wavering between being 'not much inclined to superstition' and being 'afraid that something' will come true is typical of many of his long-held attitudes on this subject. The tension between his labelling of prophetic potentialities as superstitious in his letter to Mary Evans, and his belief in the validity of his father's prophetic dream of death, is never entirely resolved. Years later, he displayed a negative attitude to the prospect of prophecy in dreams, while at the same time admitting it to be plausible. As was often the case with a dream of Coleridge's, the strongest agent in the formation of its character and of the dreamatis personæ was an intense emotion felt for Sara Hutchinson. Doubts, jealousies, half-expressed sexual tensions and insecurities surrounding his relationship with Sara are the ingredients of the following dream, which he fears will be realised in the future. He dreams

that W. W. and D. W. were going down to Wales to *give her away* – I am persuaded, that the Sharpness of Sense will not, cannot, be greater in the agony of my Death, than at the moment when the insufferable Anguish awoke me. N.B. I could detect on awaking no bodily pain or uncomfortable sensation, in stomach, or bowel, or side, as giving origin to it/it was the entire offspring of *Thought* – O mercy, of *prophetic* Thought? O no! no! no! let me die – tho' in the rack of the Stone – only let me die before I suspect it, broad-awake! (*CN* III 3912)

The suggestion that the dream is caused by a condition of the bowels is a common enough feature of Coleridge's dreams, but in this one he can detect 'no bodily pain or uncomfortable sensation'. This absence of usual dream features forces him to consider that the dream was entirely caused by thought. This instantly leads him to the terrifying prospect that it may be prophetic: 'O mercy, of *prophetic* Thought?' The 'insufferable' anguish of his jealousy of Wordsworth, and his insecurity regarding his relations with Sara, are distressing enough for Coleridge to conclude that the dream may indeed be prophetic. What can only be suspected 'broad-awake' is fully realised in the dream, and is experienced as real. This curious characteristic, of the dream as more real or as having the potential to be more real than waking perceptions and understandings, is one which he often mentions in his notebooks: it is a part of the dream's prophetic potential. The thought, the sensation, the hypnagogic process, all acquire a degree of reality which suggests that what is dreamt might actually happen.

Coleridge's belief in the prophetic potential of dreams became more sophisticated as he thought more deeply about theology and the truth of divine miracles. In the same notebook entry of May 1818 in which he articulates his thoughts on the problematic nature of the language of dreams, he also notes that in some dreams (what he terms a 'deeper' dream, or Ὑπεροveιpoζ) there is an 'imageless but profound Presentiment or Boding'. Not content to leave it at this, he continues: 'Prophetic combinations, *if* there be such, = the instincts previous to the use and to the organ' (*CN* III 4409). That this kind of presentiment is imageless may be due to the fact that the predominant sensual mode in the 'deeper dream' is touch rather than sight. This tactile emphasis draws attention back to the body, and an awareness of it in relation not only to its environment, but to its own internal workings. The ability of a dream to be prophetic depends upon the 'instincts', on the use of 'the organ' (which, he suggests, refers to the nervous system as a whole), but also on the type of dream that is being experienced:

Even 'the visions of the night' speak to us of powers within us that are not dreamt of in their day-dream of philosophy. The dreams, which we most often remember, are produced by the nascent sensations and inward motiunculae (the fluxions) of the waking state . . . when the nervous system is approaching to the waking state, a sort of under-consciousness blends with our dreams, that in all, we imagine as seen or heard, our own self is the ventriloquist, and moves the slides in the magic-lanthorn. We dream *about* things! (*LS* 80)

Coleridge refuses to confine his explanations to a philosophy grounded only in material senses and impressions: he argues that such strange things as the visions of the night cannot possibly be explained within the limits of philosophy, particularly Lockean or Hartleian philosophies (*CN* III 3825). The allusion to *Hamlet* is pertinent: Hamlet must explain to Horatio that the wondrous appearance of ghosts and other unworldly phenomena is beyond his restrictive, rational philosophy: 'there are more things in heaven and earth, Horatio, / Than are dreamt of in your philosophy'.[9] So Coleridge must approach the visions of the night with a novel attitude, in order to understand them. It is via the workings of the waking nervous system, the 'nascent sensations and inward motiun-culae', that 'things' are dreamt about at all. The body thus comes to figure in the prophetic nature of the dream, somehow containing within its own internal functionings a 'profound' power of prophecy. It thus becomes plausible to dream of a certain diseased bodily organ and to find a means for its cure in the dream's symbols or events.

This curious influence of organ on dream and dream on organ is further compounded as Coleridge uses distinctions of consciousness as a way of offering a single explanation for the origin of dreams. Those dreams which are most likely to be remembered, the 'deeper dreams', are in fact *produced* by the combined waking motions of the nervous system, or 'organ'. Only certain species or genera of dream, when combined with certain circumstances, have the potential to be prophetic. But he hesitates to commit himself completely either way, preferring to explore the connections between dream species and the operation of specific bodily organs rather than to define the connec-tions in themselves:

there are few persons of tender feelings and reflecting habits, who have not, more or less often in the course of their lives, experienced dreams of a very different kind, and during the profoundest sleep that is compatible with after-recollection – states, of which it would be scarcely too bold to say we *dream the things themselves;* so exact, minute, and vivid beyond all power of ordinary memory is the portraiture, so marvellously perfect is our brief metempsychosis into the very *being,* as it were, of the person who seems to address us . . . Not only may we expect, that men of strong religious feelings, but little religious knowledge, will occasionally be tempted to regard such occurrences as supernatural visitations; but it ought not to surprize us, if such dreams should sometimes be confirmed by the event, as they had actually possessed a character of divination. For who shall decide, how far a perfect reminiscence of past experiences, (of many perhaps that had escaped our reflex consciousness at the time) who shall determine, to what extent this reproductive imagination, unsophisticated by the will, and undistracted by intrusions from the senses, may or may not be concentrated and sublimed into foresight and presentiment? – there would be nothing herein either to foster superstition on the one hand, or to justify contemptuous disbelief on the other. (*LS* 80–1)

Coleridge's uncertainty is indicated by the restrained and at times constricted syntax of this extract: dreams of future events are only sometimes confirmed, as if some types of dream when dreamt by certain types of people 'actually possessed a character of divination', and those partially constructed experiences from the past 'may or may not be concentrated and sublimed into foresight and presentiment'. He perceives the need for a concentration of fertile imaginative, intellectual activity with the power to feel the most subtle emotions and thoughts before experiencing the depth of the profound dream. Feeling and intellectual fervour must be united. It is this type of intense dream that has the potential to be prophetic. He is tempted to regard some dreams as 'supernatural', but reluctant to dismiss altogether, with 'contemptuous disbelief', the mantic possibilities of dreams.

That this explanation held great attraction for Coleridge over many years of his life is evident from his poetical and dramatic works.[10] Bracy's visionary dream of the dove and the snake in *Christabel* is an exquisite illustration of the poet's use of the dream as a prophetic agency. As with all of the regular inhabitants of Sir Leoline's home, Bracy reports the morning after Geraldine's arrival that he has had an uneasy rest and a disturbing dream. What he sees in his dream is not only distressing, but prophetic:

> This day my journey should not be,
> So strange a dream hath come to me:
> That I had vow'd with music loud
> To clear yon wood from thing unblest,
> Warn'd by a vision in my rest!
> For in my sleep I saw that dove,
> That gentle bird, whom thou dost love,
> And call'st by thy own daughter's name –
> Sir Leoline! I saw the same,
> Fluttering, and uttering fearful moan,
> Among the green herbs in the forest alone.   (*CKK* 39)

That Leoline and Bracy should agree that the dream is significant, yet read and understand it so differently, is both the tragedy and the triumph of the poem. Leoline immediately turns to Geraldine and assures her that the 'snake' will be crushed, for he perceives the dove to be Geraldine. But Bracy reads the images of the dove and the snake very differently. An inability to read the actions and images of the dream is typical of the poem's ambiguities and its slippery metamorphoses of the central characters, Christabel and Geraldine. At the same time, however, the dream is taken to be prophetic: Leoline acts to prevent it from being fulfilled, according to his own understanding of its meaning. Bracy also understands his dream to be prophetic, but suggests an alternative course of action. There may be disagreement as to who is the dove and who is the snake, but that the dream is a warning, a prophecy sent from somewhere, goes unquestioned.

The uncertainty surrounding the interpretation of Bracy's dream gives it a poetic and tragic poignancy. The use of the prophetic dream as a tragic device is also seen in Coleridge's *Osorio* and *Remorse*. The main characters of these two plays, both hero and villain, are frequently haunted and influenced by dreams, which bespeak ill omens, thwarted justice or guilty consciences. Alvar, thought to be dead, returns to his beloved country in a Moresco disguise.[11] He knows that his young brother plotted his murder, and he seeks to discover his beloved Teresa's involvement or innocence in the plot against his life:

> ALV. (*aside*)   She deems me dead, yet wears no mourning
>   garment!
>   Why should my brother's – wife – wear mourning garments?
>   (*To Teresa*)   Your pardon, noble dame! that I disturb'd
>   you:
>   I had just started from a frightful dream.
> TER.   Dreams tell but of the past, and yet, 'tis said,
>   They prophecy –
> ALV.   The Past lives o'er again
>   In it's effects, and to the guilty spirit
>   The ever frowning Present is it's image.   (Remorse I ii 15)

Teresa's admission that dreams can tell of the past, but also that they have a hand in the future, is crucial to the tragic development of *Remorse*. Her admission is also one that once again posits the language of dreams as one of reminiscence and anticipation. Coleridge establishes, very early in his play, the foreboding dream as an atmospheric and technical device. Prophetic dreams are also used as an indication of a character's worth. Teresa's reply to Alvar that dreams can hold an element of 'prophecy' was added to the 1813 version of the play, and does not appear at all in the *Osorio* versions. For whatever reasons, in the years between the writing of *Osorio* (draft completed in October 1797) and its redrafting as *Remorse* (performed January 1813), Coleridge decided to include prophetic dreams within his dramatic framework.

After Teresa's encouraging and sympathetic comment, Alvar describes his dream to her. What he recounts partakes both of prophecy and reminiscence, and her response to it is one means by which her innocence and their mutual love are revealed, for they share a similar view of dreams:

> ALV.   I dreamt I had a friend, on whom I leant
>   With blindest trust, and a betrothed maid,
>   Whom I was wont to call not mine, but me:
>   For mine own self seem'd nothing, lacking her.
>   This maid so idolized that trusted friend
>   Dishonour'd in my absence, soul and body!
>   Fear, following guilt, tempted to blacker guilt,
>   And murderers were suborned against my life.
>   But by my looks, and most impassion'd words,
>   I rous'd the virtues that are dead in no man,
>   Even in the assassins' hearts! they made their terms
>   And thank'd me for redeeming them from murder.
> ALHAD.   You are lost in thought: hear him no more,
>   sweet Lady!
> TER.   From morn to night I am myself a dreamer,
>   And slight things bring on me the idle mood!
>   Well sir, what happen'd then?
>   . . .   My soul is full of visions all as wild! . . .
>   Stranger farewell! I guess not, who you are,
>   Nor why you so addressed your tale to me . . .
>   If, as it sometimes happens, our rude startling
>   Whilst your full heart was shaping out its dream,
>   Drove you to this, your not ungentle, wildness –
>   You have my sympathy, and so farewell!
>
> (*Remorse* I ii lines 15–17)

The empathetic exchanges between Teresa and Alvar are central to the play's dramatic tension and psychological richness. Alvar's dream acquires a prophetic power over the fate of the characters, and tinges the play with a hint of impending tragedy. The narrative

and emotional details of his dream are part of its visionary quality.
His descriptions of the stormy night, the mingling of 'sounds of
fear' in the language of the dream, and his 'tumultuous' exclama-
tion that remorse might 'fasten' on his enemies' hearts, are both
wild and prophetic. The placing of this dream in the first act
creates a darkly foreboding atmosphere while simultaneously stres-
sing the dramatic and psychological importance of the two lovers'
understanding of the psychological and divine significance of
dreams. The rationalistic Alhadra dismisses Alvar's dream as the
rantings of a deluded man dangerously immersed in his own
thoughts. But Teresa instantly responds to the sentiment, power and
experience inherent in it.

That a belief in the prophetic potential of dreams is central to the
drama is confirmed in a MS note to the prison scene in *Osorio*. In Act
IV Ferdinand tells the villainous Osorio of a dream he has had in
prison:

> My last night's sleep was very sorely haunted
> By what had pass'd between us in the morning.
> I saw you in a thousand hideous ways,
> And doz'd and started, doz'd again and started.
> I do entreat your lordship to believe me,
> In my last dream –
> OSORIO.   Well?
> FERDINAND.   I was in the act
> Of falling down that chasm, when Alhadra
> Waked me. She heard my heart beat!
> OSORIO.
>   Strange enough!
> Had you been here before?
> FERDINAND.   Never, my lord!
> But my eyes do not see it nor more clearly
> Than in my dream I saw that very chasm.
>   (*Osorio* IV i lines 50–63, *PW* II 565–6)

By the end of this scene Ferdinand has been slaughtered, and Osorio
exclaims triumphantly: 'Now – this was luck! No bloodstains, no
dead body! His dream, too, is made out' (lines 149–50). Rewritten,
these lines read:

> He dreamt of it, henceforward let him sleep,
> A dreamless sleep, from which no wife can wake him.
> His dream too is made out.   (*PW* II 570)

Ferdinand's dream becomes dramatic reality; Coleridge's note to his dream speech seeks to differentiate his dream from other dramatic dreams:

This will be held by many for a mere Tragedy-dream – by many who have never given themselves the trouble to ask themselves from what grounds dreams pleased in Tragedy, and wherefore they have been so common. I believe, however, that in the present case, the whole is psychologically true and accurate. Prophetical dreams are things of nature, and explicable by that law of the mind in which dim ideas are connected with vivid feelings, Perception and Imagination insinuate themselves and mix with the forms of Recollection, till the Present appears to exactly correspond with the Past. (*PW* II 565–6)

Although he is discussing prophetic dreams, Coleridge's approach to his subject is rational, detached and logical. Two fundamental assumptions are made: that in certain situations dreams are extremely pleasing in tragedies, and not at all misplaced, and that such dreams are psychologically 'true and accurate'. They are representative of a certain 'law of the mind', capable of collapsing conventional understandings of time: the present becomes the past, the past becomes the present, and the present becomes the future. Ferdinand's nightmare becomes immediate and prophetic; he sees 'it now more clearly, / Than in my dream I saw – that very chasm' (IV i 80–1). The 'psychologically true and accurate' component of prophetic dreams can be explained by the fact that this particular species of dreams is a thing of nature (*CN* I 576). Coleridge believes that the dream becomes analogous to other states of mind in which not only are 'dim ideas connected with vivid feelings' but they are also connected with some thread of divine action and potential. This aligning of the prophetic dream with the natural order also suggests that there is a sympathy between mind and environment, between what the mind can experience and comprehend, and what exists outside it.

Coleridge's undated note on the inclusion of prophetical dreams in his play was perhaps a response to a review of *Remorse* by Francis Hodgson, in the *Monthly Review* (May 1813).[12] Hodgson complains that Coleridge needs to 'put some rein on his fancy', that there is 'throughout the play too much dreaming, and allusion to dreams'.[13] He is 'tempted to imagine', he writes, that the plethoric references to and use of dreams indicate that Coleridge's own 'will was suspended (as is the case in dreams) and that he was mechanically forced to dwell on such airy subjects by some involuntary impulse'. But

Teresa's and Ferdinand's dream experiences and opinions are very much a part of their characterisations, and of the play's overall tenor. Coleridge's support for the inclusion of dreams in the theatre is based on the view that prophetic dreams are both pleasing and common. And the reason they are common is not, as Hodgson would suggest, because they are trivial or instances of flighty escapism. Rather, prophetic and other dreams too have properties inherent in them which are psychologically 'true and accurate'. The power of dreams to reflect, interpret, contradict, warn, and sometimes predict is one that Coleridge sees as belonging perfectly to tragedy and other forms of drama. He would have remembered that Shakespeare frequently used dreams as a means of warning and prophetic insight (as in *Richard II, Richard III, Macbeth* and *Julius Caesar*), and he supported the principle behind Shakespeare's inclusion of dreams in his tragic and dramatic framework. Furthermore, the powerful connections he believed to exist between drama and dreaming ensured that dreams were important structural and thematic features of his own dramas.

At various times throughout his life, but particularly in his young adulthood, Coleridge did subscribe to the belief that dreams have the potential for prophecy. But he also often inclined to another well-known dream theory: the spirit theory, which argues that dreams are caused by certain spirits, who enter the dreamer's mind and shape a dream at will. This 'spirit theory' (*CN* IV 5360), particularly as espoused by Andrew Baxter, carried with it serious moral and intellectual implications. Coleridge often maintained, for instance, that the terrible nightmares he experienced could never originate from his own consciousness. It followed that they must be caused by some external form, a kind of spirit that could act on his consciousness and memory.

This belief was a popular one during the latter part of the eighteenth century, and was also widely held within Coleridge's circle of friends.[14] The appealing aspect of a spirit dream theory was that it could easily explain a range of cultural and physical phenomena, including dreams, illness and disease.[15] In 'The Pains of Sleep', Coleridge writes:

> yester-night I prayed aloud
> In Anguish and in agony,
> Up-starting from the fiendish crowd
> Of shapes and thoughts that tortured me.   (*CKK* 62)

While the torturing process must inevitably come from within the poet's own psyche, from 'the unfathomable hell within' (line 46), it is often easier to ascribe causation to an outside force. Nothing within the mind appears to be the cause of such nightly horrors, but instead, a 'fiendish crowd / Of shapes and thoughts' is blamed. That the dreamer in 'The Pains of Sleep' is able to identify *both* shapes and thoughts as originating from the 'fiendish crowd' suggests that the nightmares are an unmerciful physical and moral assault. Coleridge's desire to believe that they were the work of an invasive, evil spirit, rather than the 'sediment of the unconscious mind', was rendered relatively safe because there already existed a popular theory that dreams were caused by spirits. The shapes and thoughts experienced in the nightmare torture the dreamer, who is left a passive instrument, delirious with fear and bewilderment: 'all confused I could not know / Whether I suffered, or I did', and the pains of sleep themselves are heaped *on*, or fall on, the dreamer.

The emphasis upon the dreamer's passiveness is indicated in the draft versions of the same lines. Coleridge claims that the griefs of his nightmares 'with such men well agree', but he questions why *he* should have them. His despairing question, 'wherefore, wherefore fall on me?', is a cry of disbelief that such dreadful dreams should haunt him so persistently. It is understandable that men who are evil, whose consciences are heavy with guilt – murderers, thieves, liars – should be visited by nightly torments. But Coleridge cannot see himself as one of those. He believes he has committed no major crime, and yet the guilt and suffering he encounters during his sleeping hours would seem to indicate that he too should be counted amongst the lowest of criminals. What is experienced in dreams is often disturbing and inexplicable: he sees himself 'in chains, or in rags, shunned or passed by, with looks of horror blended with sadness, by friends and acquaintance', convinced that in some 'alienation of mind' he 'must have perpetrated some crime', which he tries to recollect 'in vain' (*CL* VI 716). The attempt to recollect or to articulate an unspoken but deeply felt sin, irrespective of whether any sin had been committed, was a feature of other notebook entries (*CN* IV 5008) and of *Christabel*, written within a few years of 'The Pains of Sleep'. Christabel awakes and exclaims, 'Sure I have sinn'd! . . . Now heaven be prais'd if all be well!' (*CKK* 30). This theme of not knowing why the sinful feeling arises, of being spellbound and unable to articulate why the guilt is felt, was a recurrent feature of

Coleridge's quest to comprehend his dreams. It is a feeling that arises from the 'what, if' scenario posited in the Conclusion to the second part of *Christabel*:

> And what, if in a world of sin
> (O sorrow and shame should this be true!)   (*CKK* 48)

The 'world of sin' is precariously close to the world of consciousness and conscience. In his enquiry into the origin of his nightmares, Coleridge was frequently confronted with the possibility that the deep feeling of having sinned might be 'true', that his dreams were entirely the troubled outpourings or reflections of his psyche. Yet, as in 'The Pains of Sleep', he also entertained the possibility that it was something or someone else who caused them.

The distressing nature of the nightmare in 'The Pains of Sleep' and its potential to reveal a morally stained soul are just as important as the possibility that it is caused by spirits. In a letter to Southey in which he alters some of the lines to the poem, the acutely perceived disparity between Coleridge and the criminals who should have horrible dreams is again one of the most perplexing features of his somnial experience. But the comparison of criminals with the poet raises another, equally compelling question:

> With such let fiends make mockery –
> But I – Oh, wherefore this *on me?*
> Frail is my soul, yea, strengthless wholly,
> Unequal, restless, melancholy,
> But free from Hate and Sensual Folly.   (*PW* I 391)

The self-justificatory 'free from Hate and Sensual Folly' indicates the tangle of deep anxieties and insecurities which surface in the wake of the nightmare. The admission of certain weaknesses such as restlessness and melancholy almost obscures the apparently simple question: 'wherefore this *on me?*' The 'me' of these lines is entirely helpless against the assaulting 'fiends'. The final question-mark adds to the ineffectualness of 'me', joining with the exasperated 'Oh' to create a sense of complete bewilderment as to the reasons for the nightmare and its accompanying feelings.

To say that something has fallen on or been heaped upon the dreamer implies that all action and origin are, grammatically and ontologically, removed from the dreamer and ascribed to an external force. Such, then, is the bewilderment and horror of Coleridge's question, 'wherefore this *on me?*' Writing to Thomas Poole in

September 1799, he exclaims: 'As to Stutfield, I could almost wish that some Incubus would get into Bed with him, & blow with a bellows the Wind of cold colic against his Posteriors' (*CL* I 526). The Incubus, that ancient and malignant creature, is here comically described, but its power to cause nightmares is unquestioned. It is the Incubus who gets into bed with Stutfield, and blows a violent colic wind against the dreaming body. The sexual implications of the bed-raiding Incubus would not have been lost on Coleridge, as he knew Fuseli's 'Nightmare' paintings. The disturbing image of the creature insidiously squatting on the bed of a defenceless woman looks forward to Coleridge's own cries, in 'The Pains of Sleep', of a fiendish crowd of shapes and thoughts tormenting the dreamer. Once again, it is significant that the dreamer, Stutfield, is acted against, and that the originating force behind the nightmare is imagined as hopping into bed with him. The complete passivity of the dreamer is, however, something which Coleridge could only partially accept. He believed that volition and will were partially suspended during sleep, but that the dreamer retained some form of volitionary power. For Coleridge, the dreamer must have some kind of active role in the dream. Still, much of the light-hearted malice of his wish that 'some Incubus would get into Bed' with Stutfield derives from the assumed total passivity of the dreaming state, and the potential for any spirit, but especially a malignant incubus creature, to terrify the dreamer and cause nightmares.

Coleridge's emphasis on the passivity experienced in dreams is clearly seen in those letters written in times of illness. This passivity is usually accompanied by the assumption that the dream is beyond the control of the dreamer, and caused by a spirit or some other force. The dream possesses the dreamer, and whatever causes the dream by implication also possesses the dreamer. In October 1797 Coleridge complains of nightmare-ridden nights and illness, adding that when half-awake and half-asleep he has frequently 'seen armies of ugly Things bursting in' upon him (*CL* I 348). Those 'armies' are dreamatis personæ but their presence also suggests that it is something else that causes the dream, something external to the dreamer. Coleridge often complained that

with Sleep my Horrors commence, & they are such, three nights out of four, as literally to *stun* the intervening Day, so that more often than otherwise I fall asleep, struggling to remain awake. Believe me . . . Dreams are no Shadows with me; but the real, substantial miseries of Life. If in

consequence of your Medicine I should be at length delivered from these
sore Visitations, my greatest uneasiness will then [be], how best & most
fully I can evince my gratitude. (*CL* II 986)

Because he seeks to be *delivered from* the horrors of sleep, he cannot be
seen as the agent in the formation of the dream. The onus for its
formation and content falls outside the dreamer, on to some kind of
strange being, who seems to be dissevered from Coleridge's psyche
but who also, regardless of the contrary effort, must belong to some
part of that psyche. Such a being is nameless, and it would be easy to
read Coleridge's letter as merely a description of a bout of illness.
Yet embedded within that description is the view that those nightmares are caused by something or someone else. The horrors of
sleep are continuous and unrelenting, and the dreamer is helpless
against his own dreams. For this reason, Coleridge wishes to be
'delivered from these sore Visitations'. Dreams become so 'real' and
'substantial' that he describes them as the 'miseries' of his life,
terrors and torments beyond his own control. They become the
'very Substances & foot-thick Calamities' of both waking and
dreaming life (*CL* II 991).

Why such visitations literally besieged Coleridge is a question he
continued to ask. Any answer he could devise was inextricably tied
up with the problem of evil itself. He does, however, suggest at one
stage that he has at times 'derived a comfort from the notion, that
possibly these horrid Dreams with all their mockery of Crimes, &
Remorse, & Shame, & Terror, might have been sent upon me to
arouse me of that proud & stoical Apathy, into which I had fallen'
(*CL* II 1008). These comments, written to his brother George in 1803,
beg the question as to the exact nature of his 'proud & stoical
Apathy'. The dreams are sent by a benevolent force as a chastise-
ment for moral shortcomings; they are described as 'sent upon' him,
in order to stun him into a more religious mode of living, or thinking.
Or perhaps they are an encouragement to be more disciplined with
opium. Coleridge's questionings into the origin(s) of evil remained
incomplete, despite consideration of many differing suggestions and
theories. After an argument with William Hazlitt, he wrote that he
had solved 'the whole business of the Origin of Evil satisfactorily'
(*CN* I 1622). But this 'business' was far from ended. He repeatedly
returned to it throughout his lifetime, and always his dreams played
a prominent part in his inability to offer a convincing explanation of
evil.

It was not surprising that Coleridge was drawn to a theory of dreams which ascribed all evil, all fears, anxieties and terror to an external cause. The attraction of such a theory partially stemmed from his reading of Andrew Baxter, who writes: 'How delightful is it to think that there is a *world* of spirits; that we are surrounded with intelligent living Beings, rather than in a *lonely, unconscious Universe* – . . . It is a *pledge* given us of *immortality itself.*'[16] Baxter maintains that presiding over this distinct world of spirits, souls and dreams incorporeal and infinite 'matter' – is an infinite, all-powerful being, a God whose presence not only justifies but also redeems human existence. The 'shame and terror' of nightmares, for instance, become a kind of punishment, a retribution for past (moral) indiscretions, for the spirits are one and the same with God himself. The intimate religious implications of a theory of dreams which posited spirits as their cause were not lost on Coleridge. Only a few years after reading Baxter, he created a mariner who seemed not only beyond the presence of God, but beyond the grace of Christ in particular:

> Alone, alone, all all alone
>   Alone on a wide wide Sea;
> And Christ would take no pity on
>   My soul in agony.   (*LB* 19 lines 224–7)

In the 1798 and 1800 editions of *The Rime of the Ancient Mariner* Coleridge wrote that 'Christ would take no pity' on the mariner. But in the 1817 edition, he altered that line to 'never a saint took pity' (*PW* 1 196 lines 232–6). In early versions, the desolation and isolation of the mariner are more potent, because it is Christ, the son of God, who will not pity him. If Coleridge accepted Baxter's argument that there were spirits in the universe and that some of those spirits caused dreams, and that the existence of such spirits was proof of an immortal and spiritually comforting universe, he also had to contemplate the possibility of a universe that was not immortal, and a theory of dreams that did not suggest that they were caused by spirits.

As late as 1826, Coleridge was still explicitly drawing attention to the existence of nocturnal spirit-creatures, while at the same time qualifying his belief in such spirits:

Since I first read Swedenborg's De Coelo et de Inferno ex Auditis et Visis . . . every horrid Dream, that I have, my thoughts involuntarily turn to the passage in p. 119 § .299 (indeed to the whole Book I am indebted for imagining myself always in Hell, i. e. imagining all the wild Chambers, Ruins, Prisons, Bridewells, to be in Hell) – Sunt Spiritus, qui nondum in conjunctione cum Inferno sunt: illi amant indigesta et maligna, qualie sunt sordescentium Ciborum in Ventriculo – Swedenborg had often talked with them, and driven them away, & immediately the poor Sleeper's frightful Dreams were removed, they being the spiritual Linguifacture of these Toad-Imps' whispers. – Only that I ~~frame~~ modify this Miltonic theory by supposing the Figures in my Dream to *be*, or to be assumed by, the Malignant Spirits themselves – for it is very curious, that they are more or less malicious. – ... But in serious whole Earnest, and however hypochondrical the Spirit-theory may be, I dare avow, that no explanation of Dreams or attempt to explain them, that I have seen or heard, has in the least degree satisfied my judgement, or appeared to solve any part of the mysterious Problem. (*CN* IV 5360)

Coleridge simultaneously accepts and partially rejects the 'Spirit-theory' of dreams. He seeks to modify it such that the 'Malignant Spirits' assume the forms and personages within the dream. But he does not seem to doubt that the spirits exist – their existence is taken for granted. Nevertheless he decides that, whether 'hypochondrical' or attractive, the theory is insufficient to explain the 'mysterious Problem' of dreams.[17]

In coming to this tentative conclusion in which he cannot offer a comprehensive alternative to the theory he has just rejected, Coleridge establishes an intertextual discourse which draws from both Swedenborg's *Heaven and Hell* (*De Coelo et de Inferno ex Auditis et Visis*) and Milton's *Paradise Lost*. Both texts read dreams as being caused by spirits. Swedenborg is mentioned first, because Coleridge claims that 'every horrid Dream' that he has had reminds him of the theologian's *Heaven and Hell*, section 299 (see also *CL* V 216). Despite Coleridge's uncertainty regarding the validity and exact nature of Swedenborg's visions (*CN* III 3474, *CM* III 983–91), his power over Coleridge's imagination is so compelling that the poet's thoughts repeatedly and 'involuntarily', he writes, turn to that particular passage. The passage that so infiltrated and 'haunted' (N35, fo. 35v) his dreams and his imagination is one in which Swedenborg describes his experiences with devilish spirits in the stomach:

There are certain Spirits, that are not yet joined to Hell, as being newly departed from the body . . . which take delight in things indigested and putrid, such as meats corrupted in the stomach, and hold their confabulations in such sinks of uncleanness in Man, as suitable to their impure affections . . . These Spirits appear near to the stomach, some to the right, some to the left of it, some higher, some lower, some nearer, some more distant, according to their different kinds of affection: and that they cause uneasiness of mind, I am fully convinced by much experience; I have seen and heard them, and felt the uneasiness caused by them, and I have also conversed with them: upon their removal, the uneasiness has ceased, and returned upon their return; and I have also been sensible of its increase and decrease, according to the degrees of their approach or removal respectively: and hence I have learnt whence it comes, that they who have no notion of conscience, from not having any themselves, ascribe the anguish of it to disorders in the stomach or bowels.[18]

For Swedenborg, these spirits are a very real presence, and he is 'fully convinced by much experience' that they exist. Not only are they found in 'things undigested and putrid', but they have allegiances with 'impure' affections. In this way, they are suited to the moral nature of the body in which they occur. He does not doubt that those who 'have no notion of conscience . . . ascribe the anguish' of these spirits' actions to 'disorders in the stomach or bowels'. Those who have no moral standards will believe that their stomach or bowels are the cause of their abdominal pains. But Swedenborg knows that the pains are caused by 'certain Spirits' that 'appear near to the stomach, some to the right, some to the left'. Coleridge also proclaims that the minute the spirits are confronted and expelled (by force of faith?), the 'frightful Dreams' disappear.

The reasons for Coleridge's simultaneous attraction to and rejection of Swedenborg's ideas strike at the heart of the moral implications of his readings of dreams. The concepts that Coleridge utilises in an effort to understand his dreams are as dependent upon issues of morality and theology as upon personal opinions and feelings. The central dilemma he faced in accepting or rejecting Swedenborg's spirit theory is succinctly expressed in a letter to James Gillman, of November 1824:

Upon my seriousness, I do declare that I cannot make out certain dream-devils or damned Souls that play pranks with me, whenever by the operation of a cathartic Pill or from the want of one, a ci devant Dinner in it's feculent metempsychosis is struggling in the mid fold of the lower intestines. I cannot comprehend, how any thoughts, the offspring or product of my own Reflection, Conscience, or Fancy, could be translated into such images, and Agents and actions – and am half tempted (n. b. between sleeping and waking) to regard with some favor Swedenborg's assertion, that certain foul Spirits of the lowest order are attracted by the precious Ex-viands, whose conversations the Soul half-appropriates to itself, and which they contrive to whisper into the Sensorium. The Honorable Emanuel has repeatedly caught them in the act, in that part of the Spiritual World corresponding to the Guts in the World of Bodies, and driven them away. (*CL* v 391–2)

Once again, Coleridge's argument is one based on default. Because he cannot 'make out' the 'dream-devils' whom he thinks responsible for his dreams, and cannot 'comprehend, how any thoughts' could be the 'offspring or product' of his own 'Reflection, Conscience or Fancy', he is 'tempted' to regard Swedenborg's theory favourably. It is worth remembering that these comments are made in a letter to his protector and friend, to whom Coleridge would not like to allude even vaguely to any moral weaknesses or failings. The attraction of Swedenborg's theory is undeniable, removing the onus for bad dreams from the conscience of the dreamer to his eating habits before retiring. His falling back on such an inadequate theory, one that locates the origin of dreams in external spirits, is couched in hesitant terms, but the perplexing struggle to both admit and deny what is uncomfortable is still palpable. Coleridge claims he is only 'half-tempted' to 'regard with some favor' Swedenborg's spirit theory. His choice of the word 'tempted' is revealing, for it suggests that to be tempted by the spirit theory is to see the 'dream-devils' as entirely separate from the self. The fact that he *is* half-tempted to consider the idea is testimony to the theological issues bound up in his dream explorations, and to the difficulty of recognising and accepting the moral implications of his dreams.

The problem of Coleridge's awareness of his own moral nature is further compounded by the admission that 'the Soul half-appropriates to itself' (*CL* v 392) those foul spirits which cause the dream. If the soul is half-appropriating foulness, it must be held at least partially responsible for the torments it suffers. It is both appropriated by and appropriating the foul spirits, and both soul and foul spirits engage in 'conversations'. But Coleridge cannot conceive how this can be (morally) possible. His attempt to deny the possibility for self-generated pain or guilt is also a recognition of the complex processes of dreams. The dream-devils must undergo some kind of transformation – they cannot be part of the waking moral consciousness – and that transformation is metaphorically described as whispers and conversations between spirits and body, denoting 'that part of the Spiritual World' which corresponds and empathises with 'the Guts in the World of Bodies'. These conversations are heightened by the 'operation of a cathartic Pill', or, significantly, 'from the want of one'. The need for a pill is both physical and psychological.

That the question of a dream's origin becomes deeply enmeshed in issues of personal morality is principally due to the theological repercussions of Coleridge's vocabulary. The significance of his understanding of the translation of the conscience or the fancy into the images of the dream-devils cannot be underestimated. The use of the term 'translation' in the immediate context of the letter to Gillman implies not only some kind of interaction between the dream-devils and the dreamer's stomach, but a transference of spiritual or cerebral activities into the bodily realm, into the 'Guts in the World of Bodies' (*CL* v 392). Concepts of a spiritual translation, or of translations from the body and blood of Christ into bread and wine, and the religious aspects of a translation between cerebral or spiritual states and human or bodily states, are all implicitly present within Coleridge's dream discourses. Part of the bewilderment expressed in the letter to Gillman relates to the translation of the conscience, the reason and other intellectual activities into the 'Guts' of bodily existence. The soul 'whispers' and consorts with the foul spirits, in a sense prostituting itself in the dream. Coleridge describes Swedenborg as catching the foul spirits 'in the act', a phrase not borrowed from section 299 of *Heaven and Hell* but one which Coleridge supplies, a phrase resonant with echoes of adulterous discovery (*in delicto flagrante*). This movement between the higher, spiritual plane and the lower or bodily plane was one which he continually tried to side-step. But in his own ill-health and particularly in his nightmares, the bodily and 'lowest order' of his existence would not and could not be denied. The issues of personal morality were bound to emerge eventually, in the 'dreadful labyrinth of strangling, hell-pretending Dreams' (*CN* IV 5375).

The 'spirit theory' conveniently solved these moral questions. If the most 'evil and distempered dreams' (N44, fo. 52) were caused by creatures in the body, then the moral nature of the soul could escape scrutiny. Coleridge still had to admit that Swedenborg's explanation was, in the final analysis, inadequate: 'no explanation', including the 'spirit-theory', satisfied his judgement as to the origin of dreams. This complex question, so fundamentally fused with the question of the origin of evil, is given added weight by the second text Coleridge engages with in the *CN* IV 5360 entry: *Paradise Lost*. This poem is an influence throughout his dream explorations. He argues, for instance, that the 'frightful dreams' are 'Linguifacture' of malignant spirits, 'Toad-imps' whispers'. The image of the whispering toad is from *Paradise Lost*. Upon the orders of Gabriel, the angels Uzziel, Ithuriel, Zephon and others search for Satan in the Garden of Eden:

> him [Satan] there they found
> Squat like a toad, close at the ear of Eve;
> Assaying by his devilish art to reach
> The organs of her fancy, and with them forge
> Illusions as he list, phantasms and dreams,
> Or, if, inspiring venom, he might taint
> Th' animal spirits that from pure blood arise
> Like gentle breaths from rivers pure, thence raise
> At least distempered, discontented thoughts,
> Vain hopes, vain aims, inordinate desires
> Blown up with high conceits engend'ring pride.[19]

In many ways, Satan's whispers are equivalent to the fall from God's grace. The ideas Satan infuses into Eve's mind are the very thoughts and actions which prompt her to eat of the forbidden fruit. These ideas – 'discontented thoughts', 'vain hopes', 'vain aims', 'inordinate desires' and 'pride' – also earlier caused Satan's expulsion from Heaven.

That the dream functions as a rehearsal of the temptation and fall is further suggested by Adam, who awakes 'pure' from his slumbers (*Paradise Lost* V lines 1–14) and discovers Eve's 'unquiet rest' (lines 10–11). That Eve's rest is 'unquiet' suggests that she is not as innocent and chaste as would be expected. Adam needs to explain why her cheek glows, and why her hair is 'discomposed'. His task is rendered more difficult because Eve first tells him that her dream is different from any other she has ever had. She is puzzled by a feeling of having sinned, of experiencing 'offense and trouble' which her mind 'knew never till this irksome night' (*Paradise Lost* V lines 30–1). Without knowing what she has done, she feels as though she has sinned, just as Christabel feels when she awakens from sleep with Geraldine (*CKK* 30). Adam's explanation is an attempt to convince himself that things are not as bad as they seem to be. Their marital bed is described as 'undefiled and chaste' (*Paradise Lost* IV line 761), yet somehow an evil and disruptive force has found its way there. Adam replies to Eve's unease with an argument that is partially valid, but not convincing:

'Best image of myself and dearer half,
The trouble of thy thoughts this night in sleep
Affects me equally; nor can I like
This uncouth dream, of evil sprung I fear:
Yet evil whence? in thee can harbor none,
Created pure. But know that in the soul
Are many lesser faculties that serve
Reason as chief; among these fancy next
Her office holds; of all external things,
Which the five watchful senses represent,
She forms imaginations, aery shapes,
Which reason joining or disjoining, frames
All what we affirm or what deny, and call
Our knowledge or opinion; then retires
Into her private cell when nature rests.
Oft in her absence mimic fancy wakes
To imitate her; but misjoining shapes,
Wild work produces oft, and most in dreams,
Ill matching words and deeds long past or late . . .
Evil into the mind of god or man
May come and go, so unapproved, and leave
No spot or blame behind: which gives me hope
That what in sleep thou didst abhor to dream,
Waking thou never wilt consent to do.'

(*Paradise Lost* V lines 95–121)

Adam can only 'hope' that what Eve dreams she would never do while waking. Her temptation has been prefigured in her dream, and the dream acquires a prophetic element.[20] What Adam thinks she would never consent to do whilst awake, she has had images and sensations of whilst dreaming. He tells her that this is a 'mimic fancy' which misjoins shapes and deeds, thereby creating visions and ideas which would not normally be experienced. Reason is exalted as the 'chief' faculty of the mind, but the powers of reason are greatly diminished in sleep. Because reason is absent, mimic fancy is able to perform the mischief which characterises Eve's 'uncouth dream'. But even if that dream were an evil one, or at least evil in intent, Adam claims that it 'may come and go, so unapproved, and leave / No spot or blame behind'. His rhetorical argument is not very convincing, and although Coleridge may have found the 'no spot or blame' aspect of Adam's theory very consoling, he could not have endorsed it any more than Milton did.[21]

In an unpublished notebook entry dated 1827, Coleridge sought to modify this 'Miltonic theory' by focussing on Adam's speech upon awakening as a means of questioning the latter's explanation of Eve's dream and Milton's reading of dreams. After a dinner party at which the conversation turned, as it often did, to the subject of dreams, Coleridge retired to bed.[22] He was later awoken by a troubling dream, which he promptly recorded in his notebook. The recording of that dream reminds him of the dinner conversation, and the ways in which cognitive faculties are disturbed during dreams:

> It is *Fancy* / says Milton's Adam, in his explanation of Dreams to Eve – & an excellent *Lady* explanation, a theory for the [?ladies], it *is!* . . . – but when the Ladys had retired I agreed that Adam had not put the Question to the [?Sociable] Angels – It is Fancy – and her Dr*eama*tis Personæ are Fancies – but what is *Fancy* – or rather *who* is Fancy. They have the same [?form] of our *own feelings* in these dreams; but those of the Dreamfolk we *infer* from their looks & actions, and most often infer malignant feelings at least (in my experience, probably depending on my ill health) . . . that they in some way are the products and the same language – the Symbols & exponents of local Sensations. (N35, fos. 37v–38)

While adding that he has 'little doubt' that his ill-health shapes his dreams, he is nevertheless intrigued by the 'particular process' by which the spirits conjure up forms in them, a process which conflates objective and subjective fears and feelings with local sensations. Coleridge is troubled by Adam's lack of curiosity: Adam does not 'put the question' to the angels on the origin or the meaning of Eve's dream. He does not seem aware of the implications of his statement that evil can appear in the 'mind of god or man' without leaving 'spot or blame behind'. The modifications to Miltonic dream theory that Coleridge wished to make led him into his own speculations as to the effects of ill-health on the formation of dreams and dreamatis personæ. Milton's suggestion that Satan attempted by devilish arts 'to reach the organs of [Eve's] fancy' (*Paradise Lost* IV lines 781–2), and Adam's belief that 'mimic' fancy was responsible for the evil of her dream, are two accounts which place great emphasis on spirits as the originating powers of the dream. This emphasis Coleridge found both attractive and unsatisfactory.

Coleridge seeks to differentiate between the faculties of memory and fancy, as well as to determine what Milton actually means by mimic fancy. Arguing that Fancy is a 'who' and not a 'what', Coleridge perceives dreamatis personæ as the 'who' products of fancy. Dreamatis personæ have the same 'inward form' as the dreamer's feelings, but their feelings, motivations and emotions must be inferred. The spirits mentioned by Coleridge are again the focus of a question he frames towards the end of Notebook 35, regarding the nature of good and evil spirits. He wonders 'in what sense the Dream persons may be demon spirits' (N35, fo. 48). This question, scrawled in a tiny margin on the last page of the notebook, reflects his wavering stance regarding the validity or otherwise of a Miltonic or Swedenborgian 'Spirit-theory' (*CN* IV 5360). He queries in 'what sense' the dreamatis personæ may be malignant or 'demon spirits'. The figures in his dreams are the 'malignant spirits' themselves – partially fictionalised from Swedenborg and from Milton, partially realised – and Coleridge wonders what form their existence may take. He does not wonder whether they exist, for he knows that they do. The querying of the 'sense' of the demon spirits is also a querying of the origins of evil feelings, of guilt, remorse, shame – of what Milton describes as 'inordinate desires / Blown up with high conceits engend'ring pride' (*Paradise Lost* IV lines 808–9).

Coleridge would also have liked to modify this spirit theory, as it is expressed in Adam's conversation with Eve and in the description of Satan's whisperings. He could not ignore the fact that his dreams often revealed a darker side to his character and that he sometimes thought himself evil or beyond the reach of God's redeeming love: for whatever reasons, he often felt 'a deep sense of the exclusion of God's Presence' (*CN* IV 5360). If the presence of some spirits causes dreams, then the *absence* of one spirit in particular (God) could be seen as the most agonising aspect of a troubling dream. Coleridge had a life-long struggle to realise and to perceive the presence of God, especially when he contemplated his dreams and nightmares. But such uncertainties should also be seen in contrast to the confident, if only occasional, later notebook entries in which he could exclaim that he was assured of God's love and forgiveness (N55, fo. 24). That dreams 'betoken or betray the innate moral character out of which they proceed' (*CL* III 303) was a possibility that was easier to write and intellectualise about than to apply to his own life.

The theory of spirits was not only a widely popular belief in Coleridge's society and therefore easy to embrace, it was also comforting. It was a theory compatible with faith and belief. Such compatibility can be seen in an unpublished notebook entry of 1827, where he agonises over the nature of apostolic writings and whether

or not the miracles described therein actually occurred. If miracles
did exist, and if the eye-witness reports were honest, what influence
must popular culture and superstitions have had on those reports?
His discussion of the truth of the gospels raises issues highly relevant
to his understanding of the origin of dreams. If the accounts in the
gospels are true, Coleridge suggests a faithful Christian would
neither 'call into question' those eye-witness accounts nor countenance the possibility that those who witnessed them might have been
'bewildered by terror' or 'driven into exaggeration' (N35, fo. 7). On
the other hand, however, he considers the possibility that the
witnesses may have been swayed by other factors:

supposing them to have been of the lower and uneducated classes of their
countrymen and it would be idle and in the face of the clearest evidence to
the contrary, to imagine them exempt from the current superstitions,
prejudices and popular notions of their age and country. That Epilepsy, for
instance, [. . .] aggravated cases of Hysteria, lycanthropy and similar forms
of insanity and nervous derangement were produced by Devils and
malignant Spirits tormenting the bodies of the unhappy Patients was ~~an
opinion~~ Persuasion so universally entertained, as to be in their minds
equivalent to a known fact. Any reason for believing it was as foreign to
their thoughts, as the fact of any one's doubting it was unknown. So widely
was the Belief, the unconscious habit of taking the truth of it for granted,
diffused that/a most important feature in this question/it has entered *into
the Language of the Country*. Inobservant and utterly unreflecting [. . .] must
the man be, who has not noticed the proneness in every one, and almost
the *necessity* in uneducated men, to confound ~~the fact~~ and as far as their
Consciousness extends to identify the fact or phoenomenon and its
supposed immediate cause and agent, whence the latter has supplied the
common name & appellation of the former, in the language of the Country.
And this will so blend with and color the description and account which
the honestest man, and the most desirous to relate the truth . . . and
nothing but the truth, of any case of this kind which he has seen, as to
~~produce it~~ render it little less than impossible for him not to lend what he
had ~~actually~~ really seen and heard with what he had with the same *sensation*
of certainty taken for granted. The most watchful analyst of his own mind
cannot at all times separate ~~his~~ the *objective* portion of what he seems to see
or hear from the subtle additional and interpolations of subjective activity.
It is not only in Sleep or in Delirium or Hypochondriasis that men *actually*
see and hear what is not *really* to be seen or heard . . . equally inevitable
and innocent is the confounding of the narrator's interpretation of what he
has witnessed with the words or actions of a superior . . . in application to
the Reports of the Eye-Witness of our Lord's Miracles . . . in weighing their
testimony we must carefully distinguish, as much as is possible, the *inferences*

of the Relation from the facts themselves . . . the Critic must be guided by the known laws of Psychology and by similar cases in the common experience of Men. (N35, fos. 7–10)

The 'universally entertained' conception of a spirit theory is clearly stated: that 'Epilepsy . . . aggravated cases of Hysteria, lycanthropy and similar forms of insanity and nervous derangement' are 'produced by Devils and malignant Spirits'. So strong is this belief that it actually enters into the 'Language of the Country'. The parallels between particular diseases, dreams and spiritual faith are drawn throughout the rest of the entry. Faithful apostles must at times suspend certain beliefs in order to be faithful. Similarly, dreams require a degree of temporary suspension of disbelief (*CL* IV 641–2) in an analogous way to that of poetry (*BL* II 6) and dramatic illusion (*Lectures* II 265–6; *BL* II 214). For Coleridge, particular species of dreams were also classic illustrations of the conflation of objective and subjective phenomena.

In attempting to construct a psychological explanation of theological and spiritual phenomena, Coleridge draws from his knowledge of dreams and dreaming. It is an attempt which must be guided by the 'known laws of Psychology' as well as by the 'common experience' of mankind. He is aware that even the 'most watchful analyst of his own mind cannot at all times' be certain of cause and effect, of what is subjective and what is objective. In this complex entry from Notebook 35, he simultaneously and implicitly affirms and denies aspects of his own moral and dreaming life. He states that it is in 'uneducated' men that the conflation of consciousness and superstition is most apparent; that it is a wise man who can perceive the differences between what is seen, what is thought to have been seen, and what was never actually seen. What he presents in this entry can be taken as an analogy for his own deeply problematic understanding of his dreams. In dreams, it is also possible to see and hear things which are not 'really' there to be seen or heard. The understanding of the dream is 'equally inevitable and innocent', but carries with it complex possibilities which may confirm or deny an important fact or personal truth. Perhaps there are spirits or gods who have the power to perform miracles; and perhaps there are spirits who cause dreams. Both cases permit the possibility of facts and phenomena having a 'supposed immediate cause and agent', and that a supposed cause can be easily and happily substituted for any number of other causes. One explanation for what is seen and heard is that 'Devils and malignant Spirits' are 'tormenting the bodies of the unhappy' dreamers.

Coleridge's deliberations over the spirit theory reveal another modification he wished to make to the Miltonic 'fancy' theory of dreams: the 'Dreamfolk' are the 'Symbols & exponents of local Sensations', he writes, and are related furthermore to his 'ill health' (N35, fo. 38). The language of pain which was the vehicle of expression in his dreams is cited as an integral component of the origin. Wondering what the 'particular process' is that enables the spirits to be 'conjured up with forms' in his dreams, he ponders the exact relationship between his body and his dreams, between bodily sensations and dream sensations. His explorations into the nature of that relationship led him to consider that his health and his body played significant roles in the formation of his dreams.

CHAPTER SEVEN

Translations of dream and body

Coleridge often suggests that his body, diseased and suffering from numerous complaints, causes his dreams and is intimately involved in many dreaming processes (*CL* v 385–6; N35, fos. 37v–38). His understanding of his body and of its role in dreams was significantly determined by his infirmities and the ways in which they were expressed in his dreams. Pain and disease underscore all of his enquiries into dreams and dreaming. In his efforts to account for both the origin and the nature of his dreams, he explored the fundamental properties that dreams and disease had in common. His deliberations on the body's role in causing dreams led him to examine the complex processes between his body and his mind during dreams. These processes he termed a translation or a transmutation, and for Coleridge they elucidated some of the most important phenomena of sleep and disease. They also revealed to him the many complex and exciting ways in which the imagination acts in dreaming states.

When he was sixty years old, Coleridge wrote in his notebook: 'I am tied down, and strait-waisted by Disease, & driven inward on my own unworthy *Self*, fighting with my own sensations, listening to my own moans & groans, & imploring God's mercy on my*self*, on my miserable *Self*' (N50, fo. 35v, 21 February 1832). This entry epitomises an ageing man's weariness as well as Coleridge's perception of his body as a vehicle for suffering, defined by pain and disease. The presence of continual illness meant that he was 'driven inward' on himself, forced to fight his 'own sensations'. When the body is well, it is not often a subject for contemplation; but when sick and harassed by its own organs, it mercilessly forces attention upon itself. This ailing body was particularly evident in dreams, the result both of the language of dreams and of the important role the body played in their cause. Coleridge often partially rejected his own organs and his body as identifiable with himself. His body often seemed to rise up against him, to torment him through illness, through his use of opium, through sexual awareness and the relentless occurrence of nightmares. The body seems not to constitute the self, – it is so far distanced from the concept of self that the two seem entirely disparate entities.[1]

Many of the illnesses from which Coleridge suffered were the result of either his continued use of opium or his efforts to stop taking it. That his body was incessantly troubled by disease and other minor discomforts is (almost too) readily discerned: in June 1801 he complains of weeks of 'blood-shot eyes & swoln Eyelids . . . followed by large Boils in my neck & shoulders – these by Rheumatic Fever – this by a distressing & tedious Hydrocele & since then by irregular Gout, which promises at this moment to ripen into a legitimate Fit' (*CL* II 735–6). Almost thirty years later, he is still troubled by his bodily processes. In a notebook entry of September 1829, he describes the daily experience of his body thus:

After a disturbed Doze was forced to get up, a little before 1, having retired in prayer for rather than in hope of Rest, a little after 10, Monday Night – & soon after obliged to call up the servant – & from this time till near 9 this morning – O misery. The [?dyspnoa] & the sharp scream – [. . .] pain in the right-Shoulder, & so down to the knees had converted into pain and miserable sensation . . . looseness in the lower Bowels, aching across the umbilical region & distressful Sickness at the Stomach, and confusion in the Head. (N41, fo. 53v)

There is no possible refuge from the onslaught of these pains, and sleep itself becomes impossible. Dreams become manifestations of this painful body which, for hour upon hour, aches across the stomach and endures shooting pains in the shoulder. 'Damnable' dreams follow ingestions of 'mercurial purgatives', intended to relieve various sufferings, and those dreams are always characterised by a strong pressure and discomfort around the umbilical region (N39, fo. 85v).

Such tortuous descriptions provide foundations for the presentation of what he terms a 'Morbid Sleep', a 'disturbed Imagination' which forms dreams yet also torments the body:

One of the most horrible of these states of Morbid Sleep is the Sensation that counterfeits Remorse – & actual Remorse we know, when intense, ~~takes the~~ realizes all the horrors of sleep & seems indeed the identity or co-inherence of Sleep & Wake, Reality and Imagination. – If then Hell mean,

& I know no more rational meaning, the state & natural consequences of a diseased Soul, abandoned to itself or additionally tortured by the very organic case which had before sheltered it, and the force of the blows & blunted the point and edge of the daggers – it must contain – & surpass all the descriptions of Hell, that were the portraits of the disturbed imagination – (*CN* IV 4846)

What is most disturbing about morbid sleep is that it is accompanied by a sensation that 'counterfeits' remorse. This realisation prompts Coleridge to contemplate the meaning of Hell: but he suggests that the experience of Hell must contain, but cannot 'surpass', the portraits and sensations that a disturbed and dreaming imagination can create. His alternative vision of Hell is closely aligned with his views of the relationships between dreaming mind and diseased body, 'the organic case' which shelters the soul. The 'sensation' that he identifies as counterfeiting remorse during dreams could be caused by either a physical or an emotional sense. The torments he experiences become self-conflicting and contradictory: the 'portraits of the disturbed imagination'. The combination of pain experienced in dreams, the realisation that his body could be experienced in sleep and dreams, and an interest in the physiology of specific organs, produced a formidable horror that not even Hell could match.

What particularly perplexed Coleridge about the experience of his body in dreams was that the sensation of pain seemed to be qualitatively different from pain experienced while awake. The imposition of the body during dreaming states varies, depending on the state of consciousness:

This astonishing multiplication of Pain into itself, in dreams, – I do not understand it. This Evening sleeping I – for the first time I recollect, had a most intolerable sense of *Pain* as *Pain*, without affright or disgustful Ideas – a sense of an excruciating patience-mocking Rheumatism in my right arm . . . the astonishing difference in the degrees of the Pain felt or supposed when asleep & when awaked. (*CN* II 2838)

He becomes even more aware of his body, because the pain experienced is multiplied. His comment that there is an 'astonishing difference in the degrees of the Pain felt or supposed when asleep & when awaked' helps to explain why sleeping and dreaming becomes so terrifying, psychologically as well as physically. In particular, nightmares have the potential to become physical realities. Pain seems to be even more intense because it is experienced without

'affright or disgustful Ideas'. It is a purified pain, a pain so different
from anything previously experienced that the language employed to
express it must also be purified: 'pain as pain'. He remarks to friends
in numerous letters that he is too frightened to fall asleep, that he
struggles to remain awake (*CL* II 991), staying up late, reading, 'from
the *dread* of falling asleep . . . from being literally afraid to trust
myself again out of the leading-strings of my Will & Reason' (*CL* II
999). It was no wonder that he dreaded falling asleep – sleep was
often no escape from pain:

> when the dream of night
> Renews the phantom to my sight,
> Cold sweat-drops gather on my limbs;
> My ears throb with horrid tumult swims;
> Wild is the tempest of my heart
> And my thick and struggling breath
> Imitates the toil of death.
>
> ('Ode to the Departing Year', *PW* I 166 lines 103–12)

The constrained breathing and throbbing ears are characteristic of
the nightmare. Sleep becomes a catalogue of physical discomfort
and terror: the accessible image of the 'cold sweat-drops' provides a
physical immediacy contrasting with the potential quietude and rest
of sleep. The physical, the bodily, and the diseased component of the
dream terrify Coleridge: the cold sweat, the throbbing in the ears,
the ineluctable experience of 'pain as pain' (*CN* II 2838). The nature
of the somnial disease was perceived as both moral and physical, so
that he felt himself 'afflicted' in every possible way (*CN* IV 5360).

His body could be a site for both physical delight (as in *CN* I 1718)
and torment (as in *CN* II 2838). Physical delight and torment both
allow the body to become the primary site for the origin and
understanding of, and the metaphorical battle-ground between,
sleeping body and dreaming mind. The somatic provided Coleridge
with a point of entry for an enquiry into the origins of dreams. As
mentioned earlier, many writers in the eighteenth century, including
Erasmus Darwin, William Buchan and David Hartley, attributed the
origin of dreams at least in part to somatic or sensory causes. Many
cited the eating of a heavy meal too close to bedtime as the cause of
nightmares. Coleridge was aware of these and other similar ideas,
but his concept of his body altered his view on how the body caused
or influenced dreams. He relied on his own understanding of his
body – an understanding determined primarily by his medical

readings and his ill-health. He speculated that certain parts of the body were important players in sleep and dreams:

The importance of the Gastric and especially the hepatic – and ~~its~~ the paramouncy of the Ganglionic over the Cerebral in Sleep. The Liver, and lower Abdomen – the Engastrimuthi, and the prophetic Power of *diseased* Life in the ancient Oracles, hard by Streams & Caverns of deleterious influences . . . Liver – &c. The passions of the Day as often originate in the Dream, as the Images of the Dream in the Day. Guilt, Falsehood, traced to the Gastric Life. See my *Pains* of Sleep. (*CN* III 4409)

The shifting religious references, interspersed with comments on the nature of his dreams and his 'Pains of Sleep' poem, reveal unusual emphases in his thinking on dreams. Many of the issues with which Coleridge was confronted in relation to his dreams are crammed into this entry, including the role that he perceived his body to play in their formation. To think on the subject of dreams was to consider his body's physiology.

Through his references to the body, Coleridge draws strong connections between his dream life and his (diseased) bodily life. The gastric system in dreams is 'especially' singled out, and the ganglionic system is perceived as attaining 'paramouncy' over the brain (the 'cerebral') while he is sleeping. The roles of the lower abdomen and the liver remind him of the 'Engastrimuthi', the 'ventriloquists' of Plutarch's *De Defectu Oraculorum* (*CN* III 4409n). This reference allows him to allude to the question of prophecy in dreams. Furthermore, he notes that certain feelings in dreams, such as guilt and falsehood, can be 'traced to the Gastric Life'. Referring to his own 'Pains of Sleep', he offers further proof of the important influence of his body in his dreams: the liver '&c' are the organic source of the 'life-stifling fear, soul-stifling shame' of the poem. Coleridge uses his body in ways similar to those in which he used the 'spirit theory' (*CN* IV 5360): both the body and the spirits remove the unbearable thought that dreams tap into morally undesirable components of his character.

The figuring of his body in dreams – especially of particular organs, such as the liver, or the ganglionic system – is one of the most unusual and complex features of Coleridge's investigation into the nature of his dreaming life. He readily discerned that sometimes the mere awareness of disordered bodily parts was sufficient to cause a particular type of dream: the effect of posture (*CN* II 2064), or the 'disquieting miserableness of the Rectum' (N44, fo. 67v). In a letter

to Daniel Stuart of June 1809 he observes the role of the digestive
system in the formation of certain dreams, referring to the frightening prospect of a 'desperate experiment of abandoning all at
once' his opium usage. While realising that opium has contributed to
his suffering digestive organs, he adds that 'Sleep or even a supine
Posture does not fail to remind me that something is organically
amiss in some one or other of the Contents of the Abdomen' (*CL* III
212). Coleridge does not deny in his letter to Stuart that opium has
plagued his body, but he also suggests that while sleeping, his dreams
reveal to him that 'something is organically amiss . . .'[2] This offers
convincing proof that the mind is 'never perhaps wholly uninformed
of the circumstantia in Sleep' (*CN* III 4396; *Lectures* II 207). Body
posture was not the sole determining factor in the creation of
dreamatis personæ and the dream's action: pressure on the thigh, or
any slight alteration in body position or feeling could also cause a
change in the dream's character, whether it was a day-dream or a
nightmare (*CN* I 1765).

One of the earliest mentions of the possibility of dreams being
caused by the body comes from a May 1804 notebook entry:

A really important Hint suggested itself to me, as I was falling into my first
Sleep – the effect of the posture of the Body, *open mouth* for instance, on first
Dreams – & perhaps on all. White Teeth in behind a̶ ̶d̶i̶m̶ open mouth of a
dim face – / My Mind is not vigorous enough to pursue it – but I see, that
it leads to a developement of the effects of continued Indistinctness of
Impressions on the Imagination according to laws of Likeness & what ever
that may solve itself into. (*CN* II 2064)

The posture of the body at the time of falling asleep affects the types
of images seen and experienced in the dream, particularly the first
dream of the night. Coleridge implies that we dream many dreams
every night, and that depending on when it occurs, each will be
influenced by the body in a slightly different manner. The face in
this entry is of primary importance. He had complained of being
'desperately sick, ill, abed', possibly as a result of eating rhubarb.
The open mouth in this entry has its origin in a physical activity
prior to falling asleep, and it is this that ushers in the dream of 'white
teeth in behind . . . open mouth of a dim face'. Coleridge admits
that his mind is 'not vigorous enough' to pursue the question of the
effects of the body's posture on dreams, and he will take it no
further. His perception of his intellect as inadequate to the task

prevents him following up the associations he perceives, and provides a convenient excuse to opt out of a complex problem.

Coleridge calls on the imagination to explain, partially at least, how it is that the 'effect of the posture of the Body' can be discerned as it relates to dreams: 'according to laws of Likeness', posture seems to weave its way into the dream's contents and character. The imagination is stimulated by the state of the body during sleeping and dreaming states. Differing levels of awareness – semi--consciousness, pre-consciousness, unconsciousness – all have the power to form images, or 'impressions', and feelings: 'Query as to the Posture of the Body we being semi-demi-conscious of it in falling to sleep, does it not act sometimes by suggesting the postures of Objects, of inanimates so that *I* could see them, of the animate partly so & partly so as they could see me? & would look in on me' (*CN* II 2073). The body 'act[s] sometimes' in an imaginative realm: the way it is positioned at the moment of falling asleep suggests 'the postures of Objects' in the dream. The body is said to 'act sometimes' in an imaginative realm, powerfully 'suggesting' how objects are positioned. Body and dream object are both said to be positioned such that what is experienced in the dream and what the body is aware of are one and the same. The problem of how it is that an awareness of the body, even if only a dim semi-awareness, enters into the imaginative activity of his dreams fundamentally concerns Coleridge.

He repeatedly claims that a particular organ, or awareness of an organ, has caused a disturbing dream or series of events within a dream. This conflation of body and mind is a specific characteristic of the dreaming state, accounting for the origin of many dreams. The imagination is not merely responsible for poetic visions and dreams of Kubla Khan: in sleep it is connected with the 'motions of the blood and nerves', and the images that are seen in dreams are 'forced into the mind by the feelings that arise out of the position & state of the Body and its different members' (*CN* II 2543). One part that continually presents itself as having a strong role to play in dreams is the rectum. In an entry from 1827, Coleridge asserts that the 'lowest abdomen, in and near the Rectum', has 'so manifest an influence in Dreams' (N36, fo. 5v) that he cannot deny its importance. In a later entry, of 19 August 1830, he exclaims that a restful sleep, free from tormenting dreams, is next to impossible when the digestive organs are in revolt:

Wedn. night, gained Sleep against the *subsultus* of the Stomach, and the disquieting miserableness of the Rectum (*mem.*! what can go *right* when the Rectum itself goes wrong?) . . . / But awake to an anxious day, as stressful & restless – and wretched as well can be with my degree of inward peace – as much, I mean, as is compatible with the conviction that my bodily pains, langour, and depression have been the consequences and ought to be regarded as the deserved [?penance] of my own transgressing & culpable weakness & Indiscretions. (N44, fo. 67v)

The admission of his own role in causing his misery (by continuing to take opium) is given equal weight in his realisation that the stomach's spasms and discomforts intrude into dreams. That Coleridge describes himself as eventually conquering the subsultus of the stomach is indicative of the aggressive nature of the battle between the different organs of the body and the need for sleep. The rectum is in a state of revolt against other organs, and although he believes he has won the battle of the night, he awakes to find that his day is 'anxious', 'stressful & restless – and wretched as well'.

'Morbid' sensations in dreams are ascribed by Coleridge to the accumulation of wind in the bowels, so that by turning to one side, and discharging the 'oppressive air from the stomach or lower Bowels'[3], it was possible to alter the dream sensation and the dream-images seen: 'Misery of a bad stomach from intemperance causing the Dream of a full highly ~~stored~~ set out Table, not as an object of Appetite, but of disgust and terror with remorse. a most *striking fact* this!' (*CN* II 2457). The origin of 'terror with remorse' seems obscure, but perhaps the appetite to which he refers is a sexual appetite, and one that if 'highly stored' may demand some feelings of remorse. He may also have felt remorse at wanting to eat so indulgently in the dream when he was aware that his stomach was already 'bad'. Interestingly, he labels his observation a 'fact', which seems to suggest that there could be no question as to the origin and the character of this particular dream.

Coleridge's perception of his body as the cause of his dreams placed a somewhat unfortunate emphasis on the body in his thinking on dreams, because it could never be the whole body, but only parts of it, variously experiencing pain at different times and continually subject to some form of unease. One of the many consequences of this emphasis is that the body and its organs repeatedly become the centre of interest, and when this happens it is often the result of a specific absence: what is absent is a 'desired or ordinary state'.[4]

Once the body has been accentuated in this manner, Coleridge often sees the symptoms of his bodily ailments in relation to his dreams (*CL* VI 606–7). Dreams become a special type of disease, and can be conceptualised in ways similar to that of physical illness. In one of his 1808 lectures he suggests that during sleep, images are the 'mere effects & exponents' of an active nervous system. The entire nervous system is 'brought into a certain state, the sensation of which is ~~grossly~~ exaggerated during Sleep' (*Lectures* II 135). The excitement of the nervous system, all the internal functionings of the body, are said to cause certain dream images and experiences. This is to be seen in stark contrast to the appearance of a ghost, or apparition, when the image seen is said to rush 'thro' the senses upon . . . a nervous system wholly unprepared'. The condition of the nervous system as 'unprepared' is posited as a state that, Coleridge believes, actually causes the sensation of seeing an apparition (*Lectures* II 135; *PLect* 319). His differentiation between images seen in dreams and those seen as apparitions is one that also acknowledges the role of the nervous system in differing states of consciousness.

The emergence of certain emotions and feelings in dreams, and the suggestion that this is due to (usually diseased) body organs or positions, is central to Coleridge's approach to dreams.[5] His observations that his bodily pains initiate a 'dunning' pain, 'like a bad conscience', as soon as his head reaches a 'few inches for the doubled Pillow', and that his entire body 'throughout the night is intolerant even of the upper Sheet, and on quarrelsome terms even with Night-shirt' (*CL* V 253; also *PW* I 304–5), are fundamental to the perceived relationship between his dreams and his body. This physical responsiveness between body and dream was dependent on processes that he strove to understand throughout his life: those of transmutation and translation. Coleridge's ideas on these processes are inextricable from his thoughts on dreams and the role of his diseased body in dreams. His insight into the existence of translation and transmutation processes resulted in the recognition that certain intellectual and psychological faculties could be translated and transformed into bodily functions; that bodily functions could be translated into dream emotions, thoughts and passions: into dreamatis personæ.

He often struggled for the exact terminology to describe what he believed was going on between his mind and his body, between his illnesses and his dreams. He used various terms in his attempt to define and articulate a complex process of interactions, mutations, and relations between psychological and physiological experiences: the words 'translation' and 'transmutation' were freely used, often interchangeably. Frustrated at the inadequacy of language to provide an appropriate term, he coined one that is now in current usage: 'psychosomatic' (*SWF* II 1444). Simply defined, translations and transformations are intense and complex processes exhibiting the mind's power to act on the body. If the mind can act on the body, Coleridge saw no reason why it would not be possible that 'the purest . . . Impulse can introduce itself to our consciousness no otherwise than by *speaking to us* in some bodily feeling' (*CN* II 2495). The bodily feeling that speaks to the consciousness was evidence of a translation process, a psychosomatic relationship between mind and body which could also be seen as one of the most complex and crucial features of dreams.

One of the primary characteristics of both dreams and disease is the 'conversion of Pain into mental *affections*' (N36, fo. 6). In many dreams, Coleridge described his pain as 'transmuted' into various '*mental* passions', such as 'Grief, Fear, Remorse, Hate, Revenge &c' (*CN* IV 5377). The 'first moments of awaking from a Dream' provide a perfect opportunity to study the 'dependence of ideas' on the 'state of bodily or mental *Feeling*' (*CN* II 2638). He does not distinguish between these two feelings: both are dependent on ideas. The body interacts with the mind and modifies, alters and translates psychological and physiological experiences into the dream (*CN* IV 5033).

A letter that Coleridge wrote to Southey in August 1803 raises issues concerning the nature of transmutation, the properties of the imagination, and the intimate connections he perceived between sleep, dreams and disease. Both disease and dreams shared a peculiar 'state of mind'. This state of mind was another of the species of dream that he identified, one which he believed could explain the connections between 'frightful Dreams' and some diseases (*CL* II 976). The most striking feature of this state of mind was its capacity for enacting or allowing transmutations. Coleridge's medical knowledge is crucial in the formation of his concept of a translation, as is clear from this letter to Southey in which, after reading the entry on gout in the *Encyclopedia Britannica*, he explains his one point of disagreement with it:

Of my disease there now remains no Shade of Doubt: it is a compleat & almost heartless case of Atonic Gout. If you would look into the Article Medicine, in the Encyc. Britt. . . . you will read almost the very words, in which, before I had seen the Article, I had described my case to Wordsworth. – The only non-agreement is – 'an imaginary aggravation of the slightest Feelings, & an apprehension of danger from them.' – The first sentence is unphilosophically expressed / there is a state of mind, wholly unnoticed, as far as I know, by any Physical or Metaphysical Writer hitherto, & which is necessary to the explanation of some of the most important phaenomena of Sleep & Disease / it is a transmutation of the *succession* of *Time* into the *Juxtaposition* of *Space*, by which the smallest Impulses, if quickly & regularly recurrent, *aggregate* themselves – & attain a kind of visual magnitude with a correspondent Intensity of general Feeling. – The simplest Illustration would be the *circle* of Fire made by whirling round a live Coal – only here the mind is passive. Suppose the same effect produced ab intra – & you have a clue to the whole mystery of frightful Dreams, & Hypochondriacal delusions. – I merely hint at this; but I could detail the whole process, complex as it is. – (*CL* II 974)

The 'process' was indeed complex, and one which Coleridge tried to understand throughout his life. There is a 'state of mind' – a species of dream – that can be explained by processes of transmutation. The conscious recognition of likenesses between sleep and disease is unquestioned in this letter. Not *all* the phenomena of the two conditions are explained by this 'state of mind', but 'some of the most important' are. The 'transmutation' is based on cardinal qualities of time and space. That disease and dreams are partially explained in terms of an 'aggregation' illustrates the existence of a 'somnial or Morphean space' (*CN* IV 5360), and once again places the diseased body at the centre of dream explorations. Through the medium of space, over certain periods of time, impulses of feelings accumulate in the somnial space and are then 'transmutated'. This process sheds crucial light on the 'whole mystery of frightful Dreams', and demands the attention of both medical and metaphysical thinkers.

Transmutations between mind and body were most noticeable in times of illness and frightful dreams, and were too persistent to be ignored. Part of the reason these (re)actions could not be ignored was their physically painful nature. Coleridge once stated that the 'strong feelings' experienced in dreams arise because those feelings are in fact 'bodily sensations' (*CL* IV 642). A notebook entry from October 1823 elaborates on this connection:

Awoke from a dream – sensation[6] of the intensest, deepest, bitterest agony of *Grief* respecting Derwent – a purer more condensed Grief per se Grief, without fear or anger, cannot be felt – and found in the instant of awakening a *heavy pain* across the umbilical region, probably at the pit of the stomach. – Now this (often have I noted it) this translation of pain into mental passion! (*CN* IV 5033)

The connections between pain and mental passion have not only been observed, they have also been given a name: a 'translation'. The emotional disturbance, 'a purer more condensed Grief per se Grief', is organically linked to the 'pit of the stomach' via the dream itself.

The claim that pain experienced in a dream is 'purer' and 'more condensed' than waking pain arises from Coleridge's life-long enquiry into the nature of pain as well as into the relationships between pain and dream experience. His investigations into pain significantly contributed to his understanding of his body and of what constituted a translation, and of how translations revealed the similar phenomena of sleep and disease. He systematically examined the philosophical, emotional and physical qualities of pain (*CN* III 3371, *CN* IV 5189), as well as the different responses to it that men and women experienced (N46, fo. 20).[7] A significant portion of at least two unpublished notebooks, 38 and 39, is concerned with definitions of pleasure as 'synthesis' and pain as 'compression' (N39, fo. 2). After a discussion with Charles Lamb, Coleridge raises the problem of whether or not 'persons in *frenzy* actually *suffer*' (N39, fo. 32v), and what the nature of pain might be in different illnesses:

Pain, essentially subjective, may become so intensely subjective as to swallow up all objectivity & in so doing destroy itself. One great Function of the Brain is to objectivize Pain by reflecting it, and thus to preserve its subjectivity – but it may be so vehement as to extend into the Brain itself and either to suspend the reflecting function or to convert the organ of reflection into an organ of Sensation, partially at least . . . The reflectory function being suspended in Sleep, Pain is translated into Mental passions – a fact of manifest as well as of deep interest. (N39, fos. 32v–33, late 1829)

Coleridge's interest in the nature of pain becomes more intricate when he examines the differences between waking and sleeping consciousnesses. When fully conscious, the brain is able to 'objectivize' pain by somehow 'reflecting' it. If pain is so intense that the brain has problems with this objectivisation, the 'reflectory function' may be diverted or suspended. But in sleep, that function is automatically suspended, in much the same manner as the faculties of reason or will or surprise. Because the reflectory function is suspended, pain is 'translated into Mental Passions'.

The process involves the metamorphosis – or translation – of objective pain into subjective pain, and accounts for many emotions and images experienced during some of the wildest dreams. Coleridge tries to articulate these connections in terms of the properties of somnial space, the relationships between space and time, while also drawing on the practice of animal magnetism:

The reflectory function being suspended in Sleep, Pain is translated into Mental Passions – a fact of manifest as well as of deep interest . . . Pain becomes the Positive Factor, and sets the Brain in action as music has been known to set an unsonorous body & set it a spinning, itself ceasing to be in control of the action. The Magnetizer is not conscious of the products of his agency in the System of the Patient. Pain is here the unconscious Magnetist, the Brain being the Patient i.e. it becomes objective, and causes the brain, as the Subject, to produce in its own kind, and yet in the *form* of the agent – in its own kind and therefore subjective, but in the form of the agent, and therefore formally objective and such is the character of the passions & accompanying images in my Dreams, i.e. Subjectively Object-ive / Hence [?for] the Loss of Time, and the Predominance of Space, of Heights, Depths, Expansion – for Space is in its' essence Subjectively Objective – and hence the things that fill space, as Buildings of all kinds ([?*vide*] Piranesis Dreams, the Delirium of Architectural Genius) but which make no resistance and neither occupy Space than fill it up – possibly from the suspension of *Time* as that which furnishes the element of *Resistance* – a most important, but little regarded, principle of Psychology & not without its uses in Physiology and even in Physics.

As Pain is translated into Passion, so that which would in the waking state be pleasure, losing the access of mind necessary for its [?completion], manifests a tendency to translate itself into *Appetite*. (N39, fos. 32v–33v)

Coleridge explores the confusion of subjective and objective per-ception to account for somnial mysteries. In dreams, the pain is both objective and subjective, it is more intense, more 'pure' (*CN* IV 5033). It can be translated from the body into the dream and out of the dream into the body. Dream passions and images are both their own agent and their own subject, because of the process of translation from pain into passion. This translation, as with the 'transmutation' Coleridge refers to in his letter to Southey (*CL* II 974), requires the 'suspension of *Time*'. What would be pleasure in a waking state is translated into a distinctly physical 'appetite' in the dream. There is a degree of autonomy involved in the way this translation occurs: pain is capable of setting the brain in 'motion' in an analogous manner to that in which 'music has been known to set an unsonorous body & set it a spinning'. Movement and perceived harmony become the means for the brain to subjectivise and objectivise bodily pains. The oscillations between objective and subjective experiences of pain explain the 'character of the passions & accompanying images' in Coleridge's dreams. What interests him more than Piranesian dreams of architectural delirium is the tendency of pain to be translated into an appetite in a dream, as well as the differences between the same pain experienced when sleeping and when awake. The same sensation, if the subject were awake, would be termed 'pleasure'.

The translation of pain into dream-passion, of pleasure into (lustful) appetite, is yet another example of how dreams become a part of Coleridge's somatic experience, and vice versa. The existence of somatic dream-passions is dependent on the processes of translation and transformation between body and mind, mind and body. Pain experienced in dreams testifies to the existence of a complex process between psychological sensations and physical sensations, often with little to distinguish them. The translations and conversions of pain in dreams become the 'pains of sleep', the physical realities of dreams become 'distemper's worst calamity', and the 'fiendish dream' can only be interrupted by the dreamer's 'own loud scream' ('The Pains of Sleep', *CKK* 63). These translations between body and dream explain why pain experienced in dreams is 'purer', 'more condensed' than that which is felt in waking life (*CN* IV 5033).

Sometimes Coleridge used the word 'conversion' to explain the process. The metaphor he employs in a notebook entry of 1826 is both literal and figurative; it is what he calls a 'conversion' of the physical body and its organic functions into psychic existence: 'Conversion of bodily Pain into some Passion of the Mind – Heart-burn becomes intense Grief, with bitter Weeping; Pain in the Umbilical Region becomes Terror – & in like manner, I doubt not, that bodily pleasure becomes Hope, or intense Love nullo libidine mixtus' (*CN* IV 5360). The need to translate impure, corporeal sensations into a purer, spiritual form in this entry is typical of Coleridge's attempt to idealise the body while simultaneously shrinking from it. Bodily pain can be converted into 'some Passion of the Mind', supposedly more acceptable to the waking self, but still problematic. Pain in the 'umbilical Region' becomes 'terror', and he does not 'doubt' that (sexual) bodily pleasure becomes 'Hope' when it appears in the dream.[8] The reference to an 'intense Love' and the qualification of this statement with the censoring Latin, 'nullo libidine mixtus' ('not mixed with desire'), indicate the extent of his uneasiness with his dreams and the ways in which his sexual desires could form part of them. Love, when not mixed with desire, can be (theoretically) pure, spiritual. The potential for love to be purely ideal was an attractive thought, but Coleridge's body was too dominant a presence in his thoughts and dreams for an ideal love to exist in isolation. Bodily pain undergoes a conversion into a 'passion of the mind', such that a pain in the umbilical region is converted into dream-terror. This terror is experienced as a sensation in the dream, by the dream-Coleridge, but also as a sensation experienced in and for itself by Coleridge the man. In dreams, different organs may come to represent different degrees of converted, or translated, passion:

most interesting – the apparent representative character of particular Forms and Images, repr. I mean, each of some particular organ or structure – Ex. gr. I have never of late years awaked, desiderio mingendi, but the preceding Dream had presented some water-landskip, Lake, River, Pond, or Splashes, Water-pits. . . . But I suspect, the vermiform motion of the Bowels – & the predominance of the colors, & other things in dreams, I am disposed to refer *fæcibus* accumulatis. (*CN* IV 5360)

The physical need to urinate, 'desiderio mingendi', forms part of the dream's generally stagnant but strongly aqueous landscape of lakes, rivers, ponds and water-pits. Bodily retention of fluid seems to suggest certain images and landscapes in the dream. The need to urinate often passes from the body of the dreamer and into a dream-world (but not always, as in N36, fo. 37). The act of passing from the physiological into the somnial space was an act of translation. A dream containing a multitude of colours, and 'other things', Coleridge attributes to the accumulation of faeces in the bowels. In this manner, bodily function, and bodily discomfort in the form of a need to defecate and urinate, are converted into some 'Passion of the Mind' in the dream-state.

The process of 'conversion' (*CN* IV 5360) is of particular interest when it is remembered exactly what it is that is being converted. Coleridge claims that bodily pain is converted into 'some Passion of the Mind', that specific physiological states are also represented as different, perhaps correspondent, psychological experiences. The observation of this process provides him with the grounds for his various classifications of dreams as possessing *both* a physical manifestation and a physical cause. Nightmares are terrible not merely for their disorientating psychological effects: they are as painful, threatening and substantial as an open wound, or as an attack of diarrhoea. That dreams can become so substantial is one reason for the extreme terror, the '*grasp . . . weight*, of Hate and Horror', of some dream-creatures (*CN* II 2468). The power of the process of translation or 'conversion' is such that, on one occasion, Coleridge confesses:

Even before I fall to sleep, I know what sort of dreams I am sentenced to suffer – by the rising up of ugly, often [?scabbed] & ulcerous faces, which, when I exorcise by an action of will or by turning around, instantly alternates with a sensation of pain & uneasiness at my Stomach or below – i.e. changes for an emotion – (N35, fo. 39, dated 1827)

The faces which rise up before him as he waits to fall asleep have intimate associations with processes happening in the gut. The 'sensation of pain & uneasiness' in the stomach is a manifestation of the conversion between mind and sleeping body: thoughts are translated into physical experiences. Dreams do not emerge within a vacuum: they strongly adhere to and partake of the bodily life of the dreamer. And the body, with its organs and aches and pains, also partakes in the dream-life as well as in the pre-dream life. Those ugly scabbed faces that seem to rise up spontaneously before sleep can be manipulated by the dreamer's 'will', or if he turns 'around'. But in turning around, Coleridge 'instantly' receives a 'sensation of pain & uneasiness' in his stomach. His cry that he knows even before he falls asleep what type of dream he must be 'sentenced to suffer' reveals that he perceives the dream to be a form of punishment. The ugly faces of malignant spirits need to be exorcised by an action of the will, for, since he is still awake, the will has not yet been rendered powerless. That he realises that there is a causal relationship between what *will* be dreamt 'I know what sort of dreams I am sentenced to suffer' and the presence of his body suggests that the processes of translation and conversion are once again active.

The words Coleridge chose to describe the processes he observed going on between his mind and body in dreams also have moral and religious connotations. His quest for an explanation which would satisfactorily account for the origin of dreams led him to the consideration of his own moral nature. However, his frequent rejection of a spirit theory in favour of perceiving his body as the cause of his dreams was also couched in terms which could lead him back to the perpetual problem of his moral nature (as in *CN* I 1770). The alteration from a state of sinfulness to a state of repentance and grace is one meaning of 'conversion'. The word 'translation' also has religious overtones: *The Oxford English Dictionary* gives as one meaning 'removal from earth to heaven'. What these two words – conversion and translation – imply is that a change has occurred from the bodily to the spiritual, or the cerebral. The movement is usually upwards, away from the body and to a higher state. These associated meanings of the words 'conversion', 'translation' and 'transmutation' linger in the background to Coleridge's discussion of his dreams as evidence of the exchanges between dreams and his body. The relationship he perceived between his body and his dreaming mind is, however, reciprocal: it is equally important for the body to be capable of moving into the spiritual as it is for the spiritual, or the psychological, to move, to translate, into the somatic.

The importance and potency of the process by which emotions and thoughts become related to or even become a part of the body in dreams and in illness are indicated in Coleridge's coining of two very significant words: one already mentioned, 'psychosomatic' – he refers to 'Psycho-Somatic' processes in some dreaming states' (*SWF* II 1444–47); and 'corporific' (*CM* III 949). In an unfinished essay, possibly written in 1828, he tackles the inadequacies of considering the soul and the body as 'correspondent opposites, the Positive and Negative Poles, as it were, of which the Man was the Unity' (*SWF* II 1420). Emotions, including emotions in dreams, were not to be seen in strictly psychological terms: Coleridge believed that they should also be discussed in relation to physiology, physics and anatomy. Rage, fear, anger, joy, grief and hope, all have a physiological base because they have physiological components (*SWF* II 429–30).[9] When he claims that fear has its 'birthplace in the Digestive System, especially . . . in the Sypogastric Organs', and that rage has its 'birthplace in the vasculo-muscular system, the Blood and the Muscles' (*SWF* II 430), he displays considerable insight into the relations between psychological and physiological experiences. This is a phenomenon which can readily be seen in dreams: Coleridge once described his dreamatis personæ as dying 'without a wound, from Fear' (*CN* II 2418). What he explores is the relations of psychosomatics, the translations between body and mind which are evident in waking and all varieties of dreaming states.

That Coleridge felt the need and then invented a term – 'Psycho-

somatic *Ology*' – to describe his unique discussion of the passions
reveals his originality and his insight into the problems and complexity of the relationships between body and mind. His coinage
reveals the extent to which he wished to conceptualise the psychological as having interdependencies with the somatic. The recognition of connections between psyche and soma is also evident in his
invention of the word 'corporific' in an annotation to William
Nicholson's *Journal of Natural Philosophy, Chemistry, and the Arts*.
Although Coleridge is directly commenting upon chemical changes,
his observations and his coinage of 'corporific' have significant
implications for a discussion of his dreams, particularly the process of
translation. The editors of the third volume of his *Marginalia* define
'corporific' as meaning 'body-making', 'that which causes something
to assume a body or material form' (*CM* III 949). The word
'corporific', from *corpus* (body) and *facere* (to make), has an obvious
resemblance to, and significant parallels with, the word 'soporific'
(from *sopor*, sleep and *facere*). He has taken the process of becoming
sleepy as the model for the process of making a body. He could have
used the word 'corporify' (it, too, deriving from *corpus* and *facere*), for
instance, meaning to assume a material form. But instead he uses a
term that underscores the connections between 'making sleep' and
'making body'. This coinage reflects his belief that there are discernible connections between dreams and bodies, between 'some of the
most important phaenomena of Sleep & Disease' (*CL* II 974).

Coleridge's use of the compound word 'corporific' can be taken
almost literally when seen in relation to 'soporific phenomena':
when he dreams, he does in fact make bodies. In dreams, he
encounters many different types of bodies, from pursuing demons
(*CN* I 1649, *CN* IV 5360) to representations of his family and friends
(*CN* II 2055, 2441). He also encounters *his own body*, both as an *imagined*
corporeality and as a representation of his *experience* of his waking
body. In this sense, he (re)makes his body in his dreams, but his
dreams also make and present different parts and versions of his
body. A unique type of body is created: a 'dreambody'.[10] At different
times, the various organs and processes of the Coleridgean dreambody are exaggerated. In one dream, the right eye is emphasised (*CN*
I 848); in another, his vulnerable scrotum (*CN* I 1726); in yet another,
the veins are slashed open, and 'torrents of Blood' gush from the
dreambody (*CN* II 2559).

The dreambody is also exposed during moments between sleeping and waking. In a letter to Thomas Boosey, Coleridge recalls an experience he had 'some 15 or 16 years ago' (as recorded in *CN* I 1108) in which parts of his body acquired remarkable powers:

I have myself once seen (i.e. appeared to see) my own body under the Bed cloaths flashing silver Light from whatever part I prest it – and as it were, my name, Greek words, cyphers &c on my Thigh: and instantly seen them together with the Thigh in brilliant Letters of silver Light. – It was some 15 or 16 years ago – I had left a jovial party, after much and very animated conversation, at a Mr Bellow's . . . and had drank two large Tumblers of very strong Punch. I deduced from the Phaenomenon the existence of an imitative sympathy in the nerves, so that those of the Eye copied instantaneously the impressions made on those of the Limbs. – (*CL* IV 781)

That perhaps the 'very strong punch' had something to do with this strange visual and somatic experience is of less interest to Coleridge than that the thigh could be perceived in such a way. The observations are connected with single and double touch. The body is bizarrely represented, acquiring remarkable, indeed impossible, abilities. This is a kind of dreambody, a reproduction or partial representation of the body experienced in differing species and genera of dreams. Coleridge's 'corporific' process was an especially apt one for the examination of dreams and somnial states. The process of becoming physical, tangible, applied also to feelings and emotions experienced in the many different species and genera of dreams.

The psychosomatic and corporific connections between the organs and the character of dreams are often mysterious but also undeniable. In a letter of August 1826, Coleridge laments:

I am sorry to say that since I last wrote, my health has suffered a worse than relapse – and my friend, Mr Green, does not know what to make of it. He can discover no mark of organic injury – no symptom of inflammation in Liver or Kidney, or (tho' the functions are greatly deranged) any structural ailment in the intestinal Canal – . But he is inclined to think the ganglionic System, pectoral and abdominal, to be the seat of the disorder – the more so, from the worse sufferings being in sleep, and my greatest weakness and langour during the two or three hours after my last Sleep. – These disturbances have almost forced my attention to the obscure subject of dreams – and the extraordinary tendency to a sort of allegoric personification of the processes & incidences of vital Action, that is so characteristic of Sleep when the lower Bowels are deranged. (*CL* VI 606–7)[11]

The 'worse than relapse' brings with it not only a further debilitation (the 'greatly deranged' functions in the intestinal canal) but also an increased focus on the 'obscure subject of dreams'. The associations between 'Sleep & Disease' are undeniable (*CL* II 974), and the pains of the body become the pains of sleep. It seems that Joseph Green and Coleridge agree that the 'seat of the disorder' must be within the chest and the nervous organs of the abdomen because the 'sufferings' are 'worse' in sleep. The pain and suffering go beyond the limits of consciousness, transgressing the boundaries of logic such that they are felt even when consciousness is partially if not totally absent.[12] Coleridge's pain is felt just as powerfully in sleep as it is in waking life and is often of a more intense nature in dreams (*CN* IV 5033). He and Green both discover that organic processes possess an 'extraordinary tendency to a sort of allegoric personification' in sleep and dreams (*CL* VI 607).

In a notebook entry of December 1827, Coleridge again confronts the problems of a psychosomatic existence and the relation between dreams and organs (N36, fo. 5v). He suggests in this entry that the 'Dreamatis Personæ' are 'combined with *motives* generally suggested by Passions' and that the one thing to be discovered from this is the 'locality' of each passion within the 'organic system'. He wonders if fear and terror are located in the 'vascular system', if rage is born 'in the blood', and what role the lower abdomen and its organs have to play in dreams. He writes that the lower abdomen has 'so manifest an influence in Dreams', but cannot decide if it is capable of acting by itself in this respect, or if it acts 'rather by pressure in <the> nerves of higher organs'. Either way, he is forced to exclaim that he is 'mortified and perplexed'.

Dreams create and respond to a unique 'somatosphere' (*CM* III 373, 387), a complex interplay between soma and psyche that permits transmutations between dream world and body. Coleridge hypothesises a chain of possible actions, reactions and corporific interactions in a complex relationship between the two. He continues the Notebook 36 entry with a query on the possibility of the 'potenziation'[13] of the solar plexus, then traces the possible effects on organs and on the mind if particular conditions are met. He wonders if certain parts of the solar plexus are potenziated by a 'morbid excitement or stimulus of the imperfectly digested food', and if 'acrid fæces' are in 'alliance' with nerves in the brain:

that the Organs with their integral parts thus raised into Consciousness –

each would become pro tempore a Spirit – in what way would they manifest their presence to the Spirit of the Whole – dem ich? As Men, Women, Children, Serpents, Fairies? and the inorganized Contents, the urine, Seminal Fluid, Fæces, Blood as [. . .]: Rivers, Trees, Swamps, Muddy Sloughs & the like? you may laugh with and at yourself, while you are thinking on this, if you like; but ridentem verum indagare verum Quid vetat! (N36, fos. 4v–5)

Coleridge may well have wanted to laugh at himself, at the possible results of the translations of organs into spirits, of the body into the dream – examples of transmutations between dream and body. Would men and women and fairies in dreams correspond to, or be 'in alliance' with, nerves and organs in the body?[14] Would seminal fluid be manifested as a swamp, or as a muddy slough '& the like', in the dream? Does the sequence itself suggest that the 'inorganized contents' of the bowels turn into men, that urine turns into women, seminal fluid into children, faeces into serpents, and blood into fairies? If the 'acrid fæces' ally themselves with both cerebral and ganglionic nerves, thereby raising certain organs into consciousness, then it is possible for those organs and organic processes to be manifested in a dream. This entire process fascinates Coleridge: '*in what way* would they manifest their presence to the Spirit of the Whole?' (my emphasis). It is a question not only of the nature of the organ's entry into the dream, but also the relationship to the 'spirit' of the dreamer's organs and soul. Fluids seem the most accessible bodily component, for they are mobile – fluid – and, in the case of blood, able to flow to all parts of the body. This entry reveals that dreams are poised between the benign and malignant features of sleeping life. The questions are apparently straightforward: for instance, if the organs were to become 'pro tempore' spirits, what forms would they take in the dream? There is an uneasy and implicit innocence in this question. In some dreams, the manifestation of organs and spirits is curious, non-threatening, and sometimes even pleasant (*CN* i 1718). In other dreams, the manifestation is shockingly frightful and painful (*CN* ii 2468, *CN* iii 3322). Via transmutations and corporific actions (*CN* iii 4406) 'sensations' in dreams become as much sensations of the body as of the mind. Coleridge's slight chuckle to himself at the end of this intriguing entry reveals his cautious feelings about his analysis of his dreams, but also his heartfelt conviction that he was continually plumbing the *truth* of the 'mysterious problem of dreams' (*CN* iv 5360). One of the most salient features of his investigation was his suggestion that, through processes of transmutation and corporific action, 'some of the most important phaenomena' (*CL* II 974) of both sleep and disease could be revealed and explored.

Coleridge recognised various degrees and manifestations of his transmutational processes, in relation to his dreams and his illnesses. In an annotation to Tennemann's *Geschichte der Philosophie* he defines dreams as: 'a shifting Current in the shoreless Chaos of the Fancy in which the streamy *Continuum* of passive Association is broken into zig-zag by Sensation, from within or from without – ex. gr. distension from wind in the stomach, or a knot in the bed-cloathes.'[15] His basic notion of a dream depends on the ability for sensation to interfere with the 'Chaos of the Fancy'. This interference could stem equally from a sensation within the body, or a sensation external to it. Those sensations outside the body implicitly require a translation from the touch of the 'bed-cloathes' to the dreaming mind. The sensations within the body are also translated into the dreaming mind.

The connections between the mind and the diseased body were present in all the different species of dreams and dreaming states:

I hurried down to the Necessary – vomited a little, & was finally relieved by a violent Diarrhoea – & recovered, tho' I remain somewhat feeble – . I can refer it to no imprudence or excess – I had eat nothing since breakfast . . . but this is ever the way with me / Rainy windy Weather diseases my Stomach: & if any thing happens to affect & harrass me, I have no other salvation from these or worse attacks, than to eat nothing / & how far that would answer, I cannot say / for to sleep is equally dangerous . . . But for a slight irregular Fluttering at the Heart, & a speck of *Coldness* felt there, I should not have known, that T. W.'s Letter had *got into me* . . . It should seem, as if certain Trains of Feeling acted, *on me*, underneath my own *Consciousness* . . . & so that all Feelings which particularly affect *myself, as* myself, connect & combine with my bodily sensations, especially the trains of motion in the digestive Organs, & therefore tho' I feel them *en mass*, I do not & cannot make them the objects of a distinct attention. Any one who witnessed the effects of bad news &c &c on my body, would conclude that I was a creature of diseased Sensibility. (*CL* 1045–6)

One of the most striking features of this letter is the way in which Coleridge describes it as having '*got into me*'. It is not simply that the letter has deeply affected him, either positively or negatively; he is not necessarily confining himself to a figurative meaning. The distressing nature of the letter's contents acts as an agency of dis-ease inside his digestive system. The subtle confusions of tense and grammar, and the need to refer euphemistically to certain places or bodily processes, reflect an intellectual struggle to come to terms with the precise nature of the connections between the physical attack and the emotional state preceding it: 'all Feelings . . . connect and combine with my bodily sensations', and 'to sleep is equally as dangerous'. In this letter, the suggestion is that what has happened is that the (distressing) emotional response to the letter has been 'translated' into a distressing organic reaction. 'T.W's Letter had *got into me*', because 'all Feelings . . . connect & combine with my bodily sensations'. The particular sympathy between bowels and 'feelings', possibly enhanced by opium, is also found in a fragmentary essay on animal magnetism in which Coleridge claims that the 'known sympathy of the Stomach and Bowels with the Skin' is well documented, particularly in dreaming states (*SWF* II 912). Organs can cause certain types of dreams, and certain dreams can be embodied in different organs or limbs, or in pains. The transmutations between mind and body are possible because of the exquisite sympathy between feelings, affections (both as something emotional and something which affects the body) and organic processes.[16]

Coleridge's notion of self is closely connected and combined with 'bodily sensations' (*CL* II 1045–6). He believed that his entire health was 'so intimately connected' with the state of his spirits, and these again 'so dependent' on his thoughts, that it was impossible at times to distinguish between a bodily pain originating in an organic disturbance, and a bodily pain originating in an emotional response (*CL* v 25). All that is subjective and defines the self – 'myself' – Coleridge believes 'connect[s] & combine[s] with . . . bodily sensations'. He may well be using 'sensations' in at least two different yet related applications: as both a mental feeling and the physical faculty of perceiving via the senses – through touch, hearing, sight, and so on.

It is not merely that the feelings both connect and combine with the bodily sensations, but also that the feelings seem to be distinct from the self: 'Certain Trains of Feeling acted, *on me*, underneath my own *Consciousness*' (*CL* II 1046). Coleridge seems to become a passive instrument, as was often the case with his dreams, in which both body and mind are seen as acting 'underneath' consciousness. The particular processes by which the feelings and the body connect and combine convince him not only that his body is diseased, but also that his 'Sensibility' is diseased. It is these two factors that Coleridge perceives to be the cause of many dreams. The ability of the body, the sensibilities and the emotions to be so similarly diseased depended upon the recognition of corporific, psychosomatic processes. Translations and transmutations of dream and diseased body, between dreaming body and dreaming mind, also revealed that certain cognitive faculties were extremely powerful in the formation of diseases. One of the most powerful of all these faculties was the imagination.

CHAPTER EIGHT

The dreaming medical imagination

Coleridge so often claimed that it was his diseased and ailing body which caused particular features of his dreams that it may appear impossible for the imagination to have played any role at all in the dreaming process as he understood it. But he was easily able to factor the imagination into the dreaming equation because the imagination was not only the forming power of poetry: it was also the 'true inward Creatrix' of many confusing nightmares, readily participating in them (*CN* III 4046), and in disease and illness. He perceived that the imagination was the linking faculty between the psychological and physical states of dreaming and disease, and that it displayed properties of both dreaming and diseased states of mind (*CL* II 974). There were specific diseases which Coleridge argued illustrated this particular and fascinating species of dream: gout was caused by an '*aggregation* of slight Feelings by the force of a diseasedly retentive Imagination' (*CL* II 975). Sleep and disease possessed inherently similar properties and could therefore be studied as complementary disciplines. Dreams had long been considered to be types of diseases. What united the studies of dreams, disease and sleeping in Coleridge's thinking was the imagination. This emphasis on the physical, medical imagination calls for a re-evaluation of the broader concept of the imagination as Coleridge understood it, and consequently, for a re-evaluation of the critical notion of the Romantic imagination. For Coleridge, the imagination is not only an imagination capable of producing poetry and dreams: it is also an imagination of medicine and disease. Both notions were firmly grounded in the psychology and medical science of the late eighteenth century.

Coleridge often referred to poetry as a particular species of dream (*Lectures* II 425), a 'rationalized dream' (*CN* II 2086), and maintained that the imagination was equally active in both poetry and dreaming.

That he could maintain this belief while also exploring the somatic, physical origins of his dreams demanded that the imagination itself be a physical entity. Through an intricate study of his dreams, his diseased body and the translations between dream and body, he perceived that the creative, often spiritual, imagination could be seen as an organ of the body that had a special role to play in different species and genera of dreams (*CN* II 2999). He referred to the imagination as behaving like any other organ of the body, succumbing to disease and sometimes causing disease, acting as the interpreter of translated bodily feelings and dream languages (*CN* III 3547).

Throughout his lifetime Coleridge maintained that thoughts in dreams were easily 'translated into sights and sensible impressions' (*CL* VI 616). If emotions and thought processes in dreams were connected with the 'motions of the blood and nerves', and feelings arose from the 'position & state of the Body and its different members' (*CN* II 2543), it was plausible to see the imagination as also being of the body, as physiologically based and influenced, as having physiological links with specific nervous systems – the nerves, 'or parts of nerves', being 'instrumental to the will' (*CN* IV 5341). The imagination was both a somatic and a poetic faculty. By positing the imagination as having a physical, bodily component, it was also therefore possible to recognise its importance as a causal factor in dreams.

Coleridge's poetics has often been characterised as ascribing to a theory of organic unity.[1] These readings emphasise the idea that his religion, philosophy and poetry all depend upon notions of spiritual growth, evolution and wholeness. Many such readings draw from various statements of Coleridge's that there is a 'synthetic and magical power' (*BL* II 16) which 'dissolves, diffuses, dissipates, in order to re-create', an organic power that strives to unify: that power is the imagination (*BL* I 304). This mode of criticism, itself very Coleridgean, has recently come under scrutiny.[2] Clifford Siskin has successfully argued that many critical accounts of Coleridge have been heavily influenced by a catalogue of 'characteristic Romantic behaviours: to explore mind, to undergo epiphany, to alter visions, to dream dreams, to intensify imagination, to heighten depression, to suffer ecstasy, to fragment experience, to burn out, to flower lyrically and then wither'. This catalogue, as Siskin points out, is an artificial creation of the critic rather than an inherent feature of Romantic poetry.[3]

With few exceptions, both the popular organic reading and the more recent critical readings of the imagination fail to acknowledge the physical and medical characteristics of the so-called Romantic imagination: that the imagination was also perceived as a physical and medical faculty, and that it was distinctly linked to the material, to the corporeal. It is evident that Coleridge and other writers perceived it as an intellectual, poetic faculty, but also as the expression of specific organs of the body and of specific physiological processes. This aspect of Coleridge's notion of imagination, and the debate concerning the imagination at the turn of the nineteenth century, have received little attention. One of the few exceptions to this is G. S. Rousseau's companion works which explore the interdisciplinary nature of the imagination, madness and science in the eighteenth century: *Enlightenment Crossings*, *Enlightenment Borders* and *Perilous Enlightenment*. Rousseau charts the course by which eighteenth-century physiologists and neurologists conducted their experiments on the nerves in an attempt to understand not only anatomy but also the workings of the imagination.[4] What emerges from his studies is the strong presence of the imagination in that century as both material and spiritual, medical and poetic. As he argues, Coleridge's theories of the sympathetic and esemplastic imagination can also be understood as explorations of the medical history of the discovery of the imagination rather than solely as the poetic discovery of the creative, Romantic imagination. This broader concept was pivotal in Coleridge's explorations of dreams and of the relations between dreaming states and his diseased body.

Coleridge's presentation of the imagination as a somatic, medical faculty postulates it as literally esemplastic (*BL* II 168): it shapes and coadunates both psyche and soma, emotion and organ, dream and body. The recognition that the imagination could partake in bodily experience was not particular to Coleridge; it was an emerging part of medical practice in the eighteenth century and was deeply embedded in the science of animal magnetism. It was in his essay on that subject that Coleridge claimed the imagination as one of the causal features of the whole magnetism phenomenon: it was the power by which a 'Patient's Mind produces changes in . . . in his body, without any intentional act of the Will' (*SWF* II 913). This absence of the power of the will renders it a species of dream, and the imagination becomes an inextricable part of the magnetism process, capable of causing bodily as well as emotional change.

The acceptance of the imagination as a tool of magnetism, of medicine and of poetry is readily seen in the many medical treatises written on the nature of the imagination throughout the eighteenth and early nineteenth centuries. The concept of the imagination was hotly debated at this time, which helps to explain why Coleridge, as both a poet and an analyst of his dreams, was able to conceive it as belonging both to poetry and to his very physical, very painful dreams and diseases. The wealth of material on this subject in the eighteenth century cannot be fully explored in this present study: but it is important to gauge a sense of the currency of the debate in order to understand the complex ways in which Coleridge perceived the connections between his dreaming body and dreaming imagination.

One of the most popular works was William Falconer's *A Dissertation on the Influence of the Passions Upon Disorders of the Body*.[5] Falconer claims that many common ailments are the result of an excited or dulled nervous system. Typhus provides a 'striking instance of the power of mental affections', for it was thought to be caused by 'grief, fear, and other mental affections of the debilitating kind'.[6] Falconer's dissertation was influential in a later study by the pioneering Bath physician, John Haygarth.[7] Haygarth was also interested in exploring the potential powers of the imagination, dedicating his treatise, *Of the Imagination, as a Cause and as a Cure of Disorders of the Body*, to Falconer.[8] Haygarth seeks to reveal how the mind, and most specifically the imagination, can cause and cure particular diseases:

That faculty of the mind which is denominated the Imagination, has been the subject of two very elegant compositions in the English language, in prose and poetry, by ADDISON and AKENSIDE. It has not wholly escaped the notice of medical writers, but merits their farther investigation. This slight Essay may, perhaps, incite others to prosecute this inquiry more fully, in order to extend the power of physicians to prevent and cure the maladies of mankind.[9]

Haygarth clearly establishes the place of a study of the imagination in both poetic and medical contexts. Through an examination of the effects of using real and 'false' tractors in treating patients, he attempted to show the connections between imagination and bodily health. Devised and patented by Benjamin Perkins, tractors were a relatively new medical instrument which relied on the principle of magnetism for their efficacy. Consisting of a pair of pointed rods, usually made from brass or steel, they were believed to relieve rheumatic and other pains when drawn over or rubbed on the skin.

Haygarth treated a group of patients with wooden, or false, tractors and after the experiment concluded that the false ones worked as well, and sometimes better than, the 'patent' instrument. His success in disproving the efficacy of the original tractors (by showing cures can be produced with false ones – a placebo effect) bolsters his argument, 'what powerful Influence upon diseases is produced by mere Imagination'.[10] The patients' belief in the power of the tractors is so strong that they imagine themselves to be cured.

Haygarth's conclusion was immediately refuted by Perkins, who claimed that Haygarth had misrepresented the nature of his tractors. Perkins claimed that although Haygarth was of high medical standing, he was more necromancer than physician.[11] A lively debate between the two medical men quickly ensued. However, many of Haygarth's colleagues had already documented the tremendous potential of the imagination to influence and to interact actively with the ailing body.[12] Haygarth refers to a colleague, Dr James Lind,[13] concurring with his conclusion that:

an important lesson in physick is . . . to be learned, viz. the wonderful and powerful influence of the passions of the mind upon the state and disorders of the body. This is too often overlooked in the cure of diseases; many of which are sometimes attempted by the sole mechanical operation of drugs, without calling in to assistance the strong powers of the imagination, or the concurring influences of the soul.[14]

Curative processes therefore need not necessarily be confined to the 'sole mechanical operation of drugs', but should also take into consideration powerful psychological faculties, such as the imagination. Such faculties are indeed 'strong powers', whose influence cannot be underestimated. What the debate between Perkins and Haygarth reveals is the increasing perception that mechanical explanations of disease, so prevalent in the early decades of the eighteenth century, were inadequate to account for the symptoms of many diseases. Indicative of this perception was the growing opinion that powers of the mind and emotions have fundamental roles to play in the treatment and cause of diseases.[15] Of all mental faculties, the imagination was considered to be the most powerful.

The attraction of a medical philosophy which acknowledges the power of the mind, and of the imagination in particular, to effect changes in illness, as argued by physicians such as Haygarth, would have had immense appeal for Coleridge. He had read many works written in the late eighteenth and early nineteenth centuries which presented the imagination as a disease-causing and disease-curing agency. Indeed, the concept of a 'diseased imagination' was well established as early as the 1720s, and many works were devoted to suggesting cures for such a malady.[16] Debate as to the properties of the imagination was both vigorous and widespread. Works on the subject were not confined to England. In Italy, *On the Power of the Human Imagination* (1745) by Muratori, who also wrote at length on dreams and dreaming, was extremely influential and popular,[17] and G. A. Dupasquier's *De l'imagination, et de son influence sur l'homme dans l'état de santé ou de maladie* was published in Paris in 1821. In Germany, student, colleague and successor of Boerhaave, Jerome Gaub, gave a series of significant lectures in 1763 on the 'mutual relations of mind and body in health and disease', and explicated the ways in which the mind and emotions can be both causal and potentially curative factors in bodily disease.[18] In Scotland, O. Hunter's *De imaginatione morborum causa et remedio* (1803); in Ireland, Arthur Jacob's *Essay on the Influence of the Imagination and Passions in the Production and Cure of Diseases* was published in 1823; and Grant Powers' *Essay upon the Influence of the Imagination on the Nervous System, Contributing to a False Hope in Religion* (1828). These were all well-known works, their arguments received readily in both literary and medical circles. The imagination was as relevant to medical science as it was to poetics: it had 'become a faculty of the medical arts'.[19] And because dreams and disease were often seen as one and the same, the role of the imagination in both fields of enquiry needed to be considered.

Those who studied the imagination and its powers often acknowledged the importance of recognising that '*the power of the imagination and passions extensively influences the ordinary operations of the animal economy; and that the same influence is not only capable of producing diseases but of contributing to their removal*'.[20] Coleridge also concluded this, noting in *Biographia Literaria*: 'It is within the experience of many medical practitioners, that a patient, with strange and unusual symptoms, has been more distressed in mind, more wretched, from the fact of being unintelligible to himself and others, than from the pain or danger of the disease' (*BL* II 234). Coleridge's belief in the power of the distressed mind to cause more wretchedness than 'the pain or danger of the disease' reflects his interest in the capacity of disease to be mediated, accentuated and even cured by psychological states. To support his assertion, he cites the authority of medical practitioners as well as his own theoretical ideas on dreams and the nature of the passions. Drawing upon the growing realisation in medical treatises that the imagination could be a powerful healing faculty, he claims that, in the patient's mind, the imagination 'produces changes in . . . [the] body, without any intentional act of the Will'. The most striking demonstrations of this imaginative power are witnessed when a blush creeps across the face, or when yawning becomes 'contagious', or when fevers beset the body; or in 'Palpitations of the Heart', or, most significantly, in the case of the 'Night-Mair' (*SWF* II 913). In dreams, especially the 'Night-Mair', the imagination can create physical changes in the body.

The ideas of Haygarth, Jacob and others were very popular and provided Coleridge with a framework in which poetry, sleep, dreams and disease could be discussed. The imagination could be seen as a medical tool, with strong ties to the organs of the ailing patient. Another medical and philosophical debate which provided Coleridge with food for thought was the theory of maternal impressions. He may have at times mocked the notion of such a theory, but he was fascinated by it as an example of the relationship between the imagination and the body. More importantly, the maternal impressions debate still flourished throughout the eighteenth century, at the same time that debates into the nature of the imagination and the causes of monstrous births were raging.[21] The premise of the maternal impressions theory is that a woman's imagination can produce 'impressions' upon her unborn foetus. If the impressions are negative, the baby will be deformed. If they are positive or beautiful, the baby too will be beautiful.[22] Coleridge approached this apparently strange theory with his usual blend of scepticism and belief. In an annotation to Carl Kluge's *Versuch einer Darstellung des animalischen Magnetismus* (1815), he claims that the argument should not centre on whether there is a joining nerve between mother and daughter; rather, the '*limited* number of the sorts of mother-marks, whereas they ought to be as various as the occasions acting on, and the forms excited in, the imagination of the mother: at least in some proportion' must be held accountable (*CM* III 392).

Coleridge's hesitant 'at least in some proportion' seems to have disappeared entirely in another marginal comment. The third volume of Marcus' and Schelling's *Jahrbücher der Medizin* (1805–8) presents the case of a mother who had several healthy children and then one child born with a hare-lip. She maintained that 'she was startled by a hare in a field in the fifth month of her pregnancy and could not for a long time afterwards dispel the picture of the hare's head from her imagination' (*CM* III 131). Coleridge humorously adds: 'But how many Children have been born Hare-lipped whose Mothers were never Harum-scarumed? How many whose Mothers never saw a Hare?' (*CM* III 131). However, acutely aware as he was of the potential of the imagination's physical influence, he was not always so facetious. What interested Coleridge about the maternal impressions theory was its recognition of the potential of the imagination as a somatic agency, as a cognitive faculty which could literally instigate physical change. This potential was acutely expressed in times of emotional unrest or states of semi-consciousness.

Both the maternal impressions debate and the controversy that raged between medical men such as Haygarth and Perkins were fundamentally concerned with the nature of the imagination. It is therefore surprising that such debates have received so little attention with regard to Coleridge's notion of the imagination and his understanding of dreams. Like many of his contemporaries, Coleridge viewed dreaming to be a particularly acute type of imaginative activity. And one crucial shared property of sleep and disease was the role of the imagination. Its ability to translate between somatic and psychological states was the fundamental property underlying both dreaming and diseased states. Coleridge was obviously interested in the debates about the imagination, and some of the poems in *Lyrical Ballads* and others written during the 1790s and early 1800s draw upon them. In 'The Three Graves', a poem begun by Wordsworth in early 1797 and taken over and continued by Coleridge the following year, a striking illustration of the power of the imagination as a physical agency is presented.[23] The poem was not published until 1809 (*F* II 88–96). Coleridge presents the work to the public not because of any partiality to

tragic, much less monstrous events (though at the time that I composed the verses, somewhat more than twelve years ago, I was less averse to such subjects than at present), but from finding it a striking proof of the possible effect on the imagination, from an Idea violently and suddenly imprest on it . . . I conceived the design of shewing . . . and of illustrating the mode in which the mind is affected in these cases, and the progress and symptoms of the morbid action on the fancy from the beginning. (*F* II 89)

His interest in maternal impressions contributes to one of the most enigmatic poetic tales written in that critical period, 1797–8. The 'possible effects of the imagination' are most strikingly explored in the effects of the mother's curse upon her daughter and her husband. Coleridge's apologia to the poem states that he wished to show not *if* it is affected, but 'the mode in which the mind' is affected by a curse, and most particularly, a mother's curse. This aim drew added poignancy from the fact that during the period in which Wordsworth and Coleridge wrote the poem, the essential constitution of the imagination and of the powers of mothers to effect change (voluntarily or involuntarily) in their own bodies and in their children was a subject of intense debate.

The maternal impressions theory furnishes one instance of Coleridge's participation in the debate surrounding the physical properties of the imagination. While he used the imagination debate in his enquiries into dreams, a number of poems in the *Lyrical Ballads* (1798) collection can also be seen as explorations of current discussions on the subject. These poems distinctly reveal that both Wordsworth and Coleridge conceptualised the imagination as possessing both poetic and physical properties: the most obvious example in this respect is 'Goody Blake and Harry Gill'. In his 1800 Preface to the *Lyrical Ballads*, almost apologising for the poem as 'one of the rudest' in the collection, Wordsworth nevertheless argues that he 'wished to draw attention to the truth that the power of the human imagination is sufficient to produce such changes even in our physical nature as might almost appear miraculous. The truth is an important one; the fact (for it is a *fact*) is a valuable illustration of it.'[24] It is in the reading of 'Goody Blake and Harry Gill' as an illustration of the power of the imagination to produce physical changes that the poem is to be particularly distinguished from others in the *Lyrical Ballads* collection. The desire to draw attention to the 'power of the . . . imagination . . . to produce such changes even in our physical nature' strikingly echoes the claims made by Haygarth and others in their medical works. Wordsworth strongly believed that the power of the imagination to cause physical change was a 'fact' and in all editions of his poetical works until 1845 the preface to the *Lyrical Ballads* retains the reference to miraculous powers of the imagination. Only in the revisions for the collected poetical works of 1845 and for the redrafted 1850 Preface are all references to the imagination's miraculous powers dropped. Perhaps one of the reasons why Wordsworth could boldly claim that the imagination's powers 'might almost appear miraculous' was the currency of the debate on the imagination throughout the 1790s and the particular interest generated by such debates, particularly in medical circles, throughout the early nineteenth century.

Mary Jacobus argues that poems such as 'Goody Blake and Harry Gill' arose from Wordsworth's and Coleridge's interest in 'morbid psychology', an interest particularly evident in 1798.[25] The circumstances depicted in 'Goody Blake and Harry Gill' were taken from Erasmus Darwin's *Zoonomia*, a work which Coleridge had read via his study of dreaming, and which Wordsworth had read in March 1798.[26] The fascination and appeal of the tale for both poets are evident. Although its circumstances are lifted from Darwin's work, just as influential in Wordsworth's claim for the miraculous physical powers of the imagination seems to be the ongoing debate on that subject. As a narrative, the poem is simple enough: what makes it peculiarly intriguing is what happens to Harry when he catches Goody Blake filling her apron with his sticks:

> And fiercely by the arm he shook her,
> And cried, 'I've caught you then at last!'
> Then Goody, who had nothing said,
> Her bundle from her lap let fall;
> And kneeling on the sticks, she pray'd
> To God that is the judge of all.
> She pray'd, her wither'd hand uprearing,
> While Harry held her by the arm –
> 'God! who art never out of hearing,
> 'O may he never more be warm!'
> The cold, cold moon above her head,
> Thus on her knees did Goody pray,
> Young Harry heard what she had said,
> And icy-cold he turned away.   (*LB* 57 lines 89–104)

The physical fierceness of Harry's hold on the frail woman is contrasted with the brief impassioned curse that Goody delivers, kneeling upon the sticks, beneath the 'cold, cold' moon. After she utters her curse, Harry's flesh 'fell away', he became always 'cold and very chill', and his teeth incessantly 'clattered'. Even though wearing three riding coats and wrapped in many blankets, he is unable to keep warm. His perpetual coldness and clattering teeth are testimony to the imagination's power to effect physical changes, as, in Wordsworth's terms, 'might almost appear miraculous'. The imagination's power in this poem should be seen not only as an 'agent of moral justice',[27] but as capable of effecting lasting physical change, of causing various types of diseases.

In 'The Idiot Boy', Susan's battle with her illness fluctuates considerably, depending on the state of her mind and on its particular focus at crucial moments throughout the poem. At the beginning, she is confined to her bed, 'sick . . . / As if her very life would fail' (*LB* 87 lines 30–1). But something very unusual happens to her while she is anxiously waiting for help to arrive:

> Long Susan lay deep lost in thought,
> And many dreadful fears beset her,
> Both for her messenger and nurse;
> And as her mind grew worse and worse,
> Her body it grew better.
>
> She turned, she toss'd herself in bed,
> On all sides doubts and terrors met her;
> Point after point did she discuss;
> And while her mind was fighting thus,
> Her body still grew better.
>
> 'Alas! what is become of them?
> 'These fears can never be endured,
> 'I'll to the wood,' – The word scarce said,
> Did Susan rise up from her bed,
> As if by magic cured.   (*LB* 100 lines 422–36)

In both the nature of her illness and the almost miraculous – 'magic' – cure that she experiences, Susan serves as an illustration of the ways in which the mind can influence both the cure and the cause of certain diseases. Her misery, as described at the beginning of the poem, is a very conscious misery. But when she is forced to contemplate the safety and health of those close to her, and her focus shifts from her own body to theirs, her own 'still grew better'. The word 'magic' could just as easily have been used to describe the change in Susan's constitution as the word 'miraculous'; her imagination, while constructing the worst possible scenarios that could befall Johnny and Betty, produces a change in her physical nature which effects a magical 'cure'.[28]

The experimental nature of the whole volume of *Lyrical Ballads* may have resided in the fact that Wordsworth and Coleridge were giving poetic expression to the debate on the powers of the imagination, and in so doing were embodying the idea that the imagination is both a medical and a poetic faculty. That they were seen to contribute to the debate is suggested by an anonymous contributor to the *London Magazine*, writing on 'The Phenomena of Diseased Imagination'. Although writing in 1820, he firmly places the two poets within the imagination debate:

The power of the imagination, says a great living poet, is sufficient to produce changes, even in our physical nature, which might almost appear miraculous; and Coleridge, in one of the most amusing papers contained in that most extraordinary collection, called *The Friend*, relates an anecdote of Luther, which gives the masterly Essayist an opportunity of descanting on the wonderful effect of this faculty when it is combined with a morbid state or action of the corporeal machinery.[29]

Both poets are unquestionably perceived as contributing to an understanding of the imagination as a diseased faculty, as one that can produce physical changes and, that in relation to physical states, can also explain Luther's experience. Both are cited not as experts on the poetic imagination, but as experts on an imagination which effects physical change and which, when 'combined with a morbid state or action of the corporeal machinery', displays the most unusual powers. Coleridge also believed that Luther's sighting of the ghost was an example of a specific genus of dreaming, in which the imagination played a pivotal role. The perception of Wordsworth and Coleridge as experts on the physical powers of the imagination remains relevant to the author of the *London Magazine* article in 1820, even following the publication of *Biographia Literaria*, in which Coleridge establishes himself as an expert on the imagination in its poetic manifestation.

Coleridge's concept of the imagination demands that it be truly recognised as a 'multiform power': a power that embraces both the psychological and the physiological, the medical and the poetic.[30] His claim that there is a 'state of mind . . . which is necessary to the explanation of some of the most important phaenomena of Sleep & Disease', and that this state of mind could be explained according to the processes of transmutation between body and mind, signifies that the imagination is both a cognitive and a somatic, medical faculty. It was through his life-long study of dreams that Coleridge was able to perceive the connections between his dreams, his health, his body and his moral life. He perceived the imagination to be the interpreter both of the bodily sensations in his dreams and of the language of those dreams; to be a faculty which frequently caused and cured diseases and was intimately involved in material, physiological processes.

The imagination was an interpreter of bodily feelings and sensations (*CN* III 3547) as well as of the language and dreamatis personæ of many species and genera of dreams because it was not merely a faculty of the (poetic) mind: it was also capable of causing physical, bodily change. In a letter to Southey in which he refers to the process of transmutation, Coleridge mentions the role that the imagination plays in disease and dreams. He describes it as a 'diseasedly retentive' force which, by quickly and repeatedly aggregating slight feelings, causes nightmares and diseases:

there is a state of mind . . . which is necessary to the explanation of some of the most important phaenomena of Sleep & Disease / it is a transmutation of the *succession* of Time into the *Juxtaposition* of *Space*, by which the smallest Impulses, if quickly & regularly recurrent, *aggregate* themselves – & attain a kind of visual magnitude with a correspondent Intensity of general Feeling. – The simplest Illustration would be the *circle* of Fire made by whirling round a live Coal – only here the mind is passive . . . I merely hint at this; but I could detail the whole process, complex as it is. – Instead of 'an imaginary aggravation &c' it would be better to say – 'an *aggregation* of slight Feelings by the force of a diseasedly retentive Imagination'. (*CL* II 974–5)

The process of transmutation depends upon the imagination being diseased and retentive. Coleridge disagrees with the *Encyclopedia Britannica*'s description of atonic gout as an 'imaginary aggravation' of feelings: rather, he believes it to be a case of the '*aggregation* of slight Feelings by the force of a diseasedly retentive Imagination'. An important feature of this state of mind is its capacity to permit movement within the somnial space, for the state of mind in which the mysteries of dreams and diseases are revealed is precisely one which requires movement, translation, dissolution, transmutation. The species of dream at issue here is 'essentially vital' in the same way that the poetic imagination is said to be vital, and capable of movement (*BL* I 304).

The similarities between the imagination of poetry and the medical imagination of the dreaming body (and its organs) are enlarged upon by Coleridge's qualification that the mind is passive. The transmutation that he describes as belonging to both sleep and disease requires that the mind be permissive enough to allow the process to occur. In some diseases, including nightmares, the will is present in a way analogous to its presence in acts of poetic creation and profound meditation:

a small water-insect on the surface of rivulets . . . how the little animal *wins* its way up against the stream, by alternative pulses of active and passive motion, now resisting the current, and now yielding to it in order to gather strength and a momentary *fulcrum* for a further propulsion. This is no unapt emblem of the mind's self-experience in the act of thinking. (*BL* I 124)

The small insect's progression on the water, alternatively passive and active, yielding and resisting, is an image which helps to reveal the essential paradox of the imagination's role in disease and dreams. The imagination's vital powers work in concert with the will to create and form poetic images. But it is also capable of stagnation and retention, a property that can produce such an accumulation of thoughts and feelings that it causes disease: this is the diseasedly retentive imagination Coleridge refers to in his letter to Southey.

The imagination can act as an organ of the body and, in concert with translationary processes, become a physical part of dreams. Coleridge once commented: 'Frequently have I, half-awake & half-asleep, my body diseased & fevered by my imagination, seen armies of ugly Things bursting in upon me' (*CL* I 348). Here the body's diseased state results from the 'fevered' imagination. One acts upon, influences and infiltrates the other to produce a disturbing onslaught of 'ugly Things' in a dream. Those ugly things, the dreamatis personæ, hovering between somnial and waking worlds, are dramatically described as 'bursting in' through the skin and into the dreamer's deepest recesses. Illness in which the body is 'diseased' by the imagination provides fertile ground for the armies of dream-creatures to launch their assault. The 'astounding rapidity and complexity' of many of the images and sensations in dreams prompt Coleridge to suggest that such sequences 'may depend on the suspension of the *Personal* Volition' or, equally, on the 'potential or negative state of the connexive *Life* of the Muscles'.[31] The suspension of volition was a recurring feature of dreams, but even more frequently encountered was Coleridge's perception of the potential actions of the 'connexive *Life* of the Muscles' in his dreams.

The imagination's status as an organ of the body, as an instrument and interpreter of disease and 'distempered' sleep (*CN* III 3547), is indisputable:

Strange Self-power in the Imagination, when painful sensations have made it their Interpreter, or returning Gladsomeness from convalescence, gastric and visceral, have made its chilled and evanished Figures & Landscape bud, blossom, & live in scarlet, and green, & snowy white . . . – strange power to represent the events & circumstances even to the Anguish or the triumph of the *quasi*-credent Soul, while the necessary conditions, the only possible causes of such contingencies are known to be impossible or hopeless, yea, when the pure mind would recoil from the very <eve-lengthened> shadow of an approaching hope, as from a crime – yet the effect shall have *place & Substance & living energy*, & no on a blue Islet of Ether in a whole Sky of blackest Cloudage shine, like a firstling of creation . . . I *knew* the horrid phantasm to be a mere phantasm: and yet what anguish, what gnawings of despair, what throbbings and lancinations of positive jealousy! – even to this day the undying worm of distempered Sleep or morbid Day-dreams (*CN* III 3547)[32]

In this notebook entry, the imagination has acquired a mysterious and 'strange Self-power': it is an interpreter of painful sensations which belong to the language of dreams, especially the species of dreams which allow for apparitions. The imagination also has a role to play in pleasurable sensations. In convalescence, the gastric and visceral organs use it as the agency of rejuvenation: 'evanished Figures' and a desolate landscape can suddenly 'bud, blossom, & live in scarlet, and green, & snowy white'. This blossoming and budding is part of the return to 'Gladsomeness'. But the 'strange Self-power' has a negative aspect: it can also 'represent the events & circum-stances even to the Anguish or the triumph of the *quasi*-credent Soul'. The self-power which creates a budding and colourful land-scape in the recovery from painful physiological sensations also recreates anguished psychological feelings. The effect of that power is to create a 'place & Substance & living energy'. The gastric and visceral organs are perhaps the site of the anguish.

Coleridge's love for Sara Hutchinson is seen as an illustration of the way in which the 'strange Self-power' of the imagination is able to manifest itself on many different levels of experience: waking, physiological, dreaming, imaginary. Three years before he wrote this entry (*CN* III 3547), in December 1806, he feared that Wordsworth and Sara had become intimate. These fears caused distressing – and he feared prophetic – dreams (*CN* II 2975, 3148). Acknowledging the role of his imagination, together with that of his nerves and his suspicions, he can now claim in 1809 that he '*knew* the horrid phantasm to be a mere phantasm'; yet still he cannot control the jealous and self-anguishing thoughts. Be they 'mad nonsense' or not (*CN* II 3148), those thoughts create a living and perpetual nightmare. They become the cause of many 'distempered' sleeps and 'morbid' day-dreams, characterised by emotional hurt and painful gastric and other visceral sensations.

The imagination interprets and translates physical sensations into emotional turmoil and into the language of morbid day-dreams. It is able to interpret such sensations for two primary reasons. First, it is a physical, medical faculty, and so is well placed to interpret physical sensation; second, since the language of dreams is one of images and sensations (*CN* III 4406), the imagination readily exercises its 'strange Self-power' of interpretation when the gastric and other visceral organs are diseased. To translate and transmute bodily sensations into dreams necessitates that the imagination be an active power. This dynamic potential was not always welcome: but if the imagination did not act, stasis and stagnation resulted. Many of Coleridge's nightmares are characterised by a sense of suffocation (*CN* II 2468, *CN* III 4406), or of his being poetically stagnant or 'vacant', 'bereft alike of grief and glee . . . cow'r'd o'er' with poetic vacancy ('The Garden of Boccaccio', *PW* I 478 lines 7–8). The imagination can become 'diseasedly retentive', a cause not only of atonic gout, but also of poetry, sleep and those insistent 'frightful Dreams' (*CL* II 975).

Even the smallest feelings can grow into terrifying thoughts if the imagination is called, or calls itself into action. The most minuscule pains are transformed into crippling, paralysing stomach cramps, and digestive gas becomes cause and signature of dreadful nightmares:

frightful Dreams with screaming – breezes of Terror blowing from the Stomach up thro' the Brain / always when I am awakened, I find myself stifled with wind / & the wind the manifest cause of the Dream / frequent paralytic Feelings – sometimes approaches to Convulsion fit – three times I have wakened out of these frightful Dreams, & found my legs so *locked* into each other as to have *left* a bruise. (*CL* II 976)

The body loses control of its organs and its processes during dreaming, and the aggregation of feelings and impulses is characteristic of both the diseased *and* the dreaming state. The stifling wind felt immediately upon awaking convinces him that it is the 'manifest cause of the Dream'. Frequent paralytic feelings are part both of the dream itself and of the waking moments afterwards. The dream has assumed a pressure and presence of such magnitude that his body bleeds internally. The dream and the experience of it have left a bruise, a kind of stigma testifying to the physical manifestation of the 'frightful' dream. That Coleridge describes his dream as leaving a bruise is apt, for a bruise is the visible and tangible sign of an internal rupture under the skin. Here, the translation between organs and dream is so great that his legs become locked into each other and bruises are formed. Anxious, fearful, happy, sexual or sad thoughts are all seen as 'weaving on the tissue' of the dream: the physical presence of thoughts is woven into its fabric and muscle ('The Two Founts', *PW* 1 455 line 40). Dreams that are frightful owe some of their potency to the process and progress from stomach to brain and to mind, and those delusions, literally based in the stomach, also gain strength from 'transmutations'. The imagination acts organically, but in this case it causes distressing nightmares on account of its retentive nature. Because the imagination is, paradoxically, able to act in a way that prevents action, certain dreams are caused. Coleridge once referred to the accumulation of faeces as responsible for the magnificent colours in dreams (*CN* IV 5360).

A world characterised by an imagination that is retentive, and that in dreaming states stupefies action, is powerfully seen in *The Rime of the Ancient Mariner* (1798). Many of the mariner's disturbing experiences are characterised by those moments when there is no activity, only quiet and stillness:

> Down dropt the breeze, the Sails dropt down,
>   'Twas sad as sad could be;
> And we did speak only to break
>   The silence of the Sea.
>
> All in a hot and copper sky,
>   The bloody sun at noon,
> Right up above the mast did stand,
>   No bigger than the moon.
>
> Day after day, day after day,
>   We stuck, ne breath ne motion;
> As idle as a painted Ship
> Upon a painted Ocean.   (*LB* 14 lines 103–14)

The only actions here are repeated actions, without direction or apparent purpose – 'Day after day, day after day' – and the act of speaking is reduced to one that does not communicate but only breaks 'the silence of the sea'. The mariner himself is doomed only to repeat his tale, to 'pass, like night, from land to land' (line 587), lessening but never totally relieving his suffering. His stagnation is also reproduced in the complex structure of internal rhyme and repetition in the poem.[33] The imagination has retained itself, doubled up on itself, and refuses to move on. This static, repetitive quality, combined with the interpretative power, explains the horror of a *diseasedly* retentive imagination (*CL* II 975). The mariner's experience reveals, in many ways, the true physical and spiritual horror of an imagination that has doubled up on itself and frozen, 'suspended' in time.

The imagination's power as a translational organ of the body is not always disturbing: it not only translates painful sensations, it also creates a poetic world of 'deep delight' and pleasure-domes (in 'Kubla Khan', *CKK* 58), a 'pleasurable & balmy' dream (*CN* I 1718), and sometimes a dream revealing 'sui generis Elysean Sunshine' (*CN* IV 5360). The poetic imagination is a 'fusing power, that fixing unfixes & while it melts and bedims the Images, still leaves the Soul its living meaning' (*CN* III 4066). In dreams the imagination translates and shifts images between mind and body, and within the dream itself (*CN* I 1649), so that apparently immutable images are suddenly transformed into altogether different objects (*CN* I 1649); conventional landscapes become sublime or threatening, or even ridiculous (N35 fos. 35v–37v).

The imagination's position as a translational power of poetry, of dreams and of bodily organs creates a situation in which Coleridge the poet and Coleridge the dreamer can be seen as parallel actors. It is the poet who brings 'the whole soul of man into activity, with the subordination of its faculties to each other, according to their relative worth and dignity' (*BL* II 14–16). He creates a special kind of poetry

that calls into action & gratifies the largest number of the human Faculties in Harmony with each other, & in just proportions . . . Frame a numeration table of the primary faculties of Man, as Reason, *unified per Ideas*, Mater Legum . . . Judgement, the discriminative, Fancy the aggregative, Imagination, the modifying & *fusive*, the Senses & Sensations – and from these the different Derivatives of the Agreeable from the Senses, the Beautiful, the Sublime / the Like and the Different – the spontaneous and the receptive – the Free and the Necessary – And whatever calls into consciousness the greatest number of these in due proportion & perfect harmony with each other, is the noblest Poem. – (*CN* III 3827)

The poet creates a composition which calls into action and gratifies 'the largest number of the human Faculties in Harmony with each other'. In similar ways the *dreamer* can potentially unite all that arises in consciousness, harmonise the images, and sometimes impart precious or 'useful' information (*CN* I 188) or even provide the seeds of a great epic poem (*CN* I 658). The poet's dreams may also unite all human faculties in harmony, a 'dream of blissful worlds' which are all 'true' ('Inscription for a Seat', *PW* I 350 line 40); or provide evidence of a 'sweet and indissoluble union between the intellectual and the material world' (*PW* II 1139). In dreams, the imagination brings all organs together, somatically as well as psychosomatically. Sometimes, the joining of organs in dreams is painful; at others, intensely pleasurable. When organs are somatically united in positive or pleasurable ways, the imagination illustrates poetry and dreaming at their most sublime: all faculties can be (ideally) harmonised such that 'a state of pleasurable & balmy Quietness' is created, along with 'omniform Beauty . . . the Stuff of Sleep & Dreams' (*CN* I 1718). The imagination, especially in dreams, reveals the total co-operation of all powers, all organs and faculties of the mind and the body, especially in times of disease and illness (*CN* IV 4692).

In dreams the imagination is *almost* 'incapable of combining base or low Feelings' with a loved person or object (*CN* II 2600). Coleridge's qualifying 'almost' uncovers a possible threat to the idealised view of the imagination as recreative in dreaming states. Momentarily, the ideal is a stronger presence than the threat of its destruction. Coleridge mentions a dream in which he thought himself to be in a 'state of Society, like that of those great Priests of Nature who formed the Indian Worship in its purity'. In this society, 'all things, strictly of Nature, were reverenced according to their importance, undebauched by associations of Shame' (*CN* II 2600). This dream exemplifies the idealisation of both the potential of dreams and that of the imagination: both create and modify a kind of utopia. In this dream, society is free from uncomfortable sensual feelings, and at its most exalted, the imagination seems to be a 'living Power', the 'prime Agent of all human Perception' (*BL* I 304).

However, this power is still dependent upon the recognition that the imagination has a physical and often a physiological connection with the cognitive. The operation of the imagination involves a psychosomatic translation. Once Coleridge recognised this, he increasingly perceived dreams to have physical properties and pathological causes. And it was this view of dreams that he maintained throughout the last thirty years of his life. The 'motions of the blood and nerves' literally force images into the mind 'by the feelings that arise out of the position & state of the Body and its different members' (*CN* II 2543). His dreams and nightmares belong to a physiological world of organs, the 'world of Guts' (*CL* V 392), as much as to a world of fancy, to the 'realized Faery Land' of the 'stuff of Sleep & Dreams' (*CN* I 1718). What creates both types of dreams is the imagination: an imagination that is both poetic and medical, able to effect fundamental psychosomatic translations between Coleridge's dreams and his frequently diseased body.

Conclusion

Although dreams and dreaming have been readily acknowledged as expressions of Romantic imaginative creativity, it is clear that for Coleridge dreaming was also a physical, painful experience. It was as much a bodily as a psychological experience, and Coleridge vigorously explored the relations between body and mind in dreaming states. His insistence on the corporeal, medical character of dreams challenges the notion of a purely aesthetic, idealist Romantic imagination entirely separated from material or bodily concerns. If dreams are medical, physical occurrences, then the imagination must be seen as capable of participating in physical and medical processes. But this is not to suggest that the roles of the imagination as both poetic and medical, dreaming and diseased, are mutually exclusive. Coleridge and other writers of his day were inspired to explore the mysteries and complexities of dreams because they perceived that they were not merely psychological curiosities, or the result of a large meal consumed before sleeping. Dreams were considered in the contexts of science, medicine, philosophy, superstition and prophecy.

The imagination was not restricted to an aesthetic arena: it was perceived not only as a faculty of the poetic arts, but also as a faculty of medical science. Body and mind were not easily separated, and the relations between the two were crucial in the formation of dreams and dreaming states. Coleridge's awareness of the imagination as a medical entity, capable of both curing and causing diseases, demands that the notion of the imagination as an exclusively poetic, aesthetic faculty be broadened. His engagement with so many diverse texts on dreaming and his recurrent belief in the importance of the bodily in the formation of psychological, emotional states create a more complex and at the same time more accurate portrait of what the imagination is and what its powers are.

In the eighteenth and early nineteenth centuries those powers, as physicians such as Haygarth argued, from their different perspective, belonged as much to poetry as to medical science.

Coleridge's knowledge of the medical and poetic capabilities of the imagination has been more readily recognised by nineteenth-century physiologists than by twentieth-century literary critics. Johann Blumenbach's influential and celebrated lectures on anatomy and physiology, which Coleridge attended in Germany in 1799, were later edited and translated by the English physician, John Elliotson. The first edition of Elliotson's *Human Physiology* was published in 1817. In notes to the numerous editions that followed, the author cites Coleridge's preface to 'Kubla Khan' as evidence of the complete 'disengagement' of sentiments, external surroundings and ideas so characteristic of dreams, and also as proof that in dreams the 'true relations of things are discovered'.[1] Contemporary discussions of dreams in the context of illness, disease and poetry were well known to Coleridge: it is apt that his preface to 'Kubla Khan', a self-claimed work of both somnial and waking imaginations, is acknowledged in an influential *medical* text.

Coleridge utilised the complexity of the relationships, translations and transmutations between body and mind, body and dream, as a means for deeply exploring and questioning the phenomena of dreams and dreaming states. Concepts of the physical and the medical permeate all his thinking on dreams. His conception of somnial spaces in which the dramas of his dreams are performed metaphorically requires the existence of a physical space. The language in which dreams were expressed and understood was a language of sensations, often chronic and acutely painful sensations linked to digestive processes. Nightmares were obvious illustrations of the affronting nature of dreams; but even sudden 'fits of slumber' could reveal an alarming disjunction between what was perceived and what was thought to be perceived. The posture of the body, the pain of a particular organ, the touch of the pillow upon his sleeping head: all these physical conditions contributed to the formation and character of Coleridge's dreams. The important role of the body in dreaming states was hotly debated during his lifetime, bound up as it was in a larger debate concerning the processes of life, the relations between the body and the emotions, and the powers of the mind in influencing the body. Such powers were perceived to be particularly active in times of illness and disease. Coleridge's insightful contemplation of the shifting dialectic between the physiological and the psychological is one of the most original, yet deeply problematic, features of his approach to dreaming.

Coleridge explored the intricately mysterious connections between the physicality of dreams and the role of the imagination in both dreams and diseases, but was unable to arrive at a definitive theory of dreaming. Perhaps this was partly because of the paradoxical nature of dreams themselves: dreams are ineluctably private, unfathomable experiences. The same dilemma still faces dream researchers in the late twentieth century: how can we ever be sure of the truth of what is theorised about dreams, given that we experience them in sleeping states and entirely within our own subjective worlds? How can we know for certain that dreams are the expression of unconscious wishes and desires rather than visitations from malignant spirits? Despite recent discoveries in understanding the neuronal processes involved in dreaming, we are in many ways no closer to understanding without qualification *why* we dream and what our dreams mean. Coleridge was confronted with similar uncertainties. But his ideas on dreams and dreaming reveal how closely and carefully he analysed his own dreams and sought to understand dreaming phenomena. Many of his hastily scribbled notes indicate an acute awareness of the inherent difficulty of the task of dream analysis. That he was able to explore so many differing and often uncomfortable aspects of his dreams is further credit to his tenacity in investigating the mysteries of his own subjective existence.

Coleridge's dream writings explore an astonishing array of subjects: the nature of evil and of self-identity, relations between dreams and the body, the role of fantasy and sexual desire, the type of language utilised in dreams, the ability of the imagination to participate in states of sleeping and disease. His abiding interest in different species of dreams and in the origins of dreams of all kinds never deserted him. One reason for this continued interest lay in the fact that dreams revealed so many diverse processes of both mind and body, offering the opportunity to examine in minute detail the fundamental nature of perception, physiological states, thinking, and the role of the body in forming and influencing psychological states.

The many years which Coleridge spent in 'watchful notice' of the different somnial states easily dovetailed with his many other intellectual and poetic pursuits (*CL* VI 715). From animal magnetism he discerned the power of the imagination to act in diseased and dreaming states, from Luther's and Swedenborg's religious experiences he deduced that somnial states can be sudden experiences in which subjective and objective are indistinguishable. He pondered the psychological, physical and divine origins of dreams. Drawing on his childhood and school memories, he realised that dreams can reveal deeply hidden fears and anxieties. These hidden fears were then incorporated into some of his most beautiful and enigmatic poetry, which haunted and inspired fellow poets throughout the nineteenth century. His lectures and dinner conversations on dreams and dreaming phenomena prompted others to enquire into the mysteries of dreams. Many of his own dreams, committed to the privacy of his notebooks, revealed a deal of 'true psychological Feeling' at their core (*CN* 1 1824), which he analysed and pondered over for years.

In 1827 Coleridge complained to J. Blanco White that he was still 'incapable of explaining any one Figure of all the numberless Personages' of the shadowy world of dreams. Despite this declaration of inadequacy, the breadth and volume of his writings on dreams and dreaming in his notebooks and other works confirm that he explored, with 'equal fidelity' and vigour, dreams of pain and disease as well as the most blissful and exhilarating of somnial states.

Notes

INTRODUCTION

1 Kathleen Coburn, *Experience into Thought; Perspectives in the Coleridge Note-books* (Toronto University Press, 1979), p. 20.

2 Coleridge and his friends perceived that he had a problem with opium and that he was a slave to it, but neither the word 'addict' nor the term 'addiction' would have been applied to him. Dorothy Wordsworth described Coleridge's opium taking as a 'practice': see *The Letters of William and Dorothy Wordsworth; The Early Years 1787–1805*, ed. Ernest De Selincourt (Oxford: Clarendon Press, 1967), p. 330 and *The Letters of William and Dorothy Wordsworth; The Middle Years Part I 1806–1811*, ed. Ernest De Selincourt, 2 vols. (Oxford University Press, 1969), vol. I, p. 192. Sara Hutchinson described his 'passion' for opium in letters to friends: see *The Letters of Sara Hutchinson from 1800 to 1835*, ed. Kathleen Coburn (London: Routledge & Kegan Paul, 1954), p. 105.

3 Elisabeth Schneider, *Coleridge, Opium and Kubla Khan* (New York: Octagon Books, 1953, reprint 1975).

4 Patricia M. Adair, *The Waking Dream; A Study of Coleridge's Poetry* (London: Edward Arnold, 1967).

5 Alethea Hayter, *Opium and the Romantic Imagination* (London: Faber & Faber, 1968), pp. 198–224. On the influence of opium on Coleridge's life and writings, see Joseph Cottle, *Reminiscences of Samuel Taylor Coleridge and Robert Southey* (Highgate: Lime Tree Bower Press, 1970); Molly Lefebure, *Samuel Taylor Coleridge; A Bondage of Opium* (New York: Stein & Day, 1974) and Oswald Doughty, *Perturbed Spirit: The Life and Personality of Samuel Taylor Coleridge* (London and Toronto: Associated University Presses, 1981). M. H. Abrams, *The Milk of Paradise: The Effect of Opium Visions on the Works of De Quincey, Crabbe, Francis Thompson, and Coleridge* (Cambridge, Mass.: Harvard University Press, 1934) established the mode of criticism which emphasises opium addiction as a formulating agent in the poetry and lives of Romantic writers. See also David Beres, 'A Dream, A Vision, and a Poem: A Psycho-Analytic Study of the Origins of the Ancient Mariner', *International Journal of Psychoanalysis* 32 (1951), 97–116. Clifford Siskin has recently challenged such portraits of

Coleridge as dependent upon opium and concepts of addiction in *The Historicity of Romantic Discourse* (New York: Oxford University Press, 1988). Other critics have used Coleridge's opium habit as a beginning for exploring other concerns: see Lydia Wagner's 'Coleridge's Use of Laudanum and Opium as Connected with his Interest in Contemporary Investigations Concerning Stimulation and Sensation', *Psychoanalytic Review* 25 (July 1938), 309–34. See also Nigel Leask, *British Romantic Writers and the East* (Cambridge University Press, 1992), pp. 170–228.

6 Norman Fruman, *Coleridge, the Damaged Archangel* (London: George Allen & Unwin, 1971), pp. 365–411. Psychoanalytic readings of literary dreams have been very popular: see Carol Schreier Rupprecht (ed.), *The Dream and the Text; Essays on Literature and Language* (New York: State University of New York Press, 1993) and Nicolas Kiessling, *The Incubus in English Literature: Provenance and Progeny* (Washington State University Press, 1977), pp. 75–7.

7 Paul Magnuson, *Coleridge's Nightmare Poetry* (Charlottesville: University Press of Virginia, 1974).

8 David Miall, 'The Meaning of Dreams: Coleridge's Ambivalence', *Studies in Romanticism* 21 (1982), 51–71.

9 *Ibid.*, p. 70.

10 J. R. Watson, *English Poetry of the Romantic Period 1789–1830*, 2nd edn (London and New York: Longman, 1992), pp. 65, 68.

11 On Coleridge's engagement with both materialist and idealist arguments in medical and scientific terms, see Trevor Levere, *Poetry Realized in Nature* (Cambridge University Press, 1981), pp. 201–21 especially; Christopher Lawrence, 'The Power and the Glory: Humphry Davy and Romanticism', in *Romanticism and the Sciences*, ed. Andrew Cunningham and Nicholas Jardine (Cambridge University Press, 1990), pp. 213–27.

12 Humphry Davy, *Collected Works*, ed. John Davy, 9 vols. (London: Smith & Elder, 1839), vol. I, p. 60.

13 Robert Southey, *The Correspondence of Robert Southey with Caroline Bowles; to Which are Added: Correspondence with Shelley, and Southey's Dreams*, ed. Edward Dowden (London: Longmans, Green & Co., 1881), p. 377.

14 P. B. Shelley, *The Works of Percy Bysshe Shelley in Verse and Prose*, ed. Harry Buxton Forman, 6 vols. (London: Reeves & Turner, 1880), vol. VI, pp. 295–7.

15 See Leigh Hunt, *Essays*, ed. Arthur Symons (London: Walter Scott, 1887), pp. 235–42; William Hazlitt, *The Complete Works of William Hazlitt*, ed. P. P. Howe, 21 vols. (London and Toronto: Dent & Sons, 1931), vol. XII, pp. 17–24. See also Timothy Clark and Mark Allen, 'Between Flippancy and Terror: Shelley's "Marianne's Dream"', *Romanticism* 1 (1995), 90–105.

16 John Keats, *The Letters of John Keats 1814–1821*, ed. Hyder Edward Rollins, 2 vols. (Cambridge University Press, 1958), vol. II, pp. 88–9. See also Robert J. Barth and John Mahoney (eds.), *Coleridge, Keats and the*

Dreaming Imagination: Romanticism and Adam's Dream; Essays in Honour of Walter Jackson Bate (Columbia and London: University of Missouri Press, 1990).

17 *The Bijou; or Annual of Literature and the Arts* (London, 1828). See *CL* VI 716. Some of Coleridge's poems were also published in the same issue of *The Bijou*: 'Work Without Hope', 'A Day-Dream', 'Youth and Age', 'The Two Founts' and 'The Wanderings of Cain'.

18 See Ludwig Binswanger, *Wandlungen in der Auffassung und Deutung des Traumes von den Griechen bis zur gegenwart* (Berlin: Verlag von Julius Springer, 1928).

19 Leigh Hunt, *Lord Byron and Some of his Contemporaries* (London, 1828), p. 301.

20 See the Preface to Mary Shelley's *Frankenstein; or, The Modern Prometheus; The 1818 Text*, ed. Marilyn Butler (Oxford University Press, 1994), pp. 3–4, and the Introduction, pp. xxi–xxxiii. Percy Bysshe Shelley's *Alastor*, a poem filled with dreams, visions and reverie experiences, was published in December 1816.

21 *A Diary of Thomas De Quincey, 1803*, ed. H. A. Eaton (London: Noel Douglas), entry for Wednesday 1 June 1803.

22 Hunt, *Lord Byron and Some of His Contemporaries*, p. 303.

23 See the recollections of John Payne Collier, in *Coleridge the Talker*, ed. Richard N. Armour and Raymond F. Howes (New York and London: Johnson Reprint Corporation, 1969) pp. 177–9.

24 In his essay 'Witches and Other Night-Fears', Lamb laments the poverty of his dreams and imaginative ability: he exclaims how 'tame and prosaic' his dreams are. In comparison Coleridge can 'conjure up icy domes, and pleasure-houses for Kubla Khan, and Abyssinian maids, and songs of Abara, and caverns, "Where Alph, the sacred river, runs," to solace his night solitudes': *The Works of Charles and Mary Lamb*, ed. E. V. Lucas, 6 vols. (London: Metheun & Co., 1903), vol. II, p. 69. Lamb's perception of the links between dreams and poetic ability are discussed in Gerald Monsman, *Confessions of a Prosaic Dreamer: Charles Lamb's Art of Autobiography* (Durham, NC: Duke University Press, 1984), pp. 55–73. Lamb and Coleridge also discussed their dreams in letters: see, for instance, *The Letters of Charles Lamb, to which are added those of his sister Mary Lamb*, ed. E. V. Lucas, 3 vols. (London: Dent and Metheun, 1935), vol. I, p. 94.

25 Walter Jackson Bate, *Coleridge* (London: Weidenfeld & Nicolson, 1968).

26 See for instance John Beer, *Coleridge the Visionary* (London: Chatto & Windus, 1959), Thomas McFarland, *Coleridge and the Pantheist Tradition* (Oxford University Press, 1969). An astute analysis of the implications of many readings of the Romantic imagination is offered in the opening and closing chapters of Siskin, *Historicity of Romantic Discourse*.

27 On the role of nerves and fibres in the development of perceptions of sensibility integral to Romanticism, see G. S. Rousseau, *Enlightenment*

Crossings; Pre- and Post-Modern Discourses; Anthropological (Manchester University Press, 1991), pp. 122–41.

28 John Keats also trained as a physician: Marie Mulvey Roberts and Roy Porter (eds.), *Literature and Medicine during the Eighteenth Century* (London and New York: Routledge, 1993), pp. 1–22. On the blurred boundaries between medicine and poetry, science and literature, see also the Introduction to *Nature Transfigured; Science and Literature, 1700–1900*, ed. John Christie and Sally Shuttleworth (Manchester and New York: Manchester University Press, 1989).

29 The inherent subjectivity of dreams renders definite theories of them highly problematic, and there is still no agreement as to their cause and meaning. Some late-twentieth-century theories emphasise the role of chemical and electrical changes in the brain, arguing that the 'activation of neuronal circuits within the sleeping brain' accounts for the fantastic, bizarre, frightening and beautiful experiences in dreams. According to this theory dreams are caused by the 'automatic activity' of neurons in the brain during Rapid Eye Movement (REM) sleep. See J. Allan Hobson, *Sleep and Dreams* (Burlington, NC: Scientific Publications Department, Carolina Biological Supply Company, 1992), p. 1; J. Allan Hobson, *The Dreaming Brain* (Harmondsworth: Penguin, 1988), pp. 285–99 especially. This 'activation-synthesis hypothesis' of dreaming stands in contrast to another dominant dream theory of the twentieth century: Sigmund Freud's psychoanalytic theory of dreams, expounded in *The Interpretation of Dreams*. Freud's book has been profoundly influential, canvassing theoretical issues in philosophy, literary and cultural studies, and feminism. His authority, however, is beginning to be challenged. Twentieth-century dream theories are moving away from the introspective, psychological territory of Freudian analysis into the microscopic, neuronal and electrical world of dream science. There are also now highly developed alternative accounts of dreaming, ranging from Jungian interpretations through to self-help and new-age approaches. A good summary of these differing approaches is in Robert L. van de Castle, *Our Dreaming Mind* (New York: Ballatine Books, 1994) and James L. Fosshage and Clemens A. Loew (eds.), *Dream Interpretation: A Comparative Study* (New York: PMA, 1987).

I DREAMING IN THE EIGHTEENTH AND NINETEENTH CENTURIES

1 Byron, 'The Dream', lines 5–19, *Poetical Works*, ed. Frederick Page, rev. John Jump (Oxford University Press, 1987), pp. 91–2.

2 Many critics have also commented on the connections between dreaming and poetic creativity in the Romantic period: see Frank Coyne, *Nightmare and Escape: Changing Conceptions of the Imagination in Romantic and Victorian Dream Visions* (Ann Arbor: University Microfilms

International, 1984); Norman MacKenzie, *Dreams and Dreaming* (London: Aldus Books, 1965), pp. 83–97; and Christian la Cassagnère, 'Dreams', in *A Handbook to English Romanticism*, ed. Jean Raimond and J. R. Watson (New York: St Martin's Press, 1992), pp. 97–102.

3 See Francis X. Newman, *Somnium; Medieval Theories of Dreaming and the Form of Vision Poetry* (Ann Arbor: University Microfilms International, 1962).

4 H. Wijsenbeck-Wijler, *Aristotle's Concept of Soul, Sleep and Dreams* (Amsterdam: Adolf M. Hakkert, 1978), pp. 8–10.

5 W. S. Messer, *The Dream in Homer and Greek Tragedy* (New York: Columbia University, 1918). See also C. A. Behr, *Aelius Aristides and the Sacred Tales* (Amsterdam: Adolf M. Hakkert, 1968), pp. 171–95.

6 Homer, *The Odyssey*, trans. A. T. Murray (Cambridge, Mass.: Harvard University Press, 1980), Bk xix, 559–67. The belief that dreams have two gates, one of truth and the other of deception, has been popular and enduring: see *Charmides*, in *The Works of Plato*, trans. W. R. M. Lamb, 13 vols. (Cambridge, Mass.: Harvard University Press, 1964), vol. xii, p. 173; Virgil, *Aeneid*, trans. H. Rushton Fairclough (Cambridge, Mass.: Harvard University Press, 1986), Bk vi, p. 893; Horace, *The Odes and Epodes*, trans. C. E. Bennett (Cambridge, Mass.: Harvard University Press, 1968), Bk iii, p. 27. On the history of the gates, see Leslie Highbarger, *The Gates of Dreams: An Archaeological Examination of Vergil, Aenid vi, 893–99* (Baltimore: The Johns Hopkins University Press, 1940).

7 Significant dreams included symbolic dreams, visions and oracles: see E. R. Dodds, *The Greeks and the Irrational* (Berkeley, Los Angeles, London: University of California Press, 1951), pp. 106–7.

8 Walter Addison Jayne, *The Healing Gods of Ancient Civilisations* (New York: University Books Inc., 1962), pp. 219–22.

9 The incubation temple of Asklepius, at Epidaurus, was especially popular. Asklepius was the most popular and powerful god of divine healing. See Richard Caton, *The Temples and Ritual of Asklepius at Epidaurus and Athens* (Hertford, 1899), pp. 7–44. Other methods of inducing dreams included isolation, prayer, fasting, self-mutilation and sleeping on the skin of a sacrificed animal. Later Greek practices advocated less painful methods, such as sleeping with a branch of laurel under the pillow; see Dodds, *Greeks and the Irrational*, pp. 110–11.

10 *Ibid.*, p. 118.

11 A theory of dreams was in existence long before the need to interpret them was perceived. The distinction is discussed in A. Bouché-Leclerq, *Histoire de la divination dans l'antiquité*, 2 vols. (Paris, 1879), vol. i, pp. 270–8.

12 Hippocrates, *Heracleitus: on the Universe*, Regimen iv, in *Hippocrates iv*, trans. W. H. S. Jones (Cambridge, Mass.: Harvard University Press, 1943), pp. 421–47.

13 See for example Galen, *On the Usefulness of the Parts of the Body*, trans.

Margaret Tallmadge May, 2 vols. (Ithaca, New York: Cornell University Press, 1968), vol. II, pp. 490–1.

14 Steven M. Oberhelman, 'Galen, *On Diagnosis from Dreams*', *Journal of the History of Medicine and Allied Sciences* 38 (January 1983), 39. See also Oberhelman, 'The Interpretation of Prescriptive Dreams in Ancient Greek Medicine', *Journal of Medicine and Allied Sciences* 36 (October 1981), 416–24.

15 Steven M. Oberhelman, *The Oneirocritic Literature of the Late Roman and Byzantine Eras of Greece* (Ann Arbor: University Microfilms International, 1981), p. 5. On Plato's inconsistency, see *The Republic*, Bk II and *Phaedrus*.

16 Aristotle, *On the Soul, Parva Naturalia, on Breath*, trans. W. S. Hett (London: William Heinemann, Cambridge, Mass.: Harvard University Press, 1935), pp. 456–7.

17 Dodds, *Greeks and the Irrational*, p. 121. Bouché-Leclerq lists over thirty known dream-books: see *Histoire de la divination*, vol. I, pp. 277–8. In *Oneirocritic Literature*, Oberhelman provides English translations of seven other surviving dream-books: those of the Prophet Daniel, Astrampsychos, Nikephoros, Germanos, Achmet, son of Sereim, and Manuel Palaeologos. See also A. Leo Oppenheim, 'The Interpretation of Dreams in the Ancient Near East, with a Translation of an Assyrian Dream Book', *Transactions of the American Philosophical Society* 46 (1956), 179–373.

18 Michael DePorte, '"Mere productions of the brain": Interpreting Dreams in Swift', in Roberts and Porter (eds.), *Literature and Medicine during the Eighteenth Century*, p. 118.

19 Artemidorus, *The Interpretation of Dreams*, 11th edn (London, 1644). A modern translation is available from Robert J. White (NJ: Noyes Press, 1975). Two contrasting essays on Artemidorus' work are Michel Foucault, *The History of Sexuality; the Care of the Self*, trans. Robert Hurley (London: Penguin, 1986), pp. 4–36; and S. R. F. Price, 'The Future of Dreams: From Freud to Artemidorus', *Past and Present* 113 (1986), 3–37.

20 MacKenzie, *Dreams and Dreaming*, p. 75.

21 As quoted in *ibid.*, p. 76.

22 W. C. Curry, *Chaucer and the Medieval Sciences* (New York: Barnes & Noble, 1926), pp. 203–8. On medieval dream views see J. Stephen Russell, *The English Dream Vision; Anatomy of a Form* (Columbus: Ohio State University Press, 1988), pp. 50–109 and Kathryn L. Lynch, *The High Medieval Dream Vision; Poetry, Philosophy, and Literary Form* (Stanford University Press, 1988).

23 Stephen F. Kruger, *Dreaming in the Middle Ages* (Cambridge University Press, 1992), pp. 4–5.

24 Jacques le Goff, *The Medieval Imagination*, trans. Arthur Goldhammer (University of Chicago Press, 1988), p. 193.

25 Deuteronomy 18: 9–12, as quoted in Kruger, *Dreaming in the Middle Ages*, p. 7.

26 In such plays as *Julius Caesar, Hamlet* and *Romeo and Juliet,* Shakespeare utilised dreaming as a means for creating dramatic tension and tragic prophecy. For more comprehensive surveys of the history of dreams see: Andrew Lang, *The Book of Dreams and Ghosts* (London: Longman's Green & Co., 1897); Katherine Taylor Craig, *The Fabric of Dreams; Dream Lore and Dream Interpretation, Ancient and Modern* (London: Kegan Paul, 1918); Jackson Steward Lincoln, *The Dream in Primitive Cultures* (London: Cresset Press, 1935); R. L. Mégroz, *The Dream World; A Study of the History and Mystery of Dreams* (New York: Dutton, 1939); Gustave E. von Grunebaum and Ernest Caillois, *The Dream in Human Societies* (Berkeley: University of California Press, 1966); and Nancy Parsifal-Charles, *The Dream: Four Thousand Years of Theory and Practice,* 2 vols. (West Cornwall, Conn.: Locust Hill Press, 1986).

27 On the persistence of superstition and folklore, see Michael Mac-Donald, *Mystical Bedlam: Madness, Anxiety, and Healing in Seventeenth-Century England* (Cambridge University Press, 1981).

28 As in Reverend Saalfeld, *A Philosophical Discourse on the Nature of Dreams* (London, 1764).

29 Robert Gray, *The Theory of Dreams: in which an inquiry is made into the powers and faculties of the human mind, as they are illustrated in the most remarkable dreams recorded in sacred and profane history,* 2 vols. (London, 1808), vol. II, pp. 26–8, p. 50.

30 Thomas Tryon, *A Treatise of Dreams and Visions, Wherein the Causes, Natures, and Uses of Nocturnal Representations, and the Communications both of Good and Evil Angels, as Also Departed Souls, to Mankind,* 2nd edn (London, 1689), 249.

31 See John Richardson, *Thoughts Upon Thinking, or, A New Theory of the Human Mind; Wherein a Physical Rationale of the Formation of our Ideas, the Passions, Dreaming, and every Faculty of the Soul, is attempted Upon Principles Entirely New,* 2nd edn (London, 1773), p. 20. Richardson argued that dreaming was merely another mode of thinking and could largely be explained through current theories on thinking. However, many curious features of dreams, such as why it is that we do not experience surprise, he could not explain. After lengthy deliberations, he is forced to conclude that there appears to be no other explanation for the strange creatures and scenes encountered in dreams than that 'ingenious' one offered by Baxter.

32 John Bond, *Essay on the Incubus* (London, 1753), p. 4. Another early work on the nightmare which Coleridge would have known was John Waller's *Treatise on the Incubus, or Night-mare, Disturbed Sleep, Terrific Dreams, and Nocturnal Visions: with the means of removing these distressing complaints* (London, 1815), *CN* IV 4514. Other early works outside Britain on the incubus include the influential work by Matthaeus

Huisinga, *Dissertatio Medica Inauguralis Sistens Incubi Causas Praecipuas*, (Leiden, 1734).

33 Saul Jarcho, 'Some Lost, Obsolete, or Discontinued Diseases: Serous Apoplexy, Incubus, and Retrocedent Ailments', *Transactions and Studies of the College of Physicians of Philadelphia* 1980 (Part 2, Series 5), 241–66.

34 Henri F. Ellenberger, *The Discovery of the Unconscious; the History and Evolution of Dynamic Psychiatry* (London: Allen Lane, the Penguin Press, 1970), pp. 168–70.

35 Michael V. DePorte, *Nightmares and Hobby Horses: Swift, Sterne and Augustan Ideas of Madness* (San Marino: Huntingdon Library, 1974), p. ix.

36 William Buchan, *Domestic Medicine; Or, the Family Physician*, 21st edn (London, 1813), p. 78.

37 *The English Works of Thomas Hobbes*, ed. Sir William Molesworth, 11 vols. (London, 1839–45), vol. I, p. 401.

38 Erasmus Darwin, *Zoonomia, or the Laws of Organic Life*, 2nd edn, 4 vols. (London, 1794–6), vol. IV, p. 209.

39 David Hartley, *Observations on Man, His Frame, Duty, and Expectations*, 3rd edn, 2 vols. (London, 1749), vol. I, pp. 384–6.

40 Lydia Wagner, 'Coleridge's Use of Laudanum and Opium as Connected with His Interest in Contemporary investigations concerning Stimulation and Sensation', *Psychoanalytic Review* 25 (1938), 311.

41 In his essay 'On Dreams', William Hazlitt also finds many points of disagreement with Hartley's dream theories: see 'On Dreams', in *The Complete Works of William Hazlitt*, ed. P. P. Howe, 21 vols. (London & Toronto: Dent and Sons, 1931) vol. XII, pp. 17–24.

42 John Locke, *An Essay Concerning Human Understanding*, ed. A. S. Pringle-Pattison (Sussex: Harvester Press, 1978), p. 50.

43 Hartley, *Observations on Man*, vol. I, p. 384.

44 *Ibid.*, vol. I, pp. 383–4.

45 Dugald Stewart, *Elements of the Philosophy of the Human Mind* (London, 1792), p. 283.

46 *Ibid.*, pp. 327–8.

47 *Ibid.*, p. 332.

48 John Hunter, *The Works of John Hunter, F.R.S., with Notes*, ed. James F. Palmer, 4 vols. (London, 1835–7), vol. I, p. 334.

49 Andrew Baxter, *An Enquiry into the Nature of the Human Soul*, 2nd edn, 2 vols. (London, 1737).

50 *Ibid.*, vol. II, pp. 146–7.

51 *Ibid.*, vol. II, p. 47.

52 *Ibid.*, vol. II, p. 14.

53 *Ibid.*, vol. II, p. 109.

54 See DePorte, *Nightmares and Hobby Horses*, pp. 1–48. Coleridge was familiar with at least two authoritative texts on madness: William Battie's *A Treatise on Madness* (London, 1758) and John Monro's *Remarks on Dr. Battie's Treatise on Madness* (London, 1758). William Pargeter also

commented that dreaming was an illustration of the ways in which certain parts of the body could collapse, which then led to madness: *Observations on Maniacal Disorders* (London, 1792), p. 6. Michel Foucault offers a challenging and enlightening study of the approach to madness in the eighteenth century in *Madness and Civilization: A History of Insanity in the Age of Reason*, trans. Richard Howard (New York: New American Library, 1965) and also in *The Birth of the Clinic: An Archaeology of Medical Perception*, trans. Sheridan Smith (New York: Pantheon Books; London: Tavistock Publications, 1973). See also Ida Macalpine and Richard Hunter, *Three Hundred Years of Psychiatry 1535–1800* (Oxford University Press, 1963).

55 Baxter, *Enquiry*, vol. ii, p. 145.

56 *Ibid.*, vol. ii, p. 155.

57 Entry under 'incubus': *Chambers Cyclopedia, or New Dictionary of Arts and Sciences; Containing an Explication of the Terms, and an Account of the Things Signified Thereby, in the Several Arts, both Liberal and Mechanical; and the Several Sciences, Human and Divine: The Figures, Kinds, Properties, Productions, Preparations, and Uses of Things Natural and Artificial: the Rise, Progress, and State of Things Ecclesiastical, Civil, Military, and Commercial; With the several Systems, Sects, Opinions, &c among Philosophers, Divines, Mathematicians, Physicians, Antiquarians, Critics &c. The whole Intended as a Course of Antient and Modern Learning. Extracted from the best Authors, Dictionaries, Journals, Memoirs, Transactions, Ephemerides, &c in several Languages*, 4th edn, 2 vols. (London, 1741). Coleridge also owned a copy of Chambers' work.

58 Ronald R. Thomas, *Dreams of Authority; Freud and the Fictions of the Unconscious* (Ithaca and London: Cornell University Press, 1990), pp. 48–9.

59 George Crabbe, 'The World of Dreams', in *The Complete Poetical Works*, 3 vols., ed. Norma Dalrymple-Champneys and Arthur Pollard (Oxford: Clarendon Press, 1988), vol. iii, p. 247.

60 Thomas, *Dreams of Authority*, p. 111.

61 See Jane Worthington Smyser, 'Wordsworth's Dream of Poetry and Science: *The Prelude*, v', *PMLA* 71 (1956), 269–75. On Coleridge's knowledge of Descartes, see Julian Lindsay, 'Coleridge Marginalia in a Volume of Descartes', *PMLA* 49 (1934), 184–95 and Ralph Pite, *The Circle of Our Vision; Dante's Presence in English Romantic Poetry* (Oxford: Clarendon Press, 1994), pp. 68–118. See also Mary Jacobus, 'Wordsworth and the Language of the Dream', *ELH* 46 (1979), 618–44.

62 Wordsworth, *The Prelude*, Bk v, lines 49–140, pp. 154–9.

63 One sustained negative reply to Baxter's work is by Thomas Branch, *Thoughts on Dreaming; wherein the notion of the sensory, and the opinion that it is shut up from the inspection of the soul in sleep, and that spirits supply us with all our dreams, are examined by revelation and reason* (London, 1738). As late as 1841, Baxter's notion of spirits which are in communion with the soul and which cause our nightly visions was still cited in works concerning

dreams: see Walter Cooper Dendy, *The Philosophy of Mystery* (London: Longman, Orme, Brown, Green, & Longman, 1841), p. 257.

64 Coleridge owned two copies of the *Encyclopedia*, one of the third edition (1797), the other of the supplements to the fourth, fifth and sixth editions (1824). The *Encyclopedia* was a source he regularly consulted for a wide range of information: *CL* II 974.

65 *Encyclopedia Britannica; or, a Dictionary of Arts, Sciences, and Miscellaneous Literature*, 3rd edn, 18 vols. (Edinburgh, 1797), vol. VI, pp. 118–22.

66 The *Encyclopedia*'s editors also refer to Dr James Beattie's 'excellent' essay on dreaming, in *Dissertations Moral and Critical* (London, 1783), pp. 207–30. Beattie argued that 'dreams may proceed from a variety of causes, which have nothing supernatural in them', but also that they were not 'useless or superfluous, but may, on the contrary, answer some purpose of great importance to our welfare, both in soul and in body', p. 229.

67 *Encyclopedia Britannica*, vol. VI, pp. 120–1.

68 For a discussion of the influence of Darwin on Coleridge's literary thought, see Desmond King-Hele, *Erasmus Darwin and the Romantic Poets* (London: Macmillan, 1986), pp. 88–147.

69 Coleridge's erratic attitude to Darwin is evidenced in both letters and notebooks. See for example *CL* I 214, *CL* I 305, *CN* II 2325 and *SWF* I 542.

70 Ralph J. Coffman, *Coleridge's Library: A Bibliography of Books Owned or Read by Samuel Taylor Coleridge* (Boston, G. K. Hall & Co., 1987), p. 62.

71 Clement Carlyon, *Early Years and Late Reflections*, 3 vols. (London, 1856–8), vol. I, p. 210.

72 Erasmus Darwin, *The Botanic Garden, A Poem in Two Parts*, 4th edn (London, 1799), pp. 68–9.

73 *Ibid.*, p. 69.

74 *Ibid.*, p. 70.

75 Erasmus Darwin, *Zoonomia*, 2nd edn, 4 vols. (London, 1794–6), vol. IV, p. 116.

76 Darwin, *Botanic Garden*, p. 127.

77 For a discussion of the afflicted female dreamer in Fuseli's painting, see John A. Dussinger, 'Madness and Lust in the Age of Sensibility', in *Sensibility in Transformation; Creative Resistance to Sentiment from the Augustans to the Romantics; Essays in Honor of Jean H. Hagstum*, ed. Syndy McMillen Conger (Rutherford: Associated University Presses, 1990), pp. 85–102.

78 See Michael J. Tolley, 'Words Standing in Chariots: the Literalism of Blake's Imagination', in *Imagining Romanticism; Essays on English and Australian Romanticisms*, ed. Deirdre Coleman and Peter Otto (West Cornwall, Conn.: Locust Hill Press, 1992), pp. 139–40. On the collaborative relationship between Darwin and Fuseli, see Albert Boime, *Art in an Age of Revolution 1750–1800* (University of Chicago Press, 1990), pp. 289–96. On Fuseli's influence on other dreaming and nightmare

paintings, see Albert Boime, *Art in an Age of of Bonapartism 1800–1815* (University of Chicago Press, 1990), pp. 273–8.

79 See especially G. S Rousseau's essays, 'Nerves, Spirits and Fibres: Towards an Anthropology of Sensibility', 'Rationalism and Empiricism in Enlightenment Medicine' and 'Towards a Social Anthropology of the Imagination', in G. S. Rousseau, *Enlightenment Crossings: Pre- and Post-Modern Discourses; Anthropological* (Manchester University Press, 1991). Of related interest are Rousseau's three essays, 'The Discourses of Literature and Science (1), (2), (3)', in his *Enlightenment Borders; Pre- and Post-Modern Discourses; Medical, Scientific* (Manchester University Press, 1991), pp. 202–51. See also C. Lawrence, 'The Nervous System and Society in the Scottish Enlightenment', in B. Barnes and S. Shapin (eds.), *Natural Order* (Beverly Hills and London: Sage Publications, 1980), pp. 19–40.

80 Rousseau, *Enlightenment Crossings*, p. 132.

81 As quoted by Günter B. Risse, 'The Brownian System of Medicine: Its Theoretical and Practical Implications', *Clio Medica* 5 (1970), 45.

82 John Brown, *The Elements of Medicine; or, a Translation of the Elementa Medicinæ Brunonis*, 2 vols. (London, 1788), vol. I, pp. 234–84.

83 Robert Jones, *An Inquiry into the State of Medicine on the Principles of Inductive Philosophy* (Edinburgh, 1781), p. 93. See also E. M. Tansey, 'The Physiological Tradition', in *Companion Encyclopedia of the History of Medicine*, ed. W. F. Bynum and Roy Porter, 2 vols. (Routledge: London and New York, 1993), vol. I, pp. 123–5.

84 On the controversy surrounding Brown's ideas and the near riots in Göttingen in 1802, see *CN* III 4269n and Trevor Levere, *Poetry Realized in Nature* (Cambridge University Press, 1981), p. 203. On the law forbidding duelling as a result of the debate, see Donald C. Macarther, 'The First Forty Years of the Royal Medical Society and the Part William Cullen Played in It', in *William Cullen and the Eighteenth-Century Medical World; A Bicentenary Exhibition and Symposium Arranged by the Royal College of Physicians of Edinburgh in 1990*, ed. A. Doig, J. P. S. Ferguson, I. A. Milne and R. Passmore (Edinburgh University Press, 1993), pp. 247–51.

85 John Brown, *The Elements of Medicine. A new edition, revised and corrected with a biographical preface by Thomas Beddoes MD*, 3 vols. (London, 1795), vol. I, p. cxxxvi.

86 Trevor H. Levere, *Chemists and Chemistry in Nature and Society 1770–1878*, (Hampshire and Vermont: Variorum, 1994), pp. 62–7.

87 Christopher Lawrence, 'Humphry Davy and Romanticism', in *Romanticism and the Sciences*, ed. Andrew Cunningham and Nicholas Jardine (Cambridge University Press, 1990), p. 217.

88 Levere, *Chemists and Chemistry in Nature and Society*, p. 355. The complex relationship between Beddoes, Coleridge and Brunonian medicine is discussed in Neil Vickers' essay, 'Coleridge, Thomas Beddoes and Brunonian Medicine', *European Romantic Review* 8 (Winter 1997), 47–94.

89 Nigel Leask, *British Romantic Writers and the East; Anxieties of Empire* (Cambridge University Press, 1992), pp. 183–4.

90 From Beddoes' essay, *Observation in Calculus*, as quoted in Darwin, *Zoonomia*, vol. IV, pp. 206–9.

91 Albrecht von Haller, *Physiology; Being a Course of Lectures Upon the Visceral Anatomy and Vital Oeconomy of Human Bodies: Including the Latest and Most Considerable DISCOVERIES and IMPROVEMENTS, Which Have Been Made by the Most Eminent Professors, through all parts of EUROPE, down to the present year*, 2 vols. (London, 1754), vol. II, p. 117.

92 Brown, *Elements of Medicine* (1788), vol. I, pp. 262–6.

93 In Rachel Baker, *Remarkable Sermons of Rachel Baker, and Pious Ejaculations, Delivered During Sleep, Taken Down in Shorthand, with remarks on this Extraordinary Phænomeonon, by Dr. Mitchell, the late Dr Priestley, . . . and Dr Douglas* (London, 1815), p. 206.

94 For a history of the Abernethy / Lawrence debate, see Alice Snyder, *Coleridge on Logic and Learning* (New Haven and London: Yale University Press, Oxford University Press, 1929), pp. 16–25 and Owsei Temkin, 'Basic Science, Medicine, and the Romantic Era', *Bulletin of the History of Medicine* 38 (1963), 97–129. The debate between the two men was also an influential factor in the genesis of Mary Shelley's *Frankenstein*: see Marilyn Butler's Introduction to *Frankenstein; or the Modern Prometheus; The 1818 Text* (Oxford University Press, 1994), pp. xv–xxxiii and Appendix C, pp. 229–51.

95 By the beginning of the eighteenth century, discussions of hysteria in medical circles had conceded that the disease could afflict men (it was termed hypochondriasis when diagnosed in men): see Ilza Webb, *Hysteria; the History of a Disease* (University of Chicago Press, 1965), p. 139; and Günter B. Risse, 'Hysteria at the Edinburgh Infirmary: the Construction and Treatment of a Disease, 1770–1800', *Medical History* 32 (January 1988), 1–22. On hypochondria particularly, see the reference works, *Compendious Medical Dictionary* (London, 1798) and George Motherby's *Medical Dictionary* (London, 1775).

96 John Harris, 'Coleridge's Readings in Medicine', *Wordsworth Circle* 3 (1972), 85–95; R. Guest-Gournall, 'Samuel Taylor Coleridge and the Doctors', *Medical History* 17 (October 1973), 327–42; Trevor H. Levere, 'Coleridge, Davy, Science and Poetry', in *Nature Transfigured; Science and Literature, 1700–1900*, ed. John Christie and Sally Shuttleworth (Manchester University Press, 1989), pp. 85–101; and also *TT* 1 282–4 and *CN* III 4310n.

97 Betel, wrapped around limes and chewed, reddens the gums and saliva. Marginalia as cited in Guest-Gournall, 'Samuel Taylor Coleridge and the Doctors', pp. 327–42.

98 Many critics have noted Coleridge's involvement with the nitrous oxide experiments at the Bristol Pneumatic Institute. See Suzanne R. Hoover, in 'Coleridge, Humphry Davy, and Some Early Experiments with a

Consciousness-altering Drug', *Bulletin of Research in the Humanities* 81 (1978), 9–27; and Ian Wylie, *Young Coleridge and the Philosophers of Nature* (Oxford: Clarendon Press, 1989), pp. 122–42. On the nitrous experiments, see Frederick Cartwright, *The English Pioneers of Anaesthesia: Beddoes, Davy and Hickman* (Bristol: Wright, 1952).

99 Roger French, 'Sickness and the Soul: Stahl, Hoffman and Sauvages on Pathology', in *The Medical Enlightenment of the Eighteenth Century*, ed. Andrew Cunningham and Roger French (Cambridge University Press, 1990), pp. 88–110.

100 Roy Porter, *Disease, Medicine and Society in England 1550–1860* (London: Macmillan, 1987), p. 26. See also Howard Haggard, *Devils, Drugs, and Doctors* (London: Heinemann, 1929), pp. 3–49.

101 From Caelius Aurelianus, *De Morbis Acutis et Chronicis*, as cited in Jarcho, 'Some Lost, Obsolete, or Discontinued Diseases', p. 253.

2 DRAMATIC DREAMING SPACES

1 Schneider, *Coleridge, Opium and Kubla Khan*, pp. 91–100. See also the Introduction to Coleridge's *Shakespearean Criticism*, ed. Thomas Middleton Raysor, 2 vols. (London: Constable, 1930) and Douglas B. Wilson, 'The Dreaming Imagination: Coleridge, Keats, and Wordsworth', in Barth and Mahoney (eds.) *Coleridge, Keats, and the Dreaming Imagination*, pp. 58–62.

2 See Earl Leslie Griggs, 'The Willing Suspension of Disbelief', in *Elizabethan Studies and Other Essays*, ed. E. L. Griggs (University of Colorado Press, 1945), pp. 272–83. On the tension between staging and acting and the role of illusion in Romantic theatre, see Frederick Burwick, 'Stage Illusion and the Stage Designs of Goethe and Hugo', *Word and Image* 4 (July–December 1988), 692–718. Of related interest is Julie A. Carlson, *In the Theatre of Romanticism; Coleridge, Nationalism, Women* (Cambridge University Press, 1994).

3 Although he has a psychoanalytic and therapeutic purpose, Salomon Resnik, *The Theatre of the Dream*, trans. Alan Sheridan (London and New York: Tavistock, 1987) introduces fascinating concepts into the parallel study of theatre and dreams.

4 See Donald Bond, '"Distrust" of Imagination in English Neo-Classicism', *Philological Quarterly* 16 (1937), 54–69.

5 Conceiving the mind in terms of a spatial metaphor was common enough in later eighteenth-century theories of the sublime. See Thomas Weiskel, *The Romantic Sublime: Studies in the Structure and Psychology of Transcendence* (Baltimore and London: Johns Hopkins University Press, 1976).

6 Coleridge's idea is the basis of much recent research into the effects, types and causes, and patients' perceptions, of insomnia: German Berrios and Colin Shapiro, 'I Don't Get Enough Sleep, Doctor', *British Medical Journal* 306 (27 March 1993), 843–6.

7 This pun was first commented upon by Humphry House, *Coleridge: The Clark Lectures 1951–52* (London: Rupert Hart-Davis, 1953).

8 *CN* III 3587 and also cited in Grevel Lindop, *The Opium-Eater; A Life of Thomas De Quincey* (New York: Taplinger Publishing, 1981), p. 189.

9 On De Quincey's confusion surrounding Piranesi's pictures, see Nigel Leask, *British Romantic Writers and the East* (Cambridge University Press, 1992), pp. 223–5.

10 See also *L* 155–73.

11 'The Correspondence of Poole 1765–1837', held in the British Library, Add. MS 35, 343, fo. 332. Coleridge had sent Poole a copy of the poem in a letter dated 3 October 1803, *CL* II 1009.

12 Lawrence Kramer, 'That Other Will: The Daemonic in Coleridge and Wordsworth', *Philological Quarterly* 58 (1979), 299.

13 Coleridge quotes from John Milton's *Paradise Lost*, 'whence the soul / Reason receives, and reason is her being': *Paradise Lost*, ed. Scott Elledge (New York and London: Norton & Company, 1975) Bk v, lines 487–8.

14 On Coleridge's relationship with Sara Hutchinson, see John Anthony Harding, *Coleridge and the Idea of Love; Aspects of Relationship in Coleridge's Thought and Writing* (Cambridge University Press, 1974); J. Robert Barth, *Coleridge and the Power of Love* (University of Missouri Press, 1988); and Anya Taylor, 'Coleridge, Wollstonecraft and the Rights of Women', in *Coleridge's Visionary Languages; Essays in Honour of J. B. Beer*, ed. Tim Fulford and Morton D. Paley (Cambridge: D. S. Brewer, 1993), pp. 83–109.

15 It also provides an interesting comparison to De Quincey's palimpsest passage.

3 THE LANGUAGE OF DREAMS

1 As well as the anonymous *Nocturnal Revels; Or, Universal Interpreter of Dreams and Visions* (London, 1805).

2 For a very different reading of this dream, see Fruman, *Damaged Archangel*, pp. 378–80.

3 Trevor Levere, *Poetry Realized in Nature; Samuel Taylor Coleridge and Early Nineteenth-Century Science* (Cambridge University Press, 1981), p. 30.

4 Humphry Davy, 'The Bakerian Lecture, on Some Chemical Agencies of Electricity', *Philosophical Transactions* 98 (1808), 1–44.

5 Notably, Norman Fruman, but also in such critical readings as offered by Watson, *English Poetry of the Romantic Period*, p. 65.

6 See Fruman, *Damaged Archangel*, p. 391.

7 The paths to truth or political reform were well evidenced in the case of George III's two bouts of severe delirium and 'madness' in 1789 and 1801. Public interest in the King's illness remained strong throughout the first decade of the nineteenth century. See Macalpine and Hunter, *George III and the Mad-Business*. See also *CN* IV 4691.

8 Coleridge's disillusionment with Godwinian theories is evidenced in his attack on Godwin's *Political Justice* in a lecture on revealed religion, May 1795. See *Lectures 1795* 164; also *W* 98–9, 194–8 (and pp. lxvii–lxxx of the editor's introduction).

9 Gotthilf Heinrich von Schubert, *Die Symbolik des Traumes* (Bamberg, 1821). Coleridge's copy is held in the British Library at C.43. b. 17.

10 Coleridge's annotation to *ibid.*, inserted between pp. 184 and 185, fo. 1. He seems to have held a generally negative view of Schubert's philosophy and other writings: see *CN* iii 4457n.

11 Wilhelm Gottlieb Tennemann, *Geschichte der Philosophie*, 10 vols. (Leipzig, 1799–1817). Coleridge's annotation is in vol. ii, p. 77; his copy is held in the British Library at C.43. c. 24.

12 Coleridge's annotation to *ibid.*, vol. ii, p. 77.

13 In 1826, when he wrote the comment on 'whimsical' transfers in dreams (*CN* iv 5360), the dream of 1802 was not disturbing. But in 1808 when he recalled the same dream, he described it as 'quite shocking' (*CN* iii 3404).

14 See Kathleen Coburn, Introduction to *CN* i xxix–xxxii. On the tension between public and private selves as indicated through Coleridge's writings, see Tim Fulford, *Coleridge's Figurative Language* (London: Macmillan, 1991).

15 See for instance the entries from *CN* ii 3041 to 3056, all written in May 1807.

16 Kathleen Coburn compiles a comprehensive listing of Coleridge's codes in the Appendix to the notes for the second volume of the *Notebooks*.

17 On the idealisation of Coleridge's relationship with Sara Hutchinson, see George Whalley, *Coleridge and Sara Hutchinson and the Asra Poems* (London: Routledge & Kegan Paul, 1955) and Deirdre Coleman, *Coleridge and* The Friend *(1809–1810)* (Oxford University Press, 1988), pp. 26–40.

18 On Coleridge's opinions of Böhme, see *CN* iii 3263, 3263n and Tim Fulford, 'Coleridge, Böhme, and the Language of Nature', *MLQ* 25 (March 1991), 37–53.

19 Cf the tensions between gloss and narrative in *The Rime of the Ancient Mariner*.

20 On the distinction between representation and vision in Wordsworth's dream of the Arab in *The Prelude*, see Jacobus, 'Wordsworth and the Language of the Dream', 618–44.

21 See Southey, *Correspondence of Southey*, p. 368.

22 Much has been written on the importance of childhood memories in De Quincey's development as a writer and as a dream theorist. See Charles L. Proudfit, 'Thomas De Quincey and Sigmund Freud: Sons, Fathers, Dreamers – Precursors of Psychoanalytic Developmental Psychology', in *Thomas De Quincey: Bicentenary Studies*, ed. Robert Lance Snyder (Norman and London: University of Oklahoma Press, 1985),

pp. 87–108. John Barrell has argued that De Quincey's accounts of childhood events were primal scenes which resonated throughout his life and works: John Barrell, *The Infection of Thomas De Quincey: A Psychopathology of Imperialism* (New Haven: Yale University Press, 1991).

23 In *The Life of Samuel Taylor Coleridge* (London: William Pickering, 1838), p. 33, James Gillman argues that chilly morning swims and damp environments at Christ's Hospital were formative factors in Coleridge's adult health.

24 The entry reads in part: 'There was no other way [?in] – and a villainous little dog [?came] to fly at me & bit me, with a sharp nip (the nearest exactation of proper pain, that I have found occur in Sleep [)]': N35, fo. 36.

25 See Kathleen Coburn, *Inquiring Spirit: A New Presentation of Coleridge from his Published and Unpublished Prose Writings*, rev. edn (Toronto University Press, 1979), pp. 59–60.

26 Many similarities may be found in Coleridge's life, with his constant debts, lax repayment schedules and general financial instability: see for instance *CL* I 643–4; *CL* IV 551–2, 956–7; *CL* V 804–8.

27 Coleridge's fascination with the indeterminacy of causal connections is also seen in *The Rime of the Ancient Mariner*.

28 See Elaine Scarry, *The Body in Pain; the Making and Unmaking of the World* (New York: Oxford University Press, 1985); Drew Leder, *The Absent Body* (University of Chicago Press, 1990); and Steven Bruhm, *Gothic Bodies; The Politics of Pain in Romantic Fiction* (University of Pennsylvania Press, 1994), pp. 1–29.

29 Scarry, *Body in Pain*, p. 54.

4 GENERA AND SPECIES OF DREAMS

1 Keats, *Letters*, vol. II, pp. 88–9.

2 For example, Pite, *The Circle of Our Vision*, pp. 91–2; Anya Taylor (ed.) *Coleridge's Writings*, 2 vols. (Basingstoke: Macmillan, 1994), vol. II, pp. 23–51; R. C. Bald, 'Coleridge and *The Ancient Mariner*: Addenda to *The Road to Xanadu*', in *Nineteenth-Century Studies*, ed. Herbert Davis, William C. DeVane and R. C. Bald (New York: Greenwood Press, 1968), pp. 1–45; and John Beer, *Coleridge's Poetic Intelligence* (London: Macmillan, 1979).

3 Francis Hutchinson, *An Historical Essay Concerning Witchcraft. With Observations upon Matters of Fact; Tending to Clear the Texts of the Sacred Scriptures, and Confute the Vulgar Errors About that Point* (London, 1718); Cotton Mather, *The Wonders of the Invisible World: Being an Account of the Tryals of Several Witches Lately Executed in New England: and of several remarkable curiosities therein occuring by Cotton Mather*, 3rd edn. (London, 1693); John Ferriar, *An Essay Towards a Theory of Apparitions* (London, 1813); John Cotta, *The Triall of Witch-craft, Shewing the True and Right Methode of the*

Discovery: with a Confutation of Erroneous Wayes (London, 1616); John
Stearne, *A Confirmation and Discovery of Witch-craft, Containing These Severall
Particulars; That There are Witches Called Bad Witches, and Witches Untruely
Called Good or White Witches, and What Manner of People They Be, and How
They May Bee Knowne, with Many Particulars Thereunto Tending. Together with
the Confessions of Those Executed Since May 1645 in the Severall Counties
Hereafter Mentioned. As Also Some Objections Answered* (London, 1648). See
also *CN* III 4390–6.

4 Ferriar, *Theory of Apparitions*, pp. 13–14.
5 *Coleridge's Library*, p. 117.
6 Christoph Friedrich Nicolai, 'A Memoir on the Appearance of Spectres
or Phantoms Occasioned by Disease, with Psychological Remarks.
Read by Nicolai to the Royal Society of Berlin, on the 28th of February,
1799', *Journal of Natural Philosophy, Chemistry and the Arts* 6 (November
1803), 161–79. Of related interest is William Nicholson, 'Narrative and
Explanation of the Appearance of Phantoms and other Figures in the
Exhibition of the Phantasmagoria', *Journal of Natural Philosophy, Chemistry, and the Arts* 1 (February 1802), 148–50.
7 The implications of arguments between sceptics and believers as to
whether or not ghosts were visions resulting from the mind's own
illusion or from an external sighting – the inherent conundrum of an
emerging subjectivity – are discussed in Terry Castle, *The Female
Thermometer; Eighteenth-Century Culture and the Invention of the Uncanny*
(Oxford University Press, 1995), pp. 133–85 especially. See also Mary
Weightman, *The Friendly Monitor: or, dialogues for youth against the Fear of
Ghosts, and other Irrational Apprehensions, with Reflections on the Power of the
Imagination and the Folly of Superstition* (London, 1791); Samuel Hibbert,
*Sketches of the Philosophy of Apparitions, or, an Attempt to Trace Such Illusions to
their Physical Causes* (London, 1825); and William Newnham, *Essay on
Superstition: Being an Inquiry into the Effects of Physical Influence on the Mind, in
the Production of Dreams, Visions, Ghosts, and other Supernatural Appearances*
(London, 1830).
8 Coleridge's description of these 'fits of slumber' closely parallels the
symptoms of narcolepsy. Narcoleptics suffer from an uncontrollable
need to sleep, for very short periods, and the potency of this need and
the speed of its onset are such that the sleeps are termed 'sleep attacks'.
See Bedrich Roth, *Narcolepsy and Hypersomnia*, trans. Margaret Schierlova
(Basel: Karger, 1980); and Henry Kellerman, *Sleep Disorders: Insomnia and
Narcolepsy* (New York: Brunner, 1981).
9 Wordsworth, *The Poetical Works of William Wordsworth*, ed. Ernest de
Selincourt and Helen Darbishire, 5 vols. (Oxford: Clarendon Press,
1940–9), vol. II, p. 29.
10 Coleridge quotes from Shakespeare's *Hamlet*, ed. Harold Jenkins
(London and New York: Methuen, 1986) I iv 5–6: 'It then draws near
the season / Wherein the spirit held his wont to walk.'

11 In *CN* III 4396 Coleridge defines an Ocular Spectrum as 'a deception created by the disordered imagination . . . when in a nervous, languid state'.

12 In the eleventh of his philosophical lectures, Coleridge describes Brutus' visions of Dion and Caesar as cases which 'happened under one set of circumstances; they were anxious, weary, in cold and bodily discomfort; the consequence of which is that the objects from without, weakened in their influences on the senses, and the sensations meantime, from within, being strongly excited, the thoughts convert themselves into images, the man believing himself to be awake precisely by the same law as our thoughts convert themselves into images the moment we fall asleep', *PLect* 319. See also *TT* I 52–3.

13 Because Coleridge was deeply interested in the psychology and physiology behind Swedenborg's visions, and particularly the correlations with different species and genera of dreams, he gave Swedenborg a more sympathetic hearing than other thinkers of the time, in contrast to Immanuel Kant, in his *Dreams of a Spirit-Seer, Illustrated by Dreams of Metaphysics*, trans. Emanuel Goerwitz, ed. Frank Sewall (London: Swan Sonnenschein & Co, New York: Macmillan, 1900).

14 Cf N43, fo. 155, in which Coleridge argues that 'super-natural' poetry also has this ability to 'obtain a mastery over the imagination and feelings'. He suggests that such poetry 'will tend to infect the reader . . . draw him to identify himself for the *Person* of the Drama or Tale, in proportion [to] what is True to *Nature* – i. e. where the poet of his free Will and Judgement does what the believing Narrator of a Supernatural Incident, Apparition, or Charm does from ignorance and weakness of Mind – i. e. mistake a *subjective* product . . . for an objective fact'.

15 The review is reproduced by Earl Leslie Griggs, 'An Early Defense of "Christabel"', in *Wordsworth and Coleridge; Studies in Honour of George McLean Harper*, ed. E. L. Griggs (New York: Russell & Russell, 1962), pp. 173–91.

16 This is what Jonas Spatz argues in 'The Mystery of Eros: Sexual Initiation in Coleridge's "Christabel"', *PMLA* 90 (1975), 107–16, although Spatz does not imply any connection between Coleridge's ideas on ghosts and apparitions and his notebook comment on Geraldine being a 'ghost by day time'.

17 *The Diary of John William Polidori 1816*, ed. W. M. Rossetti (London: Elkin Mathews, 1911), pp. 127–8.

18 See Nora Crook and Derek Guiton, *Shelley's Venomed Melody* (Cambridge University Press, 1986).

19 Beer, *Coleridge's Poetic Intelligence*, pp. 220–3.

20 Coleridge's annotation to John Webster, *The Displaying of Supposed Witchcraft* (London, 1677), folio inserted between pages 70 and 71. Coleridge's copy is held in the British Library at C.126. l. 10.

21 On p. 76 of *ibid.*, Coleridge comments that 'sleep and sleep-like states'

both display 'the suspension of the Volition & Comparative Power'. The qualities of reason and understanding are discussed at considerable length in *L* 89, 204. For a critical reading of Coleridge's important distinction between reason and understanding, see Thomas McFarland, 'Aspects of Coleridge's Distinction Between Reason and Understanding', in Fulford and Paley (eds.), *Coleridge's Visionary Languages*, pp. 165–80.

22 Coleridge's annotation to Webster, *Displaying of Supposed Witchcraft*, inserted between pp. 70 and 71.

23 Coleridge met Tieck in Rome in 1806, and Tieck visited him at Highgate in 1817; see *CL* IV 745. Works annotated and read by Coleridge on animal magnetism include Carl Alexander Kluge, *Versuch einer Darstellung des animalischen Magnetismus* (Berlin, 1815); Karl Christian Wolfart, *Erläuterungen zum Mesmerismus* (Berlin, 1814); Johann Passavant, *Untersuchungen über den Lebensmagnetismus und das Hellsehen* (Frankfurt, 1821); M. Loewe, *A Treatise on the Phenomena of Animal Magnetism* (London, 1822); Gotthilf Heinrich von Schubert, *Allgemeine Naturgeschichte oder Andeutungen zur Geschichte und Physiognomik der Natur* (Erlangen, 1826); and the French Commissioner's *Report of the Commissioners Charged by the King to Examine Animal Magnetism* (Paris, 1784; authors included Benjamin Franklin, the distinguished astronomer Jean Sylvain Bailly and Dr Guillotin).

24 See Trevor Levere, 'S. T. Coleridge and the Human Sciences: Anthropology, Phrenology, and Mesmerism', in *Science, Pseudo-Science and Society* ed. Marsha P. Hanen, Margaret J. Osler and Robert G. Weyant (Ontario, Canada: Wilfrid Laurier University Press, 1980), pp. 171–92.

25 Coleridge claimed that the theories of magnetism enabled him to 'explain the Oracles & a score other superstitions': see *CN* IV 4908.

26 Coleridge, *Hints Towards the Formation of a More Comprehensive Theory of Life*, ed. Seth Watson (London, 1848). See also *CM* III 872.

27 One recalcitrant follower was Benjamin Perkins, an American physician who patented 'tractors' which he used to cure his patients. See his *The Efficacy of Perkins's Patent Metallic Tractors, in Topical Diseases, on the Human Body, and Animals, Exemplified by 250 cases, From the Finest Literary Characters in Europe and America. To which is Prefixed, a Preliminary Discourse, in Which, the Fallacious Attempts of Dr. Haygarth to Detract from the Merits of the TRACTORS, are Detected, and Fully Confuted* (London and Edinburgh, 1800) and chapter 8 below.

28 Anton Mesmer, *Mémoire sur la découverte du magnétisme animal*, trans. Gilbert Frankau (London: Macdonald, 1948), pp. 54–7.

29 Barbara Stafford argues that Mesmer 'profited from the Enlightenment's sense of wonder for a tide of unseen phenomena', including electricity: *Body Criticism; Imaging the Unseen in Enlightenment Art and Medicine* (Cambridge, Mass.: Massachusetts Institute of Technology Press, 1993), p. 450. Of related interest is an essay by A. J. L. Busst,

'Scottish Second Sight: The Rise and Fall of a European Myth', *European Romantic Review* 5 (Winter 1995), 149–77.

30 George Barth, *The Mesmerist's Manual of Phenomena and Practice; with Directions for Applying Mesmerism to the Cure of Diseases*, 3rd edn. (London, 1852), pp. 2–3.

31 Robert Darnton, *Mesmerism and the End of the Enlightenment in France* (Cambridge, Mass.: Harvard University Press, 1969), p. 14.

32 Ellenberger, *Discovery of the Unconscious*, p. 62.

33 For a detailed description of the magnetic healing session, see Adam Crabtree, *From Mesmer to Freud; Magnetic Sleep and the Roots of Psychological Healing* (New Haven: Yale University Press, 1993); Robert G. Weyant, 'Protoscience, Pseudoscience, Metaphors and Animal Magnetism', in Hanen, Osler and Weyant, *Science, Pseudo-Science and Society*, pp. 77–114; and Edwin Lee, *Animal Magnetism and Magnetic Lucid Somnambulism* (London, 1866).

34 Darnton, *Mesmerism and the End of the Enlightenment*, pp. 7–8.

35 Barth, *Mesmerist's Manual*, p. 25.

36 As described by John Elliotson, *Numerous Cases of Surgical Operations Without Pain in the Mesmeric States* (London, 1843).

37 Robert Southey, *Letters from England: By Don Manuel Alvarez Espreilla. Translated from the Spanish (1807)*, ed. J. Simmons (London: Cresset Press, 1951); Thomas De Quincey, 'Animal Magnetism', *Tait's Edinburgh Magazine* 4 (October 1833–January 1834), 456–74.

38 Nigel Leask, 'Shelley's "Magnetic Ladies": Romantic Mesmerism and the Politics of the Body', in *Beyond Romanticism; New Approaches to Texts and Contexts 1780–1832*, ed. Stephen Copley and John Whale (London and New York: Routledge, 1992), pp. 53–78.

39 See also Simon Schaffer, 'Self Evidence', *Critical Inquiry* 18 (Winter 1992), 327–62.

40 As quoted in Crabtree, *From Mesmer to Freud*, pp. 41–3.

41 The emphasis on the word 'Imagination' is Coleridge's. In the manuscript of the essay, held in the British Library, Add. MS 34, 225, fo. 146v, Coleridge has written the word 'Imagination' in much larger print. This emphasis is not evident from the transcription in *SWF* II 913.

5 'NIGHTMAIRS'

1 Thomas Beddoes, *Hygeia: or Essays Moral and Medical on the Causes Affecting the Personal State of Our Middling and Affluent Classes*, 3 vols. (Bristol, 1802–3), vol. III, pp. 64–6, 130–1.

2 The painting was first exhibited in 1782: see Nicolas Powell, *Fuseli: The Nightmare* (London: Allen Lane, 1973) and Boime, *Art in an Age of Revolution*. Although not widely circulated, a contrasting image of the nightmare which Coleridge may have known is William Blake's 'With

Dreams Upon my Bed', from the *Illustrations of the Book of Job* (London, 1825), plate 11.

3 See *CN* I 954n, *CN* II 2794, *CL* I 135. Coleridge always called Fuseli 'Fuzzle' or 'Fuzly': see Armour and Howes (eds.), *Coleridge the Talker*, p. 321.

4 One obvious example of the 'mare' ending is to be found in the 1800 and later editions of *The Rime of the Ancient Mariner*: 'the Night-mare LIFE-IN-DEATH' (*PW* I 194 line 193).

5 Grevel Lindop agrees with De Quincey that the latter's central concern in the *Confessions* and related writings was not with opium but rather with 'dreams': opium was 'important to [De Quincey] as an agent of vision only indirectly, in that he believed it produced more dreams, and finer ones, than would occur otherwise': Lindop, *Opium-Eater*, p. 391.

6 See Beer, *Coleridge's Poetic Intelligence*, pp. 81–7; Raimonda Modiano, 'Coleridge's Views on Touch and Other Senses', *Bulletin of Research in the Humanities* 81 (1978), 38; and *CN* II 2399n.

7 As suggested in *CM* III 868.

8 Beer, *Coleridge's Poetic Intelligence*, pp. 81–7.

9 In *CM* III 868, the editors date Coleridge's interest in double touch from 1801, but this notebook entry clearly shows interest in the phenomenon well before 1801.

10 *CN* I 1024, 1039.

11 The effort to understand the senses in relation to such diverse topics was, according to Raimonda Modiano, one of the strongest features of Romantic science: Modiano, 'Coleridge's Views on Touch and Other Senses', pp. 31–3. Many medical texts of the day devoted substantial sections to the questions of the senses and their relationship to other faculties. See Haller, *Physiology*, vol. II, pp. 1–15. On science and Romanticism in general, see *Romanticism in Science; Science in Europe 1790–1830*, ed. Stefano Poggi and Maurizo Bossi (Dordrecht, Boston, London: Kluwer Academic Publishers, 1994); *Companion Encyclopedia of the History of Medicine*, ed. W. F. Bynum and Roy Porter, 2 vols. (London and New York: Routledge, 1993); *Romanticism and the Sciences*, ed. Andrew Cunningham and Nicholas Jardine (Cambridge University Press, 1990).

12 Coleridge's annotation to Karl Christian Wolfart, *Mesmerismus*, 2 vols. (Berlin, 1814). Annotation in vol. II, p. 296. Coleridge's copy is held in the British Library at C.43. c. 1.

13 Coburn explains the meaning of stim*ulari* (esse sub stimulo) as stimulation that is not 'exclusively subject to stimulation from without':*CN* II 2399n.

14 Modiano, 'Coleridge's Views on Touch and Other Senses', p. 39.

15 *Ibid.*, p. 38.

16 Thomas Wedgwood, 'An Enquiry into the Origin of our Notion of Distance', published in the *Quarterly Journal of Science and Arts*, vol. III. The essay is reprinted in Eliza Meteyard, *A Group of Englishmen*

(1795–1815) (London: Longmans, Green & Co., 1871), pp. 395–406; the quoted passage is from *ibid.*, p. 396. Berkeley's theories are contained chiefly in the two works, *New Theory of Vision* (1709) and the *Principles of Human Knowledge* (1710). See also Stafford, *Body Criticism*, pp. 378–85. Stafford traces the eighteenth century's fascination with visual and kinetic senses of distortion through the popularity of new inventions such as the camera obscura, invented by Giovanni Battista della Porta in the sixteenth century, and still immensely popular in the eighteenth as a means for exploring visual and retinal distortions of image: pp. 369–96.

17 From Meteyard, *A Group of Englishmen*, pp. 397–8.

18 John Keats, *Poetical Works*, ed. H. W. Garrod, 2nd edn (Oxford: Clarendon Press, 1958), p. 260. Also cf a comment of Coleridge's in an unpublished notebook: 'Perhaps, I am dreaming. Perhaps, I am awake. N'importe. In either case I am': N37, fo. 85.

19 See also *CM* III 215.

20 Edward Bostetter, 'The Nightmare World of "The Ancient Mariner" ', *Studies in Romanticism* I (1962), 351–98.

21 Robert Penn Warren, 'A Poem of Pure Imagination, An Experiment in Reading', in *New and Selected Essays* (New York: Random House, 1989), pp. 335–423; and John Livingston Lowes, *The Road to Xanadu; a Study in the Ways of the Imagination* (Boston and New York: Houghton Mifflin Company, 1927).

22 Bostetter, 'Nightmare World of "The Ancient Mariner" ', p. 390.

23 Possibly because of Charles Lamb's comments that the subtitle was as 'bad as Bottom the Weaver's declaration that he is not a Lion, but only the scenical representation of a Lion': see Lamb, *Letters*, vol. I, p. 240.

24 Coleridge's comments are inserted on 4 folios between pages 184 and 185 of Gotthilf von Schubert's *Die Symbolik des Traumes* (Bamberg, 1821). Coleridge's copy is held in the British Library at C.43. b. 17.

6 THE MYSTERIOUS PROBLEM OF DREAMS

1 Coleridge described the 'Dreams of the Old Testament' as 'for the greater part evidently poetic, the becoming drapery of Wisdom': N39 fo. 34.

2 Cicero, *De Divinatione*, trans. William Falconer (Cambridge, Mass: Harvard University Press, 1979), Bk II lxv.

3 *Ibid.*, Bk II lxiv.

4 *Ibid.*, Bk II lxvii.

5 John Aubrey, *Miscellanies Upon Various Subjects* (London, 1721). See *F* II 117 and *CN* III 4390n. Rachel Baker, *Remarkable Sermons of Rachel Baker and Pious Ejaculations, Delivered During Sleep, Taken in Shorthand by Drs. Mitchell, Priestley, and Douglas* (London, 1815). 'On Dreams', *Spectator* 487

(September 1712), pp. 123–7; and 'A Vision', *Spectator* (October 1712) 524, pp. 293–8 for example.

6 Coleridge's copy of the *Remarkable Sermons* has been lost, along with some forty-four lines of marginalia: see *CM* 1 205.

7 Baker, *Remarkable Sermons*, p. ii.

8 Crabtree, *From Mesmer to Freud*, pp. 294–8 includes Baker's sleeping sermons as part of the dual-consciousness phenomenon associated with magnetic sleeps.

9 Shakespeare, *Hamlet* I v 174–5.

10 See also *The Rime of the Ancient Mariner* (1798), the 'silly buckets' filled with rain after the Mariner's dream: *LB* 21–2, lines 284–96.

11 On Coleridge's use of illusion and delusion in *Remorse*, see Carlson, *Theatre of Romanticism*, pp. 108–15.

12 See also *SWF* 1 344.

13 *Coleridge; the Critical Heritage*, ed. J. R. de J. Jackson, 2 vols. (London: Routledge & Kegan Paul, 1970), vol. 1, p. 159.

14 See for instance Carlyon, *Early Years and Late Reflections*, vol. 1, pp. 199–234. Robert Southey, in *The Doctor, &c*, 3rd edn, 11 vols. (London: Longmans, 1839), vol. 1, pp. 10–11, also expresses a popular view of dreams, including the notion that they are caused by 'unembodied spirits'.

15 David Morris, *The Culture of Pain* (Berkeley and Los Angeles: University of California Press, 1993), pp. 45–6 remarks that nineteenth-century artists such as Honoré Daumier and George Cruikshank popularised the view that 'almost any affliction from headaches to insanity might be attributed to an influx of demons sent by an enemy (through black magic) or arrived in punishment for the violation of a tribal taboo'.

16 Baxter, *Enquiry into the Nature of the Human Soul*, 2nd edn, vol. II, p. 189.

17 Interestingly, Leigh Hunt also declared that 'the materialists and psychologists are at issue upon the subject of dreams. The latter hold them to be one among the many proofs of the existence of a soul: the former endeavour to account for them upon principles altogether corporeal. We must own that the effects of their respective arguments . . . is not so much to satisfy us with either, as to dissatisfy us with both': *Essays*, p. 235.

18 Emanuel Swedenborg, *A Treatise Concerning Heaven and Hell and of the Wonderful Things Therein*, trans. J. R. Rendell, I. Tansley and J. S. Bogg, 5th edn (London, 1805), pp. 255–6.

19 Milton, *Paradise Lost* IV lines 799–809.

20 Cf *ibid.* XII lines 611–19.

21 On Milton's use of the dream in *Paradise Lost* and other works, see Manfred Weidhorn, *Dreams in Seventeenth-Century English Literature* (Paris: Mouton, 1970), pp. 130–55.

22 See John Payne Collier's description of an earlier dinner at Highgate, in 1812, at which Coleridge turned the conversation to dreams, in Armour

and Howes (eds.), *Coleridge the Talker*, pp. 177–9. In the Introduction, pp. 78–80, the editors comment on the popularity of the Thursday evening dinners and philosophical conversations at Highgate.

7 TRANSLATIONS OF DREAM AND BODY

1 As in Notebook 47, fos. 17–17v, written in September 1830: 'The regenerate Man contemplates his animal Self as an hostile Alien, an evil ground *out* of which he is to grow & growing to loosen and extricate his roots preparatively to a final transplantation into divine ground – . He no longer endures to think of it, as *him*, but as his *Nature*, tho' with sincerest humiliation and groans that can have no *utterance*, no outward expression, he knows it to be *his*, and cries out to be delivered from "the body of this Death".'

2 The effects of opium readily account for Coleridge's singling out of the digestive systems as possible causes of his dreams, but what is even more interesting are the ways in which this physical condition led him to explore in more detail the relationship between his dreaming mind and body. Opium decreases the activity of the gastrointestinal tract, which can lead to constipation if it is taken in excess. And one of the symptoms of opiate-withdrawal is abdominal cramps, diarrhoea and nausea. His efforts to stop taking the narcotic would have enhanced and aggravated his digestive symptoms, and it is not surprising that he focussed on this part of his body.

3 Coleridge's annotation to John Webster, *The Displaying of Supposed Witch-craft* (London, 1677), p. 76. Coleridge's copy is held in the British Library at C.126. l. 10.

4 On the body's tendency to assert itself and to be noticed in times of illness see F. J. Buytendijk, *Pain: Its Modes and Functions*, trans. Eda O'Shiel (University of Chicago Press, 1962).

5 In *Delicate Subjects; Romanticism, Gender, and the Ethics of Understanding* (Ithaca, New York: Cornell University Press, 1990), p. 175, Julie Ellison argues that this somatic approach to dreams was an indication of Coleridge's 'hysteria'. But his interest in the somatic nature of dreams cannot be read entirely within the parameters of a psychoanalytic understanding of hysteria. Nor does a psychoanalytical reading take into account the features of Coleridge's (constructed) notions of the body, or the body's perceived relationship to the origin of dreams.

6 It is not clear in the notebook manuscript (N30) whether Coleridge uses a dash or a hyphen here. If a dash, it would mean that he awoke from a dream and had the sensation of grief; if a hyphen, that the grief is itself a sensation experienced within the dream.

7 Coleridge's approach to pain, and particularly to men's and women's experiences of it, is deserving of another study in itself. He maintains in

an unpublished notebook entry that women and men have different responses to pain: 'In sickness the Sexes almost change character – the Woman with more than masculine fortitude, the Man Womanish – but both [?credulatory], and from the very nature of Sickness, the Man does by the disturbing [. . .] what is the ordinary Nature of Woman – i. e. determine his judgement by his feelings': N46, fo. 20.

8 See also *CN* iv 5360n.

9 Of related interest is A. Luyendijk-Elshout, 'Of Masks and Mills; The Enlightened Doctor and His Frightened Patient', in G. S. Rousseau (ed.), *The Languages of Psyche: Mind and Body in Enlightenment Thought* (Berkeley: University of California Press, 1990), pp. 186–230 and L. J. Rather, 'Old and New Views of the Emotions and Bodily Changes: Wright and Harvey versus Descartes, James and Cannon', *Clio Medica* i (1965), 1–25.

10 I borrow the term 'dreambody' from Arnold Mindell, *Dreambody: The Body's Role in Revealing the Self*, ed. Sisa Sternback-Scott and Becky Goodman (Los Angeles: Sigo Press, 1982).

11 In this letter to Charles Tulk, Coleridge is referring to nerves located in the chest and abdomen.

12 This pain is a transgression because most concepts and studies of pain require a minimal level of consciousness. David Morris writes that 'we dream or sleepwalk in a nonconscious state, but nonconscious pain is a contradiction in terms': see *Culture of Pain*, p. 158. Coleridge's experience of his dreams and his illness would appear to differ from this idea, although he once wrote that 'As no thought can climb above Self-Consciousness, so neither can it delve below Pleasure and Pain' (*CN* iv 5197).

13 In *Biographia Literaria*, Coleridge coins the word 'potenziate' to express the 'combination or transfer of powers': *BL* i 287; see also *CN* iii 4418.

14 Coleridge ends his deliberations with a quote from Horace's *Satires*, i 24–5: 'in a laughing manner to investigate the truth'; see *Horace: Satires, Epistles and Ars Poetica*, trans. H. Rushton Fairclough (Cambridge, Mass.: Harvard University Press, 1961).

15 Coleridge's annotation to Wilhelm Gottlieb Tennemann, *Geschichte der Philosophie*, vol. ii (Leipzig, 1799–1817). The annotation is on the fly-leaf. Coleridge's copy is held in the British Library at C.43. c. 24.

16 See also *CM* i 755, *CL* iii 29.

8 THE DREAMING MEDICAL IMAGINATION

1 See John Beer, *Coleridge the Visionary* (London: Chatto & Windus, 1959); Walter Jackson Bate, *Coleridge* (London: Weidenfeld & Nicolson, 1968); Thomas McFarland, *Coleridge and the Pantheist Tradition* (Oxford University Press, 1969); Stephen Prickett, *Coleridge and Wordsworth; the Poetry of Growth* (Cambridge University Press, 1970); M. H. Abrams, *The Mirror*

and the Lamp; Romantic Theory and the Critical Tradition (Oxford University Press, 1977), pp. 168–225.

2 For instance, see Jerome McGann, *The Romantic Ideology: A Critical Investigation* (University of Chicago Press, 1983); Paul De Man, *The Rhetoric of Romanticism* (Columbia University Press, 1984); Tilottama Rajan, *The Dark Interpreter* (Ithaca, New York: Cornell University Press, 1986); Nigel Leask, *The Politics of Imagination in Coleridge's Critical Thought* (London: Macmillan, 1988); Marjorie Levinson, Marilyn Butler and Jerome McGann, *Rethinking Historicism; Critical Readings in Romantic History* (Oxford and New York: Basil Blackwell, 1989); Marlon B. Ross, *The Contours of Masculine Desire* (Oxford University Press, 1989); Sandra M. Gilbert and Susan Gubar, 'The Mirror and the Vamp: Reflections on Feminist Criticism', in *The Future of Literary Theory*, ed. Ralph Cohen (London: Routledge, 1989); Mary Jacobus, *Romanticism, Writing and Sexual Difference; Essays on 'The Prelude'* (Oxford University Press, 1989); and Anne K. Mellor, *Romanticism and Gender* (London: Routledge, 1993).

3 Siskin, *Historicity of Romantic Discourse*, pp. 174–83.

4 G. S. Rousseau, *Enlightenment Crossings; Pre- and Post-Modern Discourses; Anthropological* (Manchester University Press, 1991), pp. 2–25. See also Terry Castle, *Female Thermometer: Eighteenth-Century Culture and the Invention of the Uncanny* (Oxford University Press, 1995), pp. 168–89.

5 William Falconer, *A Dissertation on the Influence of the Passions Upon Disorders of the Body*, 3rd edn (London, 1796). It was first published in 1788.

6 *Ibid.*, p. 74.

7 Haygarth was the first to realise the need to isolate patients with fevers, and he received much acclaim for this pioneering work; he had also written on the cause and cure of hydrophobia: see John Haygarth, *Hints Towards the Investigation of the Nature, Cause and Cure of the Rabies Canina* (Manchester, 1789). Coleridge was also interested in hydrophobia, not only because James Gillman wrote upon it, but also because his dreams were littered with biting dogs. Coleridge was aware of at least one of Haygarth's works: *CN* I 258n.

8 The first edition of *Of the Imagination, as a Cause and as a Cure of the Disorders of the Body* was published in Bath, 1800. A second edition, with additional remarks, came out in 1801. I quote from the first edition.

9 *Ibid.*, p. 1.

10 *Ibid.*, p. 18.

11 Benjamin Douglas Perkins, *The Efficacy of Perkins's Patent Metallic Tractors* (London and Edinburgh, 1800), pp. xxii–xxxix.

12 Among those known to Haygarth as having documented the potential of the imagination to influence and interact with the diseased body was the Royal Physician, Sir George Baker. Baker's work with lead and health, and the relationships between mind and body in epidemical diseases, is chiefly contained in *Medical Tracts, read at the College of Physicians between the years 1767 and 1785*, 2 vols. (London, 1818). Baker

was at one stage the favoured physician to George III, until the time of his most severe attack in October 1788, and certainly had some ideas on possible treatments for the King: see Macalpine and Hunter, *George III and the Mad-Business*, pp. 1–53.

13 James Lind's contribution to medical science was largely in his *Treatise on Scurvy*, published in 1753, which recommended that citrus fruits be consumed on long sea voyages, thereby preventing and curing scurvy: reprinted in C. P. Stewart and D. Guthrie (eds.) *Lind's Treatise on Scurvy* (Edinburgh University Press, 1953). Lind was also friend and teacher, 'spiritual father and guide', to Shelley when he was at Oxford: see Richard Holmes, *Shelley; the Pursuit* (Harmondsworth: Penguin, 1987), p. 28.

14 Haygarth, *Of the Imagination*, p. 28.

15 Rousseau, *Enlightenment Crossings*, p. 17.

16 *Ibid.*, p. 9. See also Stanley W. Jackson, 'The Use of the Passions in Psychological Healing', *Journal of the History of Medicine and Allied Sciences*, 45 (1990), 150–75; C. E. McMahon, 'The Role of Imagination in the Disease Process: Pre-Cartesian History (the Role of Imagination in the Disease Process)', *Psychological Medicine* 6 (1976), 179–84; and H. M. Gardiner, Ruth Clark Metcalf, and John G. Beebe-Center, *Feeling and Emotion; A History of Theories* (New York: American Book Company, 1937).

17 Lodovico Antonio Muratori, *Della Forza Della Fantasia Umana* (Venice: Presso Giambatista Pasquali, 1745).

18 See L. J. Rather, *Mind and Body in Eighteenth-Century Medicine; A Study Based on Jerome Gaub's* De Regimine Mentis (London: The Wellcome Historical Medical Library, 1965).

19 L. M. K., 'Imagination; A Lithograph by Honoré Daumier', *Journal of the History of Medicine* 20 (October 1965), 405.

20 Arthur Jacob, *An Essay on the Influence of the Imagination and Passions in the Production and Cure of Diseases* (Dublin, 1823), p. 2.

21 Marie-Hélène Huet, *Monstrous Imagination* (Cambridge, Mass.: Harvard University Press, 1993). The energy of the debate surrounding maternal impressions throughout the eighteenth century is well illustrated in the announcement in 1726 by Mary Toft, an illiterate country woman, that she had given birth to seventeen rabbits. On this scandal, see Dennis Todd, *Imagining Monsters; Miscreations of the Self in Eighteenth-Century England* (University of Chicago Press, 1995). See also G. S Rousseau, 'Pineapples, Pregnancy, Pica, and *Peregrine Pickle*', in G. S. Rousseau and P. G. Boucé (eds.), *Tobias Smollett; Bicentennial Essays Presented to Lewis M. Knapp* (New York: Oxford University Press, 1971), pp. 79–109.

22 See Benjamin Bablot, *Dissertation sur le pouvoir de l'imagination des femmes enceintes; dans laquelle on passe successivement en revue tous les grands Hommes qui . . . ont admis l'influence de cette Faculté sur le Foetus, & dans laquelle on répond aux Objections de ceux qui combattent cette Opinion* (Paris, 1788) and James

Blondel, *The Power of the Mother's Imagination Over the Fœtus Examin'd* (London, 1729). Although earlier, of related interest is the essay by Edward Smith, 'A relation of an extraordinary effect of the power of the Imagination', *Philosophical Transactions* 16 (July / August 1687), 330–42.

23 On the complex collaborative efforts of Wordsworth and Coleridge in 'The Three Graves' see Mary Jacobus, *Tradition and Experiment in Wordsworth's Lyrical Ballads (1798)* (Oxford University Press, 1976), pp. 224–32.

24 Wordsworth, *The Prose Works of William Wordsworth*, ed. W. J. B. Owen and Jane Worthington Smyser, 3 vols. (Oxford: Clarendon Press, 1975), vol. I, p. 150.

25 Jacobus, *Tradition and Experiment*, p. 234.

26 Wordsworth and Wordsworth, *Letters; The Early Years*, pp. 199, 214.

27 Jacobus, *Tradition and Experiment*, p. 235.

28 On the debate between magic and miracles in the eighteenth century, see R. D. Stock, *The Holy and the Daemonic from Sir Thomas Browne to William Blake* (Princeton University Press, 1982), pp. 61–116.

29 Author unknown, 'The Phenomena of Diseased Imagination', *London Magazine* (March 1820), 251.

30 Coleridge's annotation to Wilhelm Tennemann, *Geschichte der Philosophie*. Annotation in vol. x on p. 183. Coleridge's copy is held in the British Library at C.43. c. 24.

31 Coleridge's annotation to Schubert, *Die Symbolik des Traumes*, between pp. 184 and 185. Coleridge's copy is held in the British Library at C.43. b. 17.

32 See also *Lectures* II 208.

33 See Arden Reed, 'The Mariner Rimed', in *Romanticism and Language*, ed. Arden Reed (Ithaca, New York: Cornell University Press, 1984), pp. 168–201. Of related interest is an essay by Michael O'Neill, ' "That Dome in Air": Coleridge and the Self-Conscious Poem', *Romanticism* 1 (1995), 252–71.

CONCLUSION

1 John Elliotson, *Human Physiology, with which is incorporated much of the elementary part of the Institutions Physiologicæ of J. F. Blumenbach*, 5th edn (London: Longman, Orme, Brown, Green, & Longman, 1840), p. 615.

Bibliography

MANUSCRIPT MATERIALS

Coleridge, S. T., Notebook 30, British Library, Add. MS 47, 527.
    Notebook 34, British Library, Add. MS 47, 529.
    Notebook 35, British Library, Add. MS 47, 530.
    Notebook 36, British Library, Add. MS 47, 531.
    Notebook 37, British Library, Add. MS 47, 532.
    Notebook 38, British Library, Add. MS 47, 533.
    Notebook 39, British Library, Add. MS 47, 534.
    Notebook 40, British Library, Add. MS 47, 535.
    Notebook 41, British Library, Add. MS 47, 536.
    Notebook 42, British Library, Add. MS 47, 537.
    Notebook 43, British Library, Add. MS 47, 538.
    Notebook 44, British Library, Add. MS 47, 539.
    Notebook 45, British Library, Add. MS 47, 540.
    Notebook 46, British Library, Add. MS 47, 541.
    Notebook 47, British Library, Add. MS 47, 542.
    Notebook 48, British Library, Add. MS 47, 543.
    Notebook 49, British Library, Add. MS 47, 544.
    Notebook 50, British Library, Add. MS 47, 545.
    Notebook 51, British Library, Add. MS 47, 546.
    Notebook 52, British Library, Add. MS 47, 547.
    Notebook 53, British Library, Add. MS 47, 548.
    Notebook 54, British Library, Add. MS 47, 549.
    Notebook 55, British Library, Add. MS 47, 550.
    'On the Passions', British Library, Egerton MS 2801, fos. 43–58.
    'Zoomagnetism', British Library, Add. MS 34, 225, fos. 146–7.
Poole, Thomas, 'The Correspondence of Poole 1765–1837', British Library,
    Add. MS 35, 343.

BOOKS CONTAINING MARGINALIA BY SAMUEL TAYLOR COLERIDGE

Schubert, Gotthilf Heinrich von, *Symbolik des Traumes von Dr. G. H. Schubert*, Bamburg: Zweite Verbesserte und Vermische Auflage, 1821. Held British Library C.43. b.17. Annotations on four leaves between pages 184 and 185.

Tennemann, Wilhelm Gottlieb, *Geschichte der Philosophie*, 10 vols., Leipzig, 1799–1817. Held British Library C.43. c.24. Annotations throughout.

Webster, John, *The Displaying of Supposed Witchcraft*, London, 1677. Held British Library C.126. l.10. Annotations throughout.

Wolfart, Karl Christian, *Erläuterungen zum Mesmerismus*, 2 vols., Berlin, 1814. Held British Library C.43. c. 1. Annotations throughout vol. II.

WORKS BY SAMUEL TAYLOR COLERIDGE

Biographia Literaria, ed. John Shawcross, 2 vols., Oxford: Clarendon Press, 1907.

Christabel; Kubla Khan, a Vision; The Pains of Sleep, London, 1816. Woodstock Facsimile, ed. Jonathan Wordsworth, Oxford and New York: Woodstock Books, 1991.

Coleridge's Writings, ed. Anya Taylor, 2 vols., Basingstoke: Macmillan, 1994.

Collected Letters of Samuel Taylor Coleridge, ed. E. L. Griggs, 6 vols., London: Oxford University Press, 1956–71.

The Collected Works of Samuel Taylor Coleridge, Bollingen Series lxxv, general editor Kathleen Coburn, London and Princeton, NJ: Routledge & Kegan Paul, 1969– .

Vol. 1 *Lectures 1795, on Politics and Religion*, ed. Lewis Patton and Peter Mann, 1971.

Vol. 2 *The Watchman*, ed. Lewis Patton, 1970.

Vol. 4 *The Friend*, ed. B. E. Rooke, 2 vols., 1969.

Vol. 5 *Lectures on Literature 1808–19*, ed. R. A. Foakes, 2 vols., 1987.

Vol. 6 *Lay Sermons*, ed. R. J. White, 1972.

Vol. 7 *Biographia Literaria*, ed. James Engell and Walter Jackson Bate, 2 vols., 1983.

Vol. 11 *Shorter Works and Fragments*, ed. H. J. Jackson and J. R. de J. Jackson, 2 vols., 1995.

Vol. 12 *Marginalia*, ed. George Whalley, 1980– .

Vol. 13 *Logic*, ed. J. R. de J. Jackson, 1981.

Vol. 14 *Table Talk*, ed. Carl R. Woodring, 2 vols., 1990.

Complete Poetical Works of Samuel Taylor Coleridge, ed. E. H. Coleridge, 2 vols., Oxford: Clarendon Press, 1912.

Hints Towards the Formation of a More Comprehensive Theory of Life, ed. Seth Watson, London, 1848.

Inquiring Spirit: A New Presentation of Coleridge from His Published and Unpublished

Prose Writings, ed. Kathleen Coburn, London: Routledge & Kegan Paul, 1951; revised edition, Toronto University Press, 1979.
The Literary Remains of Samuel Taylor Coleridge, ed. H. N. Coleridge, 4 vols., London, 1836–9.
Lyrical Ballads, Samuel Taylor Coleridge and William Wordsworth, ed. R. L. Brett and A. R. Jones, 2nd edn, London and New York: Routledge, 1991.
Notebooks of Samuel Taylor Coleridge, ed. Kathleen Coburn, London and New York: Routledge & Kegan Paul, 1957– .
Notes, Theological, Political and Miscellaneous, ed. Derwent Coleridge, London, 1853.
Omniana; or Horae Otiosiores, Samuel Taylor Coleridge and Robert Southey ed. Robert Gittings, Fontwell, Sussex: Centaur Press, 1969.
Philosophical Lectures of Samuel Taylor Coleridge, ed. Kathleen Coburn, London: Pilot Press, 1949.
Remorse; A tragedy, in Five Acts, 2nd edn, London, 1813. Woodstock Facsimile, ed. Jonathan Wordsworth, Oxford and New York: Woodstock Books, 1989.
Shakespearean Criticism, ed. Thomas Middleton Raysor, 2 vols., London: Constable, 1930.

SECONDARY SOURCES

Abrams, M., *The Milk of Paradise: The Effect of Opium Visions on the Works of De Quincey, Crabbe, Francis Thompson, and Coleridge*, Cambridge, Mass.: Harvard University Press, 1934.
The Mirror and the Lamp: Romantic Theory and the Critical Tradition, Oxford University Press, 1977.
Adair, Patricia M., *The Waking Dream: A Study of Coleridge's Poetry*, London: Edward Arnold, 1967.
Anon., *Nocturnal Revels; or Universal Interpreter of Dreams and Visions*, London, 1805.
'The Phenomena of Diseased Imagination', *London Magazine* (March 1820), 250–4.
Aristotle, *On the Soul, Parva Naturalia, on Breath*, trans. W. S. Hett, London and Cambridge, Mass.: Heinemann and Harvard University Press, 1935.
Arkin, A. M., Antrobus, J. S. and Ellman, S. J. (eds.), *The Mind in Sleep*, Hillsdale, NJ: Erlbaum, 1978.
Armour, Richard W. and Howes, Raymond F. (eds.), *Coleridge the Talker: A Series of Contemporary Descriptions and Comments*, New York and London: Johnson Reprint Corporation, 1969.
Artemidorus, *The Interpretation of Dreams*, 11th edn, London, 1644.
The Interpretation of Dreams, trans. Robert J. White, Park Ridge, NJ: Noyes Press, 1975.

Aubrey, John, *Miscellanies Upon Various Subjects*, London, 1721.

Bablot, Benjamin, *Dissertation sur le pouvoir de l'imagination des femmes enceintes; dans laquelle on passe successivement en revue tous les grands Hommes qui depuis plus de deux mille ans, ont admis l'influence de cette Faculté sur le Fœtus, & dans laquelle on répond aux Objections de ceux qui combattent cette Opinion*, Paris, 1788.

Baker, Rachel, *Remarkable Sermons of Rachel Baker, and Pious Ejaculations, Delivered During Sleep, Taken Down in Shorthand, with Remarks on this Extraordinary Phænomeonon, by Dr. Mitchell, the late Dr. Priestley . . . and Dr. Douglas*, London, 1815.

Baker, Sir George, *Medical Tracts, read at the College of Physicians Between the Years 1767 and 1785*, 2 vols., London, 1818.

Barnes, B. and Shapin, S. (eds.), *Natural Order*, Beverly Hills and London: Sage Publications, 1980.

Barrell, John, *The Infection of Thomas De Quincey; A Psychopathology of Imperialism*, New Haven: Yale University Press, 1991.

Barth, George, *The Mesmerist's Manual of Phenomena and Practice; with Directions for Applying Mesmerism to the Cure of Diseases*, 3rd edn, London, 1852.

Barth, J. Robert, *Coleridge and the Power of Love*, University of Missouri Press, 1988.

Barth, Robert J. and Mahoney, John L. (eds.), *Coleridge, Keats and the Dreaming Imagination: Romanticism and Adam's Dream; Essays in Honour of Walter Jackson Bate*, University of Missouri Press, 1990.

Bate, Walter Jackson, *Coleridge*, London: Weidenfeld & Nicolson, 1968.

Battersby, Christine, *Gender and Genius: Towards A Feminist Aesthetics*, London: The Women's Press, 1994.

Battie, William, *A Treatise on Madness*, London, 1758.

Baxter, Andrew, *An Enquiry into the Nature of the Human Soul; Wherein the Immateriality of the Soul is Evinced From the Principles of Reason and Philosophy*, 1st edn., London, 1733.

An Enquiry into the Nature of the Human Soul; Wherein the Immateriality of the Soul is Evinced From the Principles of Reason and Philosophy, 2nd edn, 2 vols., London, 1737.

Beattie, James, *Dissertations Moral and Critical*, London, 1783.

Beddoes, Thomas, *Hygeia: or Essays Moral and Medical on the Causes Affecting the Personal State of Our Middling and Affluent Classes*, 3 vols., Bristol, 1802–3.

Beer, John, *Coleridge the Visionary*, London: Chatto & Windus, 1959.

Coleridge's Poetic Intelligence, London: Macmillan, 1979.

(ed.), *Coleridge's Variety: Bicentenary Studies*, London: Macmillan, 1974.

Behr, C. A., *Aelius Aristides and the Sacred Tales*, Amsterdam: Adolf M. Hakkert, 1968.

Beres, David, 'A Dream, a Vision, a Poem: a Psycho-Analytic Study of the Origins of the Ancient Mariner', *International Journal of Psychoanalysis* 32 (1951), 97–116.

Berrios, German and Shapiro, Colin, 'I Don't Get Enough Sleep, Doctor', *British Medical Journal* 306 (27 March 1993), 843–6.

The Bijou; or Annual of Literature and the Arts, London, 1828.

Binswanger, Ludwig, *Wandlungen in der Auffassung und Deutung des Traumes von den Griechen bis zur gegenwart*, Berlin: Verlag von Julius Springer, 1928.

Blake, William, *Illustrations of the Book of Job*, London, 1825.

Blondel, James, *The Power of the Mother's Imagination Over the Fœtus Examin'd*, London, 1729.

Boime, Albert, *Art in an Age of Revolution 1750–1800*, University of Chicago Press, 1990.

Art in an Age of Bonapartism 1800–1815, University of Chicago Press, 1990.

Bond, Donald, '"Distrust" of Imagination in English Neo-Classicism', *Philological Quarterly* 16 (1937), 54–69.

Bond, John, *Essay on the Incubus*, London, 1753.

Borbély, Alexander, *Secrets of Sleep; New Light on Sleep, Dreams and Sleep Disorders*, trans. Deborah Schneider, Harlow, Essex: Longman, 1987.

Bostetter, Edward, 'The Nightmare World of "The Ancient Mariner"', *Studies in Romanticism* 1 (1962), 351–98.

Bouché-Leclerq, A., *Histoire de la divination dans l'antiquité*, 2 vols., Paris, 1879.

Bowman, W. C. and Rand, M. J., *Textbook of Pharmacology*, 2nd edn, Oxford, London, Edinburgh, Melbourne: Blackwells, 1980.

Branch, Thomas, *Thoughts on Dreaming; Wherein the Notion of the Sensory, and the Opinion that it is Shut Up From the Inspection of the Soul in Sleep, and that Spirits Supply us With all our Dreams, are Examined by Revelation and Reason*, London, 1738.

Brinkley, Robert and Hanley, Keith (eds.), *Romantic Revisions*, Cambridge University Press, 1992.

Brown, John, *The Elements of Medicine; or, a Translation of the Elementa Medicinæ Brunonis*, 2 vols., London, 1788.

The Elements of Medicine. A new edition, revised and corrected with a biographical preface by Thomas Beddoes MD, 3 vols., London, 1795.

Bruhm, Steven, *Gothic Bodies; The Politics of Pain in Romantic Fiction*, University of Pennsylvania Press, 1994.

Buchan, William, *Domestic Medicine; Or, the Family Physician*, 21st edn, London, 1813.

Bullit, John and Bate, W. Jackson, 'Distinctions between Fancy and Imagination in Eighteenth-Century English Criticism', *Modern Language Notes* 40 (1945), 8–15.

Bundy, Murray Wright, *The Theory of the Imagination in Classical and Medieval Thought*, Urbana: University of Illinois Press, 1928.

Burwick, Frederick, 'Stage Illusion and the Stage Designs of Goethe and Hugo', *Word and Image* 4 (July–December 1988), 692–718.

Busst, A. J. L., 'Scottish Second Sight: The Rise and Fall of a European Myth', *European Romantic Review* 5 (Winter 1995), 149–77.

Buytendijk, F. J., *Pain: Its Modes and Functions*, trans. Eda O'Shiel, University of Chicago Press, 1962.

Bynum, W. F. and Porter, Roy (eds.), *Companion Encyclopedia of the History of Medicine*, London and New York: Routledge, 1993.

Byron, George Gordon, *Poetical Works*, ed. Frederick Page, revised John Jump, Oxford University Press, 1987.

Carlson, Julie A., *In the Theatre of Romanticism: Coleridge, Nationalism, Women*, Cambridge University Press, 1994.

Carlyon, Clement, *Early Years and Late Reflections*, 3 vols., London, 1856–8.

Cartwright, Frederick, *The English Pioneers of Anaesthesia: Beddoes, Davy and Hickman*, Bristol: Wright, 1952.

Castle, Robert L. van de, *Our Dreaming Mind*, New York: Ballantine Books, 1994.

Castle, Terry, *The Female Thermometer; Eighteenth-Century Culture and the Invention of the Uncanny*, Oxford University Press, 1995.

Caton, Richard, *The Temples and Ritual of Asklepius at Epidaurus and Athens*, Hertford: 1899.

Chambers, Ephraim, *Chambers Cyclopedia, or New Dictionary of Arts and Sciences; Containing an Explication of the Terms, and an Account of the Things signified thereby, in the Several Arts, both Liberal and Mechanical; and the Several Sciences, Human and Divine: The Figures, Kinds, Properties, Productions, Preparations, and Uses of Things Natural and Artificial: the Rise, Progress, and State of Things Ecclesiastical, Civil, Military, and Commercial; With the several Systems, Sects, Opinions, &c among Philosophers, Divines, Mathematicians, Physicians, Antiquarians, Critics &c. The whole Intended as a Course of antient and modern learning. Extracted from the Best Authors, Dictionaries, Journals, Memoirs, Transactions, Ephemerides, &c in Several Languages*, 4th edn., 2 vols., London, 1741.

Christie, John and Shuttleworth, Sally (eds.), *Nature Transfigured: Science and Literature, 1700–1900*, Manchester University Press, 1989.

Cicero, *De Divinatione*, trans. William Falconer, Cambridge, Mass.: Harvard University Press, 1979.

Clark, Timothy and Allen, Mark, 'Between Flippancy and Terror: Shelley's "Marianne's Dream"', *Romanticism* 1 (1 1995), 90–105.

Coburn, Kathleen, *The Self-Conscious Imagination; A Study of the Coleridge Notebooks in celebration of the bi-centenary of his birth 21 October 1772*, Oxford University Press, 1974.

Experience into Thought; Perspectives in the Coleridge Notebooks, Toronto University Press, 1979.

Coffman, Ralph J., *Coleridge's Library. A Bibliography of Books Owned or Read by Samuel Taylor Coleridge*, Boston: G. K. Hall & Co., 1987.

Cohen, Ralph (ed.), *The Future of Literary Theory*, London: Routledge, 1989.

Coleman, Deirdre, *Coleridge and* The Friend *(1809–1810)*, Oxford University Press, 1988.

Coleman, Deirdre and Otto, Peter (eds.), *Imagining Romanticism; Essays on*

English and Australian Romanticisms, West Cornwall, Conn.: Locust Hill Press, 1992.

Compendious Medical Dictionary, London, 1798.

Condillac, Etienne Bonnot de, *An Essay on the Origin of Human Knowledge, Being a Supplement to Mr. Locke's Essay on the Human Understanding*, trans. Thomas Nugent, London, 1756.

Treatise on the Sensations, trans. Geraldine Carr, London, 1930.

Conger, Syndy McMillen (ed.), *Sensibility in Transformation: Creative Resistance to Sentiment from the Augustans to the Romantics; Essays in Honor of Jean H. Hagstum*, Cranbury, NJ: Associated University Presses, 1990.

Copley, Stephen and Whale, John (eds.), *Beyond Romanticism: New Approaches to Texts and Contexts 1780–1832*, London and New York: Routledge, 1992.

Cotta, John, *The Triall of Witch-craft, Shewing the True and Right Methode of the Discovery: With a Confutation of Erroneous Wayes*, London, 1616.

Cottle, Joseph, *Reminiscences of Samuel Taylor Coleridge and Robert Southey*, Highgate: Lime Tree Bower Press, 1970.

Coyne, Frank, *Nightmare and Escape: Changing Conceptions of the Imagination in Romantic and Victorian Dream Visions*, Ann Arbor: University Microfilms International, 1984.

Crabbe, George, *The Complete Poetical Works*, 3 vols., ed. Norma Dalrymple-Champneys and Arthur Pollard, Oxford: Clarendon Press, 1988.

Crabtree, Adam, *From Mesmer to Freud; Magnetic Sleep and the Roots of Psychological Healing*, New Haven: Yale University Press, 1993.

Craig, Katherine Taylor, *The Fabric of Dreams: Dream Lore and Dream Interpretation, Ancient and Modern*, London: Kegan Paul, 1918.

Crichton, Alexander, *An Inquiry into the Nature and Origin of Mental Derangement*, 2 vols., London, 1798.

Crook, Nora and Guiton, Derek, *Shelley's Venomed Melody*, Cambridge University Press, 1986.

Crumpe, Samuel, *An Inquiry into the Nature and Properties of Opium*, London, 1793.

Cunningham, Andrew and French, Roger (eds.), *The Medical Enlightenment of the Eighteenth Century*, Cambridge University Press, 1990.

Cunningham, Andrew and Jardine, Nicholas (eds.), *Romanticism and the Sciences*, Cambridge University Press, 1990.

Curry, W. C., *Chaucer and the Medieval Sciences*, New York: Barnes & Noble, 1926.

Darnton, Robert, *Mesmerism and the End of the Enlightenment in France*, Cambridge, Mass.: Harvard University Press, 1969.

Darwin, Erasmus, *Zoonomia, or the Laws of Organic Life*, 2nd edn, 4 vols., London, 1794–6.

The Botanic Garden, A Poem in Two Parts, 4th edn, London, 1799.

Davies, Browyn and Harré, Rom, 'Positioning: The Discursive Production of Selves', *Journal for the Theory of Social Behaviour* 20 (1990), 43–63.

Davis, Herbert, DeVane, William C. and Bald, R. C. (eds.), *Nineteenth-Century Studies*, New York: Greenwood Press, 1968.

Davy, Humphry, 'The Bakerian Lecture, on Some Chemical Agencies of Electricity', *Philosophical Transactions* 98 (1808), 1–44.

Collected Works, ed. John Davy, 9 vols., London: Smith & Elder, 1839.

De Quincey, Thomas, 'Animal Magnetism', *Tait's Edinburgh Magazine* 4 (October 1833–January 1834), 456–74.

Confessions of an English Opium-Eater and Other Writings, ed. Grevel Lindop, Oxford University Press, 1989.

A Diary of Thomas De Quincey, 1803, ed. H. A. Eaton, London: Noel Douglas.

Dendy, Walter Cooper, *The Philosophy of Mystery*, London: Longman, Orme, Brown, Green & Longman, 1841.

DePorte, Michael V., *Nightmares and Hobby Horses: Swift, Sterne and Augustan Ideas of Madness*, San Marino: Huntingdon Library, 1974.

Dodds, E. R., *The Greeks and the Irrational*, Berkeley: University of California Press, 1951.

Doig, A., Ferguson, J. P. S., Milne, I. A. and Passmore, R. (eds.), *William Cullen and the Eighteenth-Century Medical World; A Bicentenary Exhibition and Symposium Arranged by the Royal College of Physicians of Edinburgh in 1990*, Edinburgh University Press, 1993.

Doughty, Oswald, *Perturbed Spirit; The Life and Personality of Samuel Taylor Coleridge*, London and Toronto: Associated University Presses, 1981.

Edinburgh New Dispensatory, Edinburgh, 1797.

Ellenberger, Henri, *The Discovery of the Unconscious*, London: Allen Lane, the Penguin Press, 1970.

Elliotson, John, *The Institutes of Physiology, Translated from the Latin of Johann Friedrich Blumenbach, by John Elliotson, With Additional Notes Illustrative and Emendatory*, 3rd edn, London, 1817.

Human Physiology, with which is incorporated much of the elementary part of the Institutions Physiologicæ of J. F. Blumenbach, 5th edn., London: Longman, Orme, Brown, Green, & Longman, 1840.

Numerous Cases of Surgical Operations Without Pain in the Mesmeric States, London, 1843.

Ellison, Julie, *Delicate Subjects; Romanticism, Gender, and the Ethics of Understanding*, Ithaca, New York: Cornell University Press, 1990.

Encyclopedia Britannica; Or, a Dictionary of Arts, Sciences, and Miscellaneous Literature, 3rd edn, 18 vols., Edinburgh, 1797.

Falconer, William, *A Dissertation on the Influence of the Passions Upon Disorders of the Body*, 3rd edn, London, 1796.

Ferriar, John, *An Essay Towards a Theory of Apparitions*, London, 1813.

Fosshage, James L. and Loew, Clemens A. (eds.), *Dream Interpretation; A Comparative Study*, New York: PMA, 1987.

Foucault, Michel, *Madness and Civilization: A History of Insanity in the Age of*

Reason, trans. Richard Howard, New York: New American Library, 1965.

The Birth of the Clinic: An Archaeology of Medical Perception, trans. Sheridan Smith, New York: Pantheon Books, London: Tavistock Publications, 1973.

The History of Sexuality; The Care of the Self, trans. Robert Hurley, London: Penguin, 1986.

Freud, Sigmund, *The Interpretation of Dreams*, trans. James Strachey, Harmondsworth: Penguin, 1976.

Fruman, Norman, *Coleridge, the Damaged Archangel*, London: George Allen & Unwin, 1971.

Fulford, Tim, *Coleridge's Figurative Language*, London: Macmillan, 1991.

'Coleridge, Böhme, and the Language of Nature', *MLQ* 25 (1991), 32–53.

Fulford, Tim and Paley, Morton D. (eds.), *Coleridge's Visionary Languages; Essays in Honour of J. B. Beer*, Cambridge: D. S. Brewer, 1993.

Fuller, Francis, *Medicina Gymnastica; Or, a treatise concerning the power of exercise, with respect to the animal oeconomy; and the great necessity of it, in the cure of several Distempers*, 9th edn, London, 1777.

Galen, *On the Usefulness of the Parts of the Body*, trans. Margaret Tallmadge May, 2 vols., Ithaca, New York: Cornell University Press, 1968.

Gallagher, Catherine and Laqueur, Thomas (eds.), *The Making of the Modern Body; Sexuality and Society in the Nineteenth Century*, Berkeley, Los Angeles, London: University of California Press, 1987.

Gallant, Christine (ed.), *Coleridge's Theory of Imagination Today*, New York: AMS Press, 1989.

Gardiner, H. M., Metcalf, Ruth Clark and Beebe-Center, John G., *Feeling and Emotion; A History of Theories*, New York: American Book Company, 1937.

Gillman, James, *Dissertation on the Bite of a Rabid Animal, being the substance of an essay which received a prize from the Royal College of Surgeons in London, in the year 1811*, London, 1812.

The Life of Samuel Taylor Coleridge, London: William Pickering, 1838.

Goff, Jacques le, *The Medieval Imagination*, trans. Arthur Goldhammer, University of Chicago Press, 1988.

Gravil, Richard, Newlyn, Lucy and Rose, Nicholas (eds.), *Coleridge's Imagination: Essays in Memory of Pete Laver*, Cambridge University Press, 1985.

Gray, Robert, *The Theory of Dreams: in which an inquiry is made into the powers and faculties of the human mind, as they are illustrated in the most remarkable dreams recorded in sacred and profane history*, 2 vols., London, 1808.

Griggs, Earl Leslie, *Wordsworth and Coleridge; Studies in Honour of George McLean Harper*, New York: Russell & Russell, 1962.

(ed.), *Elizabethan Studies and Other Essays*, University of Colorado Press, 1945.

Grunebaum, Gustave E. von and Caillois, Ernest, *The Dream in Human Societies*, Berkeley: University of California Press, 1966.

Guest-Gornall, R., 'Samuel Taylor Coleridge and the Doctors', *Medical History* 17 (October 1973), 327–42.

Guilleminault, Christian and Lugaresi, Elio (eds.), *Sleep/Wake Disorders: Natural History, Epidemiology, and Long-Term Evolution*, New York: Raven Press, 1983.

Guyton, Arthur C., *Medical Physiology*, 8th edn, Philadelphia: W. B. Saunders, 1991.

Haggard, Howard, *Devils, Drugs, and Doctors*, London: Heinemann, 1929.

Haller, Albrecht, *Physiology; Being a Course of Lectures Upon the Visceral Anatomy and Vital Oeconomy of Human Bodies; Including the Latest and Most Considerable* DISCOVERIES *and* IMPROVEMENTS, *Which Have Been Made by the Most Eminent Professors, Through all Parts of* EUROPE, *Down to the Present Year*, 2 vols., London, 1754.

Hanen, Marsha P., Osler, Margaret J. and Weyant, Robert G. (eds.), *Science, Pseudo-Science and Society*, Ontario, Canada: Wilfrid Laurier University Press, 1980.

Harding, John Anthony, *Coleridge and the Idea of Love; Aspects of Relationship in Coleridge's Thought and Writing*, Cambridge University Press, 1974.

Harris, John, 'Coleridge's Readings in Medicine', *Wordsworth Circle* 3 (1972), 85–95.

Hartley, David, *Various Conjectures on the Perception, Motion, and Generation of Ideas*, London, 1746.

  Observations on Man, His Frame, Duty, and Expectations, 3rd edn, 2 vols., London, 1749.

Haygarth, John, *Hints Towards the Investigation of the Nature, Cause, and Cure of the Rabies Canina*, Manchester, 1789.

  Dr Haygarth's Rules to Prevent Infectious Fevers, London, 1800.

  Of the Imagination as a Cause and Cure of Disorders in the Body, Bath, 1800.

Hayter, Alethea, *Opium and the Romantic Imagination*, London: Faber & Faber, 1968.

Hazlitt, William, *The Complete Works of William Hazlitt*, ed. P. P. Howe, 21 vols., London and Toronto: Dent & Sons, 1931.

Hibbert, Samuel, *Sketches of the Philosophy of Apparitions, or, an Attempt to Trace Such Illusions to their Physical Causes*, London, 1825.

Highbarger, Leslie, *The Gates of Dreams: An Archaeological Examination of Vergil, Aenid* VI, 893–899, Baltimore: Johns Hopkins University Press, 1940.

Hippocrates, *Heracleitus: On the Universe, Hippocrates* IV, ed. W. H. S. Jones, Cambridge, Mass.: Harvard University Press, 1943.

Hobbes, Thomas, *The English Works of Thomas Hobbes*, ed. Sir William Molesworth, 11 vols., London, 1839–45.

Hobson, J. Allan, *The Dreaming Brain*, Harmondsworth: Penguin, 1988.

  Sleep and Dreams, Burlington, NC: Scientific Publications Department, Carolina Biological Supply Company, 1992.

Holmes, Richard, *Shelley; the Pursuit*, Harmondsworth: Penguin, 1987.
Coleridge: Early Visions, London: Hodder & Stoughton, 1989.
Home, Henry, *Elements of Criticism*, 2 vols., London, 1762–5.
Homer, *The Odyssey*, trans. A. T. Murray, Cambridge, Mass.: Harvard University Press, 1980.
Hoover, Suzanne R., 'Samuel Taylor Coleridge, Humphry Davy and Some Early Experiments with a Consciousness-Altering Drug', *Bulletin of Research in the Humanities* 81 (1978), 9–27.
Horace, *Satires, Epistles and Ars Poetica*, trans. H. Rushton Fairclough, Cambridge, Mass.: Harvard University Press, 1961.
The Odes and Epodes, trans. C. E. Bennett, Cambridge, Mass.: Harvard University Press, 1968.
House, Humphry, *Coleridge: The Clark Lectures 1951–52* London: Rupert Hart-Davis, 1953.
Huet, Marie-Hélène, *Monstrous Imagination*, Cambridge, Mass.: Harvard University Press, 1993.
Huisinga, Matthaeus, *Dissertatio Medica Inauguralis Sistens Incubi Causas Praecipuas*, Leiden, 1734.
Hunt, Leigh, *Lord Byron and Some of His Contemporaries*, London, 1828.
Essays, ed. Arthur Symons, London, 1887.
Hunter, John, *The Works of John Hunter, F. R. S., with Notes*, ed. James F. Palmer, 4 vols., London, 1835–7.
Hutchinson, Francis, *An Historical essay Concerning Witchcraft. With Observations Upon Matters of Fact: Tending to Clear the Texts of the Sacred Scriptures, and Confute the Vulgar Errors About that Point*, London, 1718.
Hutchinson, Sara, *The Letters of Sara Hutchinson from 1800 to 1835*, ed. Kathleen Coburn, London: Routledge & Kegan Paul, 1954.
Jackson, J. R. de (ed.), *Coleridge: The Critical Heritage*, 2 vols., London: Routledge & Kegan Paul, 1970.
Jackson, Stanley, 'The Use of the Passions in Psychological Healing', *Journal of the History of Medicine and Allied Sciences*, 45 (1990), 150–75.
Jacob, Arthur, *An Essay on the Influence of the Imagination and Passions in the Production and Cure of Diseases*, Dublin, 1823.
Jacobus, Mary, *Tradition and Experiment in Wordsworth's Lyrical Ballads 1798*, Oxford University Press, 1976.
'Wordsworth and the Language of the Dream', *ELH* 46 (1979), 618–44.
Romanticism, Writing and Sexual Difference; Essays on 'The Prelude', Oxford University Press, 1989.
Jarcho, Saul, 'Some Lost, Obsolete, or Discontinued Diseases: Serous Apoplexy, Incubus, and Retrocedent Ailments', *Transactions and Studies of the College of Physicians of Philadelphia*, 1980 (Part 2, Series 5), 241–66.
Jayne, Walter Addison, *The Healing Gods of Ancient Civilisations*, New York: University Books Inc., 1962.
Jones, Robert, *An Inquiry into the State of Medicine on the Principles of Inductive Philosophy*, Edinburgh, 1781.

Kant, Immanuel, *Dreams of a Spirit-Seer, Illustrated by Dreams of Metaphysics*, ed. Frank Sewall, trans. Emanuel Goerwitz, London: Swan Sonnenschein & Co., New York: Macmillan, 1900.

Katz, Mark, 'Dreams and Medical Illness', *British Medical Journal* 306 (10 April 1993), 993–5.

Katzung, Bertram G. (ed.), *Basic and Clinical Pharmacology*, 4th edn, Englewood Cliffs, NJ: Prentice-Hall, 1989.

Keats, John, *Poetical Works*, ed. H. W. Garrod, 2nd edn, Oxford University Press, 1958.

The Letters of John Keats 1814–1818, ed. Hyder Edward Rollins, 2 vols., Cambridge University Press, 1958.

Kellerman, Henry, *Sleep Disorders: Insomnia and Narcolepsy*, New York: Brunner, 1981.

Kiessling, Nicolas, *The Incubus in English Literature: Provenance and Progeny*, Washington State University Press, 1977.

King-Hele, Desmond, *Erasmus Darwin and the Romantic Poets*, London: Macmillan, 1986.

Kluge, Carl Alexander, *Versuch einer Darstellung des animalischen Magnetismus*, Berlin, 1815.

Kramer, Lawrence, 'That Other Will: The Daemonic in Coleridge and Wordsworth', *Philological Quarterly* 58 (1979), 298–320.

Kruger, Stephen F., *Dreaming in the Middle Ages*, Cambridge University Press, 1992.

L. M. K., 'Imagination; A Lithograph by Honoré Daumier', *Journal of the History of Medicine* 20 (October 1965), 405.

Lamb, Charles, *The Letters of Charles Lamb, to Which are Added Those of His Sister Mary Lamb*, ed. E. V. Lucas, 3 vols., London: Dent and Methuen, 1935.

Lamb, Charles and Lamb, Mary, *The Works of Charles and Mary Lamb*, ed E. V. Lucas, 6 vols., London: Methuen & Co., 1903.

Lang, Andrew, *The Book of Dreams and Ghosts*, London: Longman's Green & Co., 1897.

Laqueur, Thomas, *Making Sex: Body and Gender from the Greeks to Freud*, Cambridge, Mass., and London, England: Harvard University Press, 1992.

Lavie, Peretz and Hobson, J. Allan, 'Origin of Dreams: Anticipation of Modern Theories in the Philosophy and Physiology of the Eighteenth and Nineteenth Centuries', *Psychological Bulletin* 100 (1986), 229–40.

Leask, Nigel, *The Politics of Imagination in Coleridge's Critical Thought*, London: Macmillan, 1988.

British Romantic Writers and the East, Cambridge University Press, 1992.

Leder, Drew, *The Absent Body*, University of Chicago Press, 1990.

Lee, Edwin, *Animal Magnetism and Magnetic Lucid Somnambulism*, London, 1866.

Lefebure, Molly, *Samuel Taylor Coleridge: A Bondage of Opium*, New York: Stein & Day, 1974.

Levere, Trevor H., *Poetry Realized in Nature; Samuel Taylor Coleridge and Early Nineteenth-Century Science*, Cambridge University Press, 1981.

Chemists and Chemistry in Nature and Society 1770–1878, Hampshire and Vermont: Variorum, 1994.

Levinson, Marjorie, Butler, Marilyn, and McGann, Jerome, *Rethinking Historicism: Critical Readings in Romantic History*, Oxford and New York: Basil Blackwell, 1989.

Lincoln, Jackson Steward, *The Dream in Primitive Cultures*, London: Cresset Press, 1935.

Lindop, Grevel, *The Opium-Eater: A Life of Thomas De Quincey*, New York: Taplinger Publishing Company, 1981.

Lindsay, Julian, 'Coleridge Marginalia in a Volume of Descartes', *PMLA* 49 (1934), 184–95.

Locke, John, *An Essay Concerning Human Understanding*, ed. A. S. Pringle-Pattison, Sussex: Harvester Press, 1978.

Loewe, M., *A Treatise on the Phenomena of Animal Magnetism*, London, 1822.

London, Irvine, *Medical Care and the General Practitioner 1750–1850*, Oxford: Clarendon Press, 1986.

The London Medical Repository, August, 1816.

Lowes, John Livingston, *The Road to Xanadu; a Study in the Ways of the Imagination*, Boston and New York: Houghton Mifflin Company, 1927.

Lynch, Kathryn L., *The High Medieval Dream Vision: Poetry, Philosophy, and Literary Form*, Stanford University Press, 1988.

Macalpine, Ida and Hunter, Richard, *Three Hundred Years of Psychiatry 1535–1800*, Oxford University Press, 1963.

George III and the Mad-Business, London: Pimlico, 1991.

MacDonald, Michael, *Mystical Bedlam: Madness, Anxiety and Healing in Seventeenth-Century England*, Cambridge University Press, 1981.

MacKenzie, Norman, *Dreams and Dreaming*, London: Aldus Books, 1965.

Magnuson, Paul, *Coleridge's Nightmare Poetry*, Charlottesville: University Press of Virginia, 1974.

Coleridge and Wordsworth: A Lyrical Dialogue, Princeton University Press, 1988.

Man, Paul De, *The Rhetoric of Romanticism*, Columbia University Press, 1984.

Mather, Cotton, *The Wonders of the Invisible World; Being an Account of the Tryals of Several Witches Lately Executed in New England: and of Several Remarkable Curiosities Therein Occurring by Cotton Mather*, 3rd edn, London, 1693.

McFarland, Thomas, *Coleridge and the Pantheist Tradition*, Oxford University Press, 1969.

Romanticism and the Forms of Ruin, Princeton University Press, 1981.

McGann, Jerome, *The Romantic Ideology: A Critical Investigation*, University of Chicago Press, 1983.

McMahon, C. E., 'The Role of Imagination in the Disease Process: Pre-Cartesian History (the Role of Imagination in the Disease Process)', *Psychological Medicine* 6 (1976), 179–84.

Mégroz, R. L., *The Dream World; A Survey of the History and Mystery of Dreams*, New York: Dutton, 1939.

Mellor, Anne K., *Romanticism and Gender*, New York and London: Routledge, 1993.

Mesmer, Anton, *Mémoire sur la découverte du magnétisme animal*, trans. Gilbert Frankau, London: Macdonald, 1948.

Messer, W. S., *The Dream in Homer and Greek Tragedy*, New York: Columbia University, 1918.

Meteyard, Eliza, *A Group of Englishmen (1795–1815)*, London: Longmans, Green & Co., 1871.

Miall, David, 'The Meaning of Dreams: Coleridge's Ambivalence', *Studies in Romanticism* 21 (1982), 51–71.

Milton, John, *Paradise Lost*, ed. Scott Elledge, New York and London: Norton & Company, 1975.

Mindell, Arnold, *Dreambody: The Body's Role in Revealing the Self*, ed. Sisa Sternback-Scott and Becky Goodman, Los Angeles: Sigo Press, 1982.

Modiano, Raimonda, 'Coleridge's Views on Touch and Other Senses', *Bulletin of Research in the Humanities* 81 (1978), 28–41.

Monro, John, *Remarks on Dr Battie's Treatise on Madness*, London, 1758.

Monsman, Gerard, *Confessions of a Prosaic Dreamer: Charles Lamb's Art of Autobiography*, Durham, NC: Duke University Press, 1984.

Morris, David, *The Culture of Pain*, Berkeley and Los Angeles: University of California Press, 1993.

Motherby, George, *Medical Dictionary*, London, 1775.

Muratori, Lodovico Antonio, *Della Forza Della Fantasia Umana*, Venice: Presso Giambatista Pasquali, 1745.

Newlyn, Lucy, *Coleridge, Wordsworth, and the Language of Allusion*, Oxford: Clarendon Press, 1986.

Newman, Francis X., *Somnium: Medieval Theories of Dreaming and the Form of Vision Poetry*, Ann Arbor: University Microfilms International, 1962.

Newnham, William, *Essay on Superstition; Being an Inquiry into the Effects of Physical Influence on the Mind, in the Production of Dreams, Visions, Ghosts, and other Supernatural Appearances*, London, 1830.

Nicholson, William, 'Narrative and Explanation of the Appearance of Phantoms and other Figures in the Exhibition of the Phantasmagoria', *Journal of Natural Philosophy, Chemistry and the Arts* 1 (February, 1802), 148–50.

Nicolai, Christoph Friedrich, 'A Memoir on the Appearance of Spectres or Phantoms Occasioned by Disease, with Psychological Remarks. Read by Nicolai to the Royal Society of Berlin, on the 28th of February, 1799', *Journal of Natural Philosophy, Chemistry and the Arts* 6 (November 1803), 161–79.

Novalis (Georg Friedrich Philipp von Hardenberg), *Henry von Ofterdingen, a Novel*, trans. Palmer Hilty, Illinois: Waveland Press Inc., 1964.

Oberhelman, Steven M., *The Oneirocritic Literature of the Late Roman and Byzantine Eras of Greece*, Ann Arbor: University Microfilms International, 1981.

'The Interpretation of Prescriptive Dreams in Ancient Greek Medicine', *Journal of the History of Medicine and Allied Sciences* 36 (October 1981), 416–24.

'Galen, *On Diagnosis from Dreams'*, *Journal of the History of Medicine and Allied Sciences* 38 (January 1983), 36–47.

O'Neill, Michael, ' "That Dome in Air": Coleridge and the Self-Conscious Poem', *Romanticism* 1 (2 1995), 252–71.

Oppenheim, A. Leo, 'The Interpretation of Dreams in the Ancient Near East, with a Translation of an Assyrian Dream Book', *Transactions of the American Philosophical Society* 46 (1956), 179–373.

Pargeter, William, *Observations on Maniacal Disorders*, London, 1792.

Parisfal-Charles, Nancy, *The Dream: Four Thousand Years of Theory and Practice*, 2 vols., West Cornwall, Conn.: Locust Hill Press, 1986.

Passavant, Johann, *Untersuchungen über den Lebensmagnetismus und das Hellsehen*, Frankfurt, 1821.

Perkins, Benjamin Douglas, *The Efficacy of Perkins's Patent Metallic Tractors, in Topical Diseases, on the Human Body and Animals, Exemplified by 250 Cases, from the Finest Literary Characters in Europe and America*, London and Edinburgh, 1800.

Pite, Ralph, *The Circle of Our Vision: Dante's Presence in English Romantic Poetry*, Oxford: Clarendon Press, 1994.

Plato, *The Works of Plato*, trans. W. R. M. Lamb, 13 vols., Cambridge, Mass.: Harvard University Press, 1964.

Poggi, Stefano, and Bossi, Maurizo (eds.), *Romanticism in Science: Science in Europe 1790–1830*, Dordrecht, Boston, London: Kluwer Academic Publishers, 1994.

Polidori, John, *The Diary of John William Polidori 1816*, ed. W. M. Rossetti, London: Elkin Matthews, 1911.

Porter, Roy, 'The Patient's View: Doing Medical History from Below', *Theory and Society* 14 (1985), 175–98.

Disease, Medicine and Society in England 1550–1860, London: Macmillan, 1987.

Powell, Nicolas, *Fuseli: The Nightmare*, London: Allen Lane, 1973.

Powers, Grant, *Essay upon the Influence of the Imagination on the Nervous System, Contributing to a False Hope in Religion*, Andover, 1828.

Price, S. R. F., 'The Future of Dreams: From Freud to Artemidorus', *Past and Present* 113 (1986), 3–37.

Prickett, Stephen, *Coleridge and Wordsworth; the Poetry of Growth*, Cambridge University Press, 1970.

Raimond, Jean and Watson, J. R. (eds.), *A Handbook to English Romanticism*, New York: St Martin's Press, 1992.

Rajan, Tilottama, *The Dark Interpreter*, Ithaca, New York: Cornell University Press, 1986.

Rather, L. J., *Mind and Body in Eighteenth-Century Medicine; A Study Based on Jerome Gaub's* De Regimine Mentis, London: The Wellcome Historical Medical Library, 1965.

'Old and New Views of the Emotions and Bodily Changes: Wright and Harvey versus Descartes, James and Cannon', *Clio Medica* 1 (1965), 1–25.

Reed, Arden (ed.), *Romanticism and Language*, Ithaca, New York: Cornell University Press, 1984.

Report of the Commissioners Charged by the King to Examine Animal Magnetism, Paris, 1784.

Resnik, Salomon, *The Theatre of the Dream*, trans. Alan Sheridan, London and New York: Tavistock, 1987.

Richardson, John, *Thoughts Upon Thinking, or, a New Theory of the Human Mind; Wherein a Physical Rationale of the Formation of Our Ideas, the Passions, Dreaming, and Every Faculty of the Soul, is Attempted Upon Principles Entirely New*, 2nd edn, London, 1773.

Risse, Guenter B., 'The Brownian System of Medicine: Its Theoretical and Practical Implications', *Clio Medica* 5 (1970), 45–51.

'Hysteria at the Edinburgh Infirmary: the Construction and Treatment of a Disease, 1770–1800', *Medical History* 32 (January 1988), 1–22.

Roberts, Marie Mulvey and Porter, Roy (eds.) *Literature and Medicine During the Eighteenth Century*, London and New York: Routledge, 1993.

Ross, Marlon B., *The Contours of Masculine Desire*, Oxford University Press, 1989.

Roth, Bedrich, *Narcolepsy and Hypersomnia*, trans. Margaret Schierlova, Basel: Karger, 1980.

Rousseau, G. S., *Enlightenment Borders; Pre- and Post-modern Discourses; Medical, Scientific*, Manchester University Press, 1991.

Enlightenment Crossings; Pre- and Post-modern Discourses; Anthropological, Manchester University Press, 1991.

Rousseau, G. S. (ed.), *The Languages of Psyche; Mind and Body in Enlightenment Thought*, Berkeley, Los Angeles, Oxford: University of California Press, 1990.

Rousseau, G. S. and Boucé, P. G. (eds.), *Tobias Smollett; Bicentennial Essays Presented to Lewis M. Knapp*, New York: Oxford University Press, 1971.

Ruoff, Gene W., *Wordsworth and Coleridge: The Making of the Major Lyrics*, New York: Harvester Wheatsheaf, 1989.

Rupprecht, Carol Schreier (ed.), *The Dream and the Text; Essays on Literature and Language*, New York: State University of New York Press, 1993.

Russell, J. Stephen, *The English Dream Vision; Anatomy of a Form*, Columbus: Ohio State University Press, 1988.

Saalfeld, Reverend, *A Philosophical Discourse on the Nature of Dreams*, London, 1764.

Scarry, Elaine, *The Body in Pain; the Making and Unmaking of the World*, New York: Oxford University Press, 1985.

Schaffter, Simon, 'Self Evidence', *Critical Inquiry* 18 (Winter 1992), 327–62.

Schilder, Paul, *The Image and the Appearance of the Human Body; Studies in the Constructive Energies of the Psyche*, New York: United Universities Press, Inc., 1978.

Schneider, Elisabeth, *Coleridge, Opium and Kubla Khan*, New York: Octagon Books, 1953, reprint 1975.

Schubert, Gotthilf Heinrich von, *Allgemeine Naturgeschichte oder Andeutungen zur Geschichte und Physiognomik der Natur*, Erlangen, 1826.

Scott, Sir Walter, *Letters on Demonology and Witchcraft, Addressed to J. G. Lockhart, Esq.*, 2nd edn, London, 1831.

Shakespeare, William, *Hamlet*, ed. Harold Jenkins, London and New York: Methuen, 1986.

Shelley, Mary, *Frankenstein; or, The Modern Prometheus; The 1818 Text*, ed. Marilyn Butler, Oxford University Press, 1994.

Shelley, Percy Bysshe, *The Works of Percy Bysshe Shelley in Verse and Prose*, ed. Harry Buxton Forman, 6 vols., London: Reeves & Turner, 1880.

Siskin, Clifford, *The Historicity of Romantic Discourse*, Oxford University Press, 1988.

Smith, Edward, 'A relation of an extraordinary effect of the power of the imagination', *Philosophical Transactions* 16 (July/August 1687), 330–42.

Smyser, Jane Worthington, 'Wordsworth's Dream of Poetry and Science: *The Prelude*, v', *PMLA* 71 (1956), 269–75.

Snyder, Alice D., *Coleridge on Logic and Learning*, New Haven: Yale University Press, 1929.

Snyder, Robert Lance (ed.), *Thomas De Quincey: Bicentenary Studies*, Norman and London: University of Oklahoma Press, 1985.

Southey, Robert, *The Doctor, &c.*, 3rd edn., 11 vols., London: Longman, Rees, Orme, Brown, Green & Longman, 1834–7.

The Correspondence of Southey with Caroline Bowles; to Which are Added Correspondence with Shelley, and Southey's Dreams, ed. Edward Dowden, London: Longmans, Green & Co., 1881.

Letters from England: By Don Manuel Alvarez Espreilla. Translated from the Spanish (1807), ed. J. Simmons, London: Cresset Press, 1951.

Spatz, Jonas, 'The Mystery of Eros: Sexual Initiation in Coleridge's "Christabel" ', *PMLA* 90 (1975), 107–16.

The Spectator 'On Dreams', 487 (September 1712) and 'A Vision', 524 (October 1712).

Stafford, Barbara Maria, *Body Criticism: Imaging the Unseen in Enlightenment Art and Medicine*, Cambridge, Mass.: Massachusetts Institute of Technology Press, 1993.

Artful Science; Enlightenment Entertainment and the Eclipse of Visual Education, Cambridge, Mass.: Massachusetts Institute of Technology Press, 1994.

Stearne, John, *A Confirmation and Discovery of Witch-craft, Containing These Severall Particulars: That There are Witches Called Bad Witches, and Witches Untruely Called Good or White Witches, and What Manner of People They Be, and How they May Bee Knowne, with Many Particulars Thereunto Tending. Together with the Confessions of Those Executed Since May 1645 in the Severall Counties Hereafter Mentioned. As Also Some Objections Answered*, London, 1648.

Stevenson, Warren, *Poetic Friends; A Study of Literary Relations During the Romantic Period*, New York, Bern, Frankfurt, Paris: Peter Lang, 1990.

Stewart, C.P. and Guthrie, D. (eds.), *Lind's Treatise on Scurvy*, Edinburgh University Press, 1953.

Stewart, Dugald, *Elements of the Philosophy of the Human Mind*, London, 1792.

Stock, R. D., *The Holy and the Daemonic from Sir Thomas Browne to William Blake*, Princeton University Press, 1982.

Sultana, Donald (ed.), *New Approaches to Coleridge: Biographical and Critical Essays*, London: Vision Press, 1981.

Swedenborg, Emanuel, *A Treatise Concerning Heaven and Hell and of the Wonderful Things Therein*, trans. J. R. Rendell, I. Tansley and J. S. Bogg, 5th edn, London, 1805.

Temkin, Owsei, 'Basic Science, Medicine, and the Romantic Era', *Bulletin of the History of Medicine* 38 (1963), 97–129.

Thomas, Ronald R., *Dreams of Authority; Freud and the Fictions of the Unconscious*, Ithaca and London: Cornell University Press, 1990.

Todd, Dennis, *Imagining Monsters; Miscreations of the Self in Eighteenth-Century England*, University of Chicago Press, 1995.

Tryon, Thomas, *A Treatise of Dreams and Visions, Wherein the Causes, Natures, and Uses of Nocturnal Representations, and the Communications both of Good and Evil Angels, as Also Departed Souls, to Mankind*, 2nd edn, London, 1689.

Tytler, Graeme, *Physiognomy in the European Novel; Faces and Fortunes*, Princeton University Press, 1982.

Vickers, Neil, 'Coleridge, Thomas Beddoes and Brunonian Medicine', *European Romantic Review* 8 (Winter 1997).

Virgil, *Aeneid*, trans. H. Rushton Fairclough, Cambridge, Mass.: Harvard University Press, 1968.

Wagner, Lydia, 'Coleridge's Use of Laudanum and Opium as Connected with his Interest in Contemporary Investigations concerning Stimulation and Sensation', *Psychoanalytic Review* 25 (July 1938), 309–34.

Waller, John, *Treatise on the Incubus, or Night-mare, Disturbed Sleep, Terrific Dreams, and Nocturnal Visions; with the means of removing these distressing complaints*, London, 1815.

Warren, Robert Penn, *New and Selected Essays*, New York: Random House, 1989.

Watson, J. R., *English Poetry of the Romantic Period 1789–1830*, 2nd edn, London and New York: Longman, 1992.

Webb, Ilza, *Hysteria; The History of a Disease*, University of Chicago Press, 1965.

Weidhorn, Manfred, *Dreams in Seventeenth-Century English Literature*, Paris: Mouton, 1970.

Weightman, Mary, *The Friendly Monitor; or, dialogues for youth against the Fear of Ghosts, and other Irrational Apprehensions, with Reflections on the Power of the Imagination and the Folly of Superstition*, London, 1791.

Weiskel, Thomas, *The Romantic Sublime: Studies in the Structure and Psychology of Transcendence*, Baltimore and London: Johns Hopkins University Press, 1976.

Whalley, George, *Coleridge and Sara Hutchinson and the Asra Poems*, London: Routledge & Kegan Paul, 1955.

Wijsenbeck-Wijler, *Aristotle's Concept of Soul, Sleep and Dreams*, Amsterdam: Adolf M. Hakkert, 1978.

Williams, Anne, 'An I for an Eye: "Spectral Persecution" in *The Rime of the Ancient Mariner*', *PMLA* 108 (1993), 1114–27.

Wordsworth, Jonathan, *The Music of Humanity*, New York: Harper & Row, 1969.

Wordsworth, William, *The Poetical Works of William Wordsworth*, ed. Ernest De Selincourt and Helen Darbishire, 5 vols., Oxford: Clarendon Press, 1944.

   The Prose Works of William Wordsworth, ed. W. J. B. Owen and Jane Worthington Smyser, 3 vols., Oxford: Clarendon Press, 1975.

   The Prelude 1799, 1805, 1850, ed. Jonathan Wordsworth, M. H. Abrams and Stephen Gill, New York and London: W. W. Norton & Company, 1979.

Wordsworth, William and Wordsworth, Dorothy, *The Letters of William and Dorothy Wordsworth; The Early Years 1787–1805*, ed. Ernest De Selincourt, 2nd edn revised by Chester L. Shaver, Oxford: Clarendon Press, 1967.

   The Letters of William and Dorothy Wordsworth: The Middle Years Part I 1806–1811, ed. Ernest De Selincourt, 2nd edn revised by Mary Moorman, 2 vols., Oxford University Press, 1970.

Wylie, Ian, *Young Coleridge and the Philosophers of Nature*, Oxford: Clarendon Press, 1989.

Index

CAMBRIDGE STUDIES IN ROMANTICISM

GENERAL EDITORS
MARILYN BUTLER, *University of Oxford*
JAMES CHANDLER, *University of Chicago*